KATHERINE ANNE PORTER

GARLAND REFERENCE LIBRARY
OF THE HUMANITIES
(VOL. 507)

KATHERINE ANNE PORTER
"An Annotated Bibliography

Kathryn Hilt
Ruth M. Alvarez

GARLAND PUBLISHING, INC. • NEW YORK & LONDON
1990

Library of Congress Cataloging-in-Publication Data

Hilt, Kathryn, 1939–
    Katherine Anne Porter : An annotated bibliography / Kathryn Hilt,
Ruth M. Alvarez.
        p.   cm. — (Garland reference library of the humanities; vol.
507)
    ISBN 0–8240–8912–X
    1. Porter, Katherine Anne., 1890–1980—Bibliography. I. Alvarez,
Ruth M. II. Title. III. Series.
Z8705.7.H54 1990
[PS3531.0752]
016.813'52—dc20   90-43628
                                                                CIP

Printed on acid-free, 250-year-life paper
Manufactured in the United States of America

CONTENTS

Preface   vii
A Note on Porter Collections   xiii

Part I: Works by Katherine Anne Porter

A. Separate Publications: English Language   3
AA. Separate Publications: Foreign Language   13
B. Fiction Contributed to Books and Periodicals   23
C. Essays, Letters, Poems   35
D. Journalism   79
E. Book Reviews   105

Part II: Works about Katherine Anne Porter

F. Bibliographical   129
G. Biographical, Including Interviews   133
H. General Criticism   173
I. Criticism of Individual Works   219
    "The Cracked Looking-Glass"   219
    "The Downward Path to Wisdom"   220
    "The Fig Tree"   220
    "Flowering Judas"   220
    "Gertrude Stein: Three Views"   224
    "The Grave"   225
    "Hacienda"   228
    "He"   229
    "Holiday"   230

Introduction to *A Curtain of Green*   231
The Itching Parrot   232
"The Jilting of Granny Weatherall"   232
"The Leaning Tower"   235
"Magic"   236
"The Martyr"   237
"Maria Concepción"   237
"Noon Wine"   237
"Notes on the Texas I Remember"   241
"Old Mortality"   241
"Pale Horse, Pale Rider"   243
Ship of Fools   246
"Theft"   255
"A Wreath for the Gamekeeper"   257
"Xochimilco"   257
J.   Book Reviews   259
    Flowering Judas   259
    Katherine Anne Porter's French Song-Book   261
    Hacienda   262
    Flowering Judas and Other Stories   263
    Noon Wine   266
    Pale Horse, Pale Rider: Three Short Novels   267
    The Itching Parrot   271
    The Leaning Tower and Other Stories   272
    The Days Before   278
    Ship of Fools   288
    Collected Stories   304
    The Collected Essays and Occasional Writings   311
    The Never-Ending Wrong   317
K.   Ph.D. Dissertations   321
Index of Authors, Editors, and Translators   333
Index of Porter Titles   343

PREFACE

As those who have studied Katherine Anne Porter's life (1890–1980) are aware, she embellished those parts of it she thought lacked sufficient glamour and suppressed details that evoked painful memories. Apparently viewing her Methodist background as pedestrian, she claimed to have been raised a Roman Catholic. Her dirt poor rural upbringing was transformed into visions of Southern gentility.

But Porter's life—even when stripped of her embellishments—is a more eventful, exciting one than those led by most twentieth-century male writers, let alone women writers. In Mexico when Alvaro Obrégon was inaugurated, she became involved with several of the revolutionaries and artists living there. In the Greenwich Village of the twenties, she was acquainted with the leaders of the literary community, among them Edmund Wilson, John Peale Bishop, Carl Van Doren, Edna St. Vincent Millay, Elinor Wylie. In the early thirties she was in Berlin, observing at first hand and with revulsion the rise of Nazism. She even met Goering, who found her attractive. Shortly thereafter, she was in Paris, counting Sylvia Beach and Ford Madox Ford among her friends. For a time during the late thirties, she lived in Baton Rouge and associated with the *Southern Review* staff, including Robert Penn Warren. Her relationships with men were as eventful as other parts of her life; she had four husbands and a succession of lovers. And—even though the egotism and garrulousness of her later years annoyed certain acquaintances—her charm and warmth continued to attract devoted admirers.

At the 1930 publication of *Flowering Judas,* Porter's first short story collection, she was critically accepted as an accomplished writer. Among the enthusiastic reviews was that of the *New York Times,* which declared that Porter was "of that youngest generation of American artists from which one dares to hope much." And Allen Tate, praising her style, versatility, and objectivity, concluded that Porter's was "a fully matured art." Subsequent collections—an expanded *Flowering Judas* (1935), *Pale Horse, Pale Rider* (1939), and *The Leaning Tower* (1944)—confirmed and reinforced this critical judgment.

But—despite the acclaim for Porter's skillful use of language, for her subtle handling of irony and intricate symbolism, for her nondidactic concern with moral questions— she failed to achieve a wide reading audience. Then, the 1962 publication of *Ship of Fools,* although disappointing to many critics, made her a popular success. Her *Collected Stories* (1965) brought her both a Pulitzer Prize and a National Book Award. Generally, reviews of this volume echoed the critical praise she had received throughout most of her literary career. Granville Hicks asserted that "one has the feeling, with almost every story, that it is absolutely right," while V.S. Pritchett held that Porter had solved the basic problem of a short story writer: "how to satisfy exhaustively in writing briefly."

If interest in Porter had waned during the 1970s, the 1982 appearance of Joan Givner's widely reviewed *Katherine Anne Porter: A Life* brought her once again to the attention of the literate public, as has the recently published *Letters of Katherine Anne Porter.*

There has been no recent book-length Porter bibliography. The last book to attempt a full listing of Porter's writing was Waldrip and Bauer's *A Bibliography of the Works of Katherine Anne Porter and a Bibliography of the Criticism of Katherine Anne Porter* (1969). The last extensive annotated bibliography of works about Porter was the first part of Robert F. Kiernan's *Katherine Anne Porter and Carson McCullers: A*

Reference Guide (1976). This work gives Porter criticism through 1973 (with one entry for 1974). As helpful as these books have been, the fact that they are dated and that many more of Porter's writings have been found makes necessary another.

This bibliography is divided into two parts, Primary and Secondary, with each of these further divided.

In Part One, primary, we have divided Porter's writing into (A) books, (AA) translations of these books, (B) stories published individually in books and periodicals, (C) essays, letters, poems, (D) journalism, and (E) book reviews.

Each section includes entries not given in previous book-length bibliographies. Some of these—such as *The Collected Essays* and *Letters of Katherine Anne Porter*—are a matter of updating prior works. But we have also added many earlier Porter works unknown to other compilers.

The most significant addition to this primary portion of the book is the compilation of Porter's journalism. Still, some of Porter's known journalism has eluded the search. There is tantalizing evidence of additional 1917–18 *Fort Worth Critic* pieces excerpted in a 1966 *Fort Worth Star-Telegram* article (G121a); there is also evidence of additional Fort Worth journalism from 1921. Appearing for the first time in a primary bibliography is a compilation of Porter's signed *Rocky Mountain News* pieces. Kathryn Adams Sexton's unpublished M.A. thesis of 1961 does list most of these but in a rather confusing and misleading manner. There are certainly 90 articles by Porter from 1919 because these contain her byline. But Porter began work on the newspaper in the late summer or the autumn of 1918; we have cited no pieces from this period. It is likely that Porter returned to the paper in early 1919 after her recovery from a nearly fatal attack of influenza and was rewarded with her own byline and the position of movie, theater, and music critic. Her signed work from 1919 does not constitute her entire contribution for this year. For example, for Sundays Porter wrote a column which included her observations and assessments, gossip and local theater news, interviews, and theater items gleaned from her reading. The first of these appears on 16 February 1919. But also in that issue and on the same page are two unsigned articles probably by Porter: "Honest Ugly Woman Is Found Refreshing" and "Joy Predominates in Bill at Orpheum." Also, two of the Sunday theater columns (from 11 May 1919 and 27 July 1919) are unsigned. A safe estimate is that there are at least 90 (perhaps almost 200) more Porter articles in the *Rocky Mountain News* of 1918–19 than we have listed.

Porter's work from such various publications as *Motion Picture Magazine*, the *Christian Science Monitor, Freeman,* and *Century* is given in Section C among her essays rather than with her journalism in Section D. She would not have considered these pieces journalism; most of her published work after her departure from Denver in autumn 1919 was done on a free-lance basis. Section C includes previously undocumented pieces from the *New York Call*, the *Magazine of Mexico*, and the *Christian Science Monitor* written in Mexico or from her experiences in Mexico.

Part Two, the secondary bibliography, lists and annotates writings about Porter and her works. This part has been organized according to type of writing: (F) bibliographical, (G) biographical (including interviews), (H) general criticism, (I) criticism of individual works, (J) book reviews, and (K) Ph.D. dissertations.

A major benefit of this part is, of course, that it brings Porter material up to date. Another benefit is that it lists many earlier works—especially interviews and book reviews—not included in previous bibliographies. This is possible because of our having had access to the numerous boxes of newspaper, magazine, and journal pieces accumulated by Porter (largely though a clipping service) and now available in the Maryland Room at the University of Maryland's McKeldin Library.

This bibliography covers Porter and Porter scholarship through 1988, with several entries for 1989 and 1990. In almost all areas, the listings are as complete as we could make them. The three exceptions are: the reprints of stories, interviews given by Porter, and reviews of Porter's books. First, there seemed no reason to attempt an exhaustive compilation of the appearances of Porter's stories, since those that are reprinted are always those that can easily be found in her *Collected*

Stories. For those that are listed, the principles of selection were significance and/or recent publication. It is worth noting, however, that almost every English-language anthology of short fiction, of American literature, of women writers, or of Southern writers has a story by Katherine Anne Porter. The majority of the Porter interviews are given. The omissions were generally for reasons of repetitive subject matter. Although the reviews of Porter's nonfiction volumes are as nearly complete as possible, the forbidding abundance of the reviews of her story collections and of *Ship of Fools* discouraged a complete listing. Persons wishing to read additional interviews and reviews can find them in the Porter Collection of the University of Maryland.

No attempt has been made to list the recordings, radio dramas, television dramas, and films made from Porter's works.

Ruth M. Alvarez has done the detective work involved in finding Porter's journalism and other hitherto undocumented nonfiction pieces. She was responsible for compiling and annotating Sections C, D, E, K, and the reviews of Porter's nonfiction volumes in Section J. In addition to compiling and annotating the material in the other sections, I have acted as editor in organizing the book and in getting it ready for publication.

Ruth and I wish to thank Dr. Donald Farren, Director for Special Collections at McKeldin Library, and Dr. Blanche Ebeling-Koning, Curator of Rare Books and Literary Manuscripts. Also, we are grateful to the entire staff of McKeldin's Maryland Room for consistent courtesy and cooperation. On a more personal note, I want to thank Sheila Spector and Wanda Avila, who at separate times graciously offered me bed and board when I had to be in College Park or Washington, D.C., for research.

Kathryn Hilt
June 15, 1990

A NOTE ON
PORTER COLLECTIONS

The resource that no Porter scholar can ignore is the large collection at the McKeldin Library, University of Maryland, College Park. In 1966 Porter sold the University many of her personal papers, her correspondence, a large number of manuscripts (of both published and unpublished works), her personal library, as well as many phonograph records and photographs. The University has continued to add to the collection.

The Beinecke Rare Book Library at Yale University and the Harry Ransom Center of the University of Texas in Austin also have noteworthy Porter material. Also, the Allen Tate and Caroline Gordon Collections at Princeton University have notable Porter letters.

PART I

WORKS BY KATHERINE ANNE PORTER

SECTION A
SEPARATE PUBLICATIONS:
ENGLISH LANGUAGE

In this section publications are given chronologically according to first edition. Subsequent editions are listed immediately following the first. Most paperbacks are identified as such.

A1. *My Chinese Marriage.* New York: Duffield, 1921.

> Author given as "M.T.F.," but ghostwritten by Porter. On a flyleaf of a copy now at the University of Maryland, Porter explains: "I wrote this book from the dictated records of Mae Taim Franking in all innocence and good faith . . . and God knows it couldn't have been more false, because she had no notion what had happened to her."

A2. *Outline of Mexican Popular Arts and Crafts.* Los Angeles: Young & McCallister, 1922.

> The catalogue for a planned "travelling Mexican popular arts exposition in the United States." Porter's discussion includes a historical survey of Mexican art.

A3. *What Price Marriage.* New York: J.H. Sears, 1927.

> Porter—as "Hamblen Sears"—compiled the contents and wrote the introduction (C21) and notes. The book consists of pieces on marriage, from Voltaire, Schopenauer, Balzac, Pepys, Tacitus, Charles Lamb, Addison, the *Koran*, Epictetus, Swift, Dostoevsky, Mary Wollstonecraft, Ibsen, J.S. Mill, I Corinthians, Laurence Sterne, Lucius Apuleius, Nietzsche, St. Augustine, Mary Wortley Montagu, Swedenborg, Thomas More, and Rabelais.

A4. *Flowering Judas.* New York: Harcourt, Brace, 1930.

> This, the first collection of Porter stories, has four fewer selections than *Flowering Judas and Other Stories* (A7). Contents: "María Concepción" (B5), "Magic" (B9), "Rope" (B10), "He" (B8), "The Jilting of Granny Weatherall" (B11), "Flowering Judas" (B13).

A5. *Katherine Anne Porter's French Song-Book.* New York: Harrison of Paris, 1933.

> Seventeen songs, ranging over a 600-year period, translated by Porter. Each song is given in both its French and its English version.

A6. *Hacienda.* New York: Harrison of Paris, 1934.

> The short novel (B15) as a separate publication, limited to 895 copies.

A7. *Flowering Judas and Other Stories.* New York: Harcourt, Brace, 1935.

> Subsequent English-language editions:
>> London: Jonathan Cape, 1936.
>> New York: Modern Library, 1940. With a two-page introduction (C37) by Porter.
>> New York and Toronto: New American Library, 1970.

An expansion of *Flowering Judas* (A4). Four stories have been added: "Theft" (B12), "That Tree" (B16), "The Cracked Looking-Glass" (B14), "Hacienda" (B15).

A8. *Noon Wine.* Detroit: Schuman's, 1937.

The short novel (B22) as a separate publication, limited to 250 copies.

A9. *Pale Horse, Pale Rider: Three Short Novels.* New York: Harcourt, Brace, 1939.

Subsequent English-language editions:
London: Jonathan Cape, 1939.
New York: The Modern Library, 1949.
New York: The New American Library (a Signet book), 1962 (paperbound).
New York: The New American Library (a Signet Classic), 1962 (paperbound). (This edition has an Afterword by Mark Schorer (H89).

Contents: "Old Mortality" (B21), "Noon Wine" (B22), "Pale Horse, Pale Rider" (B23).

A10. *Anniversary in a Country Cemetery.* New York: Arrow Music Press, [1942].

Sheet music—a Porter poem with music by David Diamond. It is a revised version of a poem she had written and buried in her mother's grave in 1936 (C36).

A11. *The Itching Parrot* (By José Joaquín Fernández de Lizárdi). Garden City, N.Y.: Doubleday, Doran, 1942.

Although Porter is named as translator of this picaresque Mexican novel, her third husband, Eugene Pressly, did the original translating. She rewrote his work and contributed a 31-page introduction (C53).

A12. *The Leaning Tower and Other Stories*. New York: Harcourt, Brace, 1944.

Subsequent English-language editions:
London: Jonathan Cape, 1945.
New York: Dell (a Delta book), 1962 (paperbound).
New York: Dell (a Laurel Edition), 1963 (paperbound).
New York and Toronto: New American Library (a Signet Modern Classic), 1970 (paperbound).

Of this third major collection of Porter stories, 20,000 copies were sold in the first two weeks. Contents: "The Source" (B26), "The Witness" (first appearance), "The Circus" (B18), "The Old Order" (B20, later "The Journey"), "The Last Leaf" (first appearance), "The Grave" (B17), "The Downward Path to Wisdom" (B24), "A Day's Work" (B25), "The Leaning Tower" (B27).

A13. *Selected Short Stories*. New York: Editions for the Armed Forces, [1945?].

This volume, with stories from all three of Porter's collections (A7, A9, A12), was printed for distribution to the United States overseas troops. Contents: "María Concepción" (B5), "That Tree" (B16), "The Grave" (B17), "The Cracked Looking-Glass" (B14), "The Downward Path to Wisdom" (B24), "The Witness" (in A12), "The Old Order" (B20, later "The Journey"), "Hacienda" (B15), "Noon Wine" (B22).

A14. *The Days Before*. New York: Harcourt, Brace, 1952.

Subsequent English-language edition:
London: Secker & Warburg, 1953.

A collection of nonfiction pieces. Contents: "The Days Before" (C59), " On a Criticism of Thomas Hardy" (C35), "Gertrude Stein: Three Views" ("Everybody is a Real One," [E19], "Second Wind," [E28], "The Wooden Umbrella," [C67]), "Reflections on Willa Cather" (C77), "'It Is Hard to Stand in the Middle'" (E61), "The Art of

Katherine Mansfield" (E46), " Orpheus in Purgatory" (E56), "'The Laughing Heat of the Sun,'" (E55), "Eudora Welty and *A Curtain of Green* (C40), "Homage to Ford Madox Ford" (C54), "Virginia Woolf" (E57), "E.M. Forster" (E62), "Three Statements about Writing" ("1939: The Situation in American Writing," [C32], "1940: Introduction to 'Flowering Judas,'" [C37], "1942: Transplanted Writers," [C48]), "No Plot, My Dear, No Story" (C46), "The Flower of Flowers"—with a note on "Pierre-Joseph Redouté" (C71, 73), "Portrait: Old South" (C60), "Audubon's Happy Land" (C33), "A House of My Own" (C39), "The Necessary Enemy" (C68), "Marriage is Belonging" (C75), "American Statement: 4 July 1942" (C47), "The Future is Now" (C74), "Notes on the Life and Death of a Hero" (C53), "Why I Write about Mexico" (C11), "Leaving the Petate" (C24), "The Mexican Trinity" (C7), "La Conquistadora" (E16), "Quetzalcoatl" (E15), "The Charmed Life" (C44).

A15. *A Defense of Circe.* New York: Harcourt, Brace, 1955.

A separate publication of the earlier *Mademoiselle* essay (C81), this little book was "limited to 1,700 copies privately printed for the friends of the author and her publishers as a New Year's greeting."

A16. *The Old Order: Stories of the South from Flowering Judas; Pale Horse, Pale Rider; and The Leaning Tower.* New York: Harcourt, Brace (a Harvest Book), 1955 (paperbound).

Contents: "The Source" (B26), "The Old Order" (B20, later "The Journey"), "The Witness" (in A12), "The Circus" (B18), "The Last Leaf" (in A12), "The Grave" (B17), "The Jilting of Granny Weatherall" (B11), "He" (B8), "Magic" (B9), "Old Mortality" (B21).

A17. *A Christmas Story.* New York: Mademoiselle, 1958.

> Subsequent English-language edition:
> New York: Delacorte Press, 1967.
>
> A separate publication of a piece that earlier appeared in *Mademoiselle* (C63). The 1967 edition has illustrations by Ben Shahn, an added note by Porter, and a photograph of her niece.

A18. *Ship of Fools.* Boston and Toronto: Little, Brown, 1962.

> Subsequent English-language editions:
> > A pirated printing of the first edition (No publishing information.)
> > London: Secker & Warburg, 1962.
> > New York: New American Library (a Signet Book), 1963 (paperbound).
> > Middlesex, Eng.: Penguin Books, 1965 (paperbound).
> > Boston: Little, Brown, 1984 (paperbound).

A19. *The Collected Stories of Katherine Anne Porter.* New York: Harcourt Brace, 1965.

> Other English-language editions:
> > London: Jonathan Cape, 1964 (not complete).
> > London: Jonathan Cape, 1967.
> > New York: New American Library (a Plume Book), 1970 (paperbound).
> > Franklin Center, Pa.: Franklin Library, 1976. (Illustrations by George Jones, Introduction by The Franklin Library.)
> > New York: Harcourt Brace Jovanovich (a Harvest/HBJ book), 1979 (paperbound).
> > London: Virago, 1985 (paperbound).

> Contents: Stories previously collected in *Flowering Judas and Other Stories* (A7), *Pale Horse, Pale Rider: Three Short Novels* (A9), *The Leaning Tower and Other Stories* (A12), Porter's Preface—"Go Little Book . . ." (C113), "The Fig Tree" (B39),

"Holiday" (B40), "Virgin Violeta" (B7), "The Martyr" (B6).

A20. *The Collected Essays and Occasional Writings of Katherine Anne Porter.* New York: Delacorte Press, 1970.

Subsequent English-language edition:
New York: Dell (a Delta book), 1973 (paperbound).

Includes the pieces collected in *The Days Before* (A14), "A Wreath for the Gamekeeper" (E68), "On Christopher Sykes" (E69), "Max Beerbohm" (E60), "Eleanor Clark" (E64), "The Winged Skull" (E51), "On Modern Fiction" (C112), "St. Augustine and the Bullfight" (C83), "A Little Incident in the Rue de l'Odéon" (C107), "A Letter to Sylvia Beach" (C105), "Letters to a Nephew" (C117), "Dylan Thomas" (E65, 66, 67), "A Defense of Circe" (C81), "Pull Dick, Pull Devil" (E53), A Letter to the Editor of *The Village Voice* (C88), A Letter to the Editor of *The Nation* (C64), "On Communism in Hollywood" (C65), A Letter to the Editor of *The Saturday Review of Literature* (C128), "Opening Speech at Paris Conference, 1952" (C76), "Remarks on the Agenda" (C91), A Letter to the Editor of *The Yale Review* (C98), A Letter to the Editor of the *Washington Post* (C101), "Speech of Acceptance" (C121), "Ole Woman River" (C118), "A Sprig of Mint for Allen" (C97), "On First Meeting T.S. Eliot" (C99), "Flannery O'Connor at Home" (C108), "From the Notebooks: Yeats, Joyce, Eliot, Pound" (C111), "Romany Marie, Joe Gould—Two Legends Come to Life" (C92), "Jacqueline Kennedy" (C106), "Affectation of Praehiminincies (*A.D.* 1663–1675)" (C45), "A Goat for Azazel (*A.D.* 1688)" (C34), "A Bright Particular Faith (*A.D.* 1700)" (C27), "Miss Porter Adds a Comment" (C58), "The Fiesta of Guadalupe" (C126), "Where Presidents Have No Friends" (C9), "My First Speech" (C129), "Notes on Writing" (C38), "On Writing" (C130), "'Noon Wine': The Sources" (C89), "Enchanted" (C12), "Two Songs from Mexico" (C13), "Little Requiem" (C14), "Winter Burial" (C19), "Anniversary in a Country

Cemetery" (C36), "November in Windham" (C84), "After a Long Journey" (C93), "Measures for Song and Dance" (C72).

A21. *He*. Cambridge, Eng.: Cambridge University Press, 1972.

A separate publication of the story (B8).

A22. *The Never-Ending Wrong*. Boston: Little, Brown, 1977.

Subsequent English-language edition:
London: Secker & Warburg, 1977.
A memoir of the Sacco-Vanzetti case and of Porter's participation in the protest, originally published in *Atlantic* (C140).

A23. *Letters of Katherine Anne Porter*. New York: Atlantic Monthly Press, 1990.

Letters ranging from April 1930 to December 1966. Selected and edited by Isabel Bayley.

A24. *Holiday*. Bielefeld, Berlin, and Hannover: Velhagen & Klasing, n.d. (paperbound).

For German students of English. (See B40.)

A25. *Old Mortality*. Tokyo: Kato Chudokan, n.d.

For Japanese students of English, edited with Introduction and notes by Kazushi Kuzumi. (See B21.)

A26. *Theft and Other Stories*. Tokyo: Sansyusya, n.d. (paperbound).

For Japanese students of English, edited with notes by Kouko Aono. Contents: "He" (B8), "Rope" (B10), "Theft" (B12), "The Jilting of Granny Weatherall," (B11), "The Circus" (B18), "The Last Leaf" (in A12), "The Grave" (B17).

A27. *Two Short Stories*. Tokyo: Kenkyusha (Kenkyusha Pocket English Series), n.d. (paperbound).

For Japanese students of English. Edited with notes by Fumi Takano. Contents: "The Cracked Looking-Glass" (B14), "Hacienda" (B15).

SECTION AA
SEPARATE PUBLICATIONS:
FOREIGN LANGUAGE

Entries in this section have been taken mainly from works in the University of Maryland's Katherine Anne Porter Room and from listings in *Index Translationum*. As these two sources have provided a lengthy and varied listing of translated Porter works and since they tend to confirm one another, no attempt has been made to search further. Also, translations of individual Porter stories are not listed. The Porter works are given chronologically according to date of first publication; translations are then given alphabetically according to language. When possible, the name of the translator is given.

AA1. *FLOWERING JUDAS AND OTHER STORIES*

AA1(a). Arabic.

[Title and publishing information in Arabic script] (paperbound).

AA1(b). Bengali.

Šiuli Majumdar. Bombay: Pearl, 1959 (paperbound).

AA1(c). French.

L'arbre de Judée. Paris: Editions du Paviois, 1945 (paperbound). Tr. by Marcelle Sibon.

AA1(d). German.

Unter heißen Himmel. Bad Wörishofen: Kindler und Schiermeyer, 1951. Tr. by Hansi Bockow-Blüthgen.

AA1(e). German.

Blühender Judasbaum und andere Erzählungen. Zurich: Diogenes, 1964 (paperbound). Tr. by Joachim Uhlmann. Rpt. 1966.

AA1(f). Greek.

[Title and publishing information in Greek alphabet].

AA1(g). Hebrew.

[Title and publishing information in Hebrew script], 1964 (paperbound).

AA1(h). Portuguese.

Árvore Florida e outres histórias. São Paulo: Editôra Cultrix, 1965 (paperbound). Tr. by Geraldo Pires do Amorim and Othon Moacyr Garcia.

AA1(i). Spanish.

Cuentos del Floreciente Judas. Buenos Aires: Plaza & Janes, 1964 (paperbound). Tr. by Maria Elvira Solá de Brinckman.

AA1(j). Tamil.

Kurutippu. Bombay: Pearl, 1958 (paperbound). Tr. by K.N. Subrahmanyam.

AA2. *PALE HORSE, PALE RIDER: THREE SHORT NOVELS.*

AA2(a). Arabic.

[Title in Arabic script]. Cairo: Akhbar Al Yom, 1954 (paperbound). Tr. by Sofie Abdullah.

AA2(b). French.

Le vin de Midi. Paris: Editions du Pavois, 1948 (paperbound). Tr. by Marcelle Sibon.

AA2(c). German.

Das dunkel Lied. Munich: Verlag Kurt Desch, 1950. Tr. by Maria von Schweinitz.

AA2(d). German.

Fahles Pferd und fahler Reiter. Zurich: Diogenes Verlag, 1963. Tr. by Maria von Schweinitz. With an essay by Robert Penn Warren.

AA2(e). German.

Fahles Pferd und fahler Reiter. Frankfurt am Main and Hamburg: Fischer Bücherei GmbH, 1968 (paperbound). Tr. by Maria von Schweinitz.

AA2(f). Indonesian.

Susunan Lama. Darkarta: Balai Pustaka, 1950. Tr. by Diterdjemahkan oleh Mochtar Lubis.

AA2(g). Italian.

Bianco cavallo, bianco cavaliere. Turin: Giulio Einaudi Editore, 1946 (paperbound). Tr. by Lidia Storoni Mazzolani.

AA2(h). Japanese.

[Title in Japanese characters]. Tokyo: Dabiddo-sha, 1954. Tr. Masao Takahashi. ("Noon Wine" is omitted.)

AA2(i). Portuguese.

Cavalo pálido, cavaleiro pálido. São Paulo: Editôra Cultrix, 1965 (paperbound). Tr. by Péricles Eugênio da Silva Ramos.

AA2(j). Spanish.

A tal caballo, tal jinete. Buenos Aires: Plaza & Janes, 1964 (paperbound). Tr. by Manuel Belaguer and Marta Acosta.

AA3. *THE LEANING TOWER AND OTHER STORIES*

AA3(a). Danish.

Det skaeve taarn. Copenhagen: Det danske Forlag, 1948 (paperbound). Tr. by Ole Jacobsen. Rpt. 1962.

AA3(b). French.

La tour penchée. Paris: Editions du Seuil, 1954. Tr. by Marcelle Sibon.

AA3(c). German.

Das letzte Blatt. Bad Wörishofen: Kindler & Schiermeyer, 1953. Tr. by Hansi Bochow-Blüthgen.

AA3(d). German.

Der schiefe Turm und andere Erzählungen. Zurich: Diogenes, 1965 (paperbound, 1967). Tr. by Joachim Uhlmann and Elizabeth Schack.

AA3(e). Portuguese.

> *A tôrre inclinada.* São Paulo: Editôra Cultrix, 1964 (paperbound). Tr. by Olivía Krähenbuhl.

AA3(f). Spanish.

> *La torre inclinada y otros relatos.* Buenos Aires: Ediciones Troquel, 1966 (paperbound). Introduction by A.D. Van Nostrand, tr. by Ana Weyland. Stories tr. by Adriane Bo.

AA3(g). Swedish.

> *Det lutande tornet.* Stockholm: Albert Bonniers, 1946 (paperbound). Tr. by Erik Sjögren.

AA3(h). Thai.

> *Ho iang lae ruang san san laeo.* Bangkok: Progress, 1970. Tr. by Arporn Chartburus.

AA4. *A CHRISTMAS STORY*

AA4(a). German.

> *Eine Weihnachtsgeschichte.* Olten und Freiburg im Breisgau: Walter Verlag, 1969. Tr. by Hannelore Placzek.

AA5. *SHIP OF FOOLS*

AA5(a). Czech.

> *Lod bláznov.* Bratislava: Pravda, 1974. Tr. by Karol Dlouhý.

AA5(b). Danish.

> *Narre skibet.* Copenhagen: Gyldendals Forlagstrykkeri, 1964 (paperbound). Tr. by Hagmund Hansen.

AA5(c). Dutch.

   Het Narrenschip. Utrecht: A.W. Bruna & Zoon, 1962
   (paperbound).

AA5(d). Finnish.

   Narrilaiva. Jyväskylä: K.J. Gummerus, 1967. Tr. by
   Kaija Kauppi.

AA5(e). French.

   La nef des fous. Paris: Editions du Seuil, 1963
   (paperbound). Tr. by Marcelle Sibon. Rpt. 1970.

AA5(f). German.

   Das Narrenschiff. Reinbek bei Hamburg: Rowohlt
   Verlag GmbH, 1963. Tr. by Susanna Rademacher. Rpts.
   1966, 1967, 1969, 1976, 1978.

AA5(g). German.

   Das Narrenschiff. Stuttgart and Hamburg: Deutscher
   Bucherbund, 1965. Tr. by Susanna Rademacher.

AA5(h). German.

   Das Narrenschiff. Zurich: Buchclub Ex Libris, 1965. Tr.
   by Susanna Rademacher.

AA5(i). Greek.

   To pliō tōn tlellon. Athens: D. Daremos, 1970. Tr. by
   D.P. Kostelenos.

AA5(j). Hungarian.

   Bolondock hajója. Budapest: Europa Könyvkiadó, 1965.
   Tr. by Róna Ilona. Paperbound rpt. 1977.

AA5(k). Hungarian.

> *Bolondock hajója.* Budapest: Kriterion, 1972. Tr. by Róna Ilona.

AA5(l). Italian.

> *La nave dei folli.* Turin: Giulio Einaudi, 1964. Tr. by Adriana Motti.

AA5(m). Italian.

> *La nave dei folli.* Milan: A. Mondadori, 1974. Tr. by Adriana Motti

AA5(n). Japanese.

> *Gusha no fune.* Tokyo: Kawado Shobo, 1965. Two vols. Tr. by Kudô Akio.

AA5(o). Norwegian.

> *Narrenes skip.* Oslo: Reistad & Sønn, 1963 (paperbound). Tr. by Trygve Greiff.

AA5(p). Portuguese.

> *A nau dos insensatos.* Rio de Janeiro, Pôrto Alegre, and São Paulo: Editòra Globo, 1964 (paperbound). Tr. by Leonel Vallandro.

AA5(q). Portuguese.

> *A nave dos loucas.* Lisbon: Livros do Brasil, 1965. Tr. by Leonel Vallandro. Rpts. 1968, 1982.

AA5(r). Portuguese.

> *A nau dos insensatos.* São Paulo: Circulo do Livro, 1973. Tr. by Leonel Vallandro.

AA5(s). Polish.

> *Statek szaleńców*. Warsaw: Czytelnik, 1966. Tr. by Krystyna Tarnowska.

AA5(t). Romanian.

> *Corabia nebunilor*. Bucharest: Cartea Românească 1975. Tr. by Eugen B. Marian.

AA5(u). Slovenian.

> *Ladja norcev*. Ljubljana: Cankarjeva zalužba, 1970. Tr. by Rapa Šuklje.

AA5(v). Spanish.

> *La nave del mal*. Barcelona: Editorial Bruguera, 1963. Tr. by Baldomero Porta. Rpts. 1966, 1973.

AA5(w). Swedish.

> *Narrskeppet*. Stockholm: Alb. Bonniers boktryckeri, 1963 (paperbound). Tr. by Torsten Blomkvist.

AA5(x). Turkish.

> *Budalalar gemisi*. Istanbul: Halk Kitabevi, 1966. Tr. by Erdem Onur.

AA6. *THE COLLECTED STORIES*

AA6(a). Italian.

> *Bianco cavallo, Bianco cavaliere e altri racconti*. Turin: Giulio Einaudi Editore, 1966. Tr. by Lidia Storoni Mazzolani.

AA6(b). Japanese.

> *Hana saka yuda no ki*. Tokyo: Shinozaki shorin, 1982. Tr. by Kenji Kobayashi and Tazuko Okada.

AA6(c). Polish.

> *Bialy koń, bialy jezdźiec.* Warsaw: Czytelnik, 1971 (not complete). Tr. by Krystyna Tarnowska.

AA6(d). Polish.

> *Wino o poludniu.* Warsaw: Czytelnik, 1971. Tr. by Maria Skroczyńska.

AA6(e). Spanish.

> *Cuentos completos.* Buenos Aires: Editorial Sudamerica, 1982 (paperbound). Tr. by Carlos Gardini.

SECTION B
FICTION CONTRIBUTED TO
BOOKS AND PERIODICALS

In this section entries are chronological according to their first appearance. Brief plot summaries are given only for those works not to appear in *Collected Stories*. (A19). Mention is made of significant reprints and of some of the more recent reprints.

Note: The title "The Order" applies to more than one Porter work. It was the original title of the story (B20) which later became "The Journey." It is also the title that Porter eventually gave to the group of Miranda stories appearing in *The Leaning Tower* (A12). And it is the title of an anthology of Porter stories set in the South (A16). Also, *No Safe Harbor* (referred to in B 29, 30, 32, 33, 36) was one of the working titles for *Ship of Fools*. The three pieces entitled "Ship of Fools" (B36, 37, 38) are separate parts of the novel.

1920

B1. "The Shattered Star." *Everyland*, Jan. 1920, pp. 422–23.

A children's story of an Eskimo girl, Nayagta, and her role in the creation of Aurora Borealis.

B2. "The Faithful Princess." *Everyland*, Feb. 1920, pp. 42–43.

   A children's story of the love of a beautiful Indian princess and a handsome rajah.

B3. "The Magic Ear Ring." *Everyland*, March 1920, pp. 86–87.

   A children's story in which an Indian bride learns magic in order to recover her abducted husband from the Fairy Queen.

B4. "The Adventures of Hadji: A Tale of a Turkish Coffee House." *Asia*, 20 (Aug. 1920), 683–84.

   A brief story "retold" by Porter. A wife acts shrewdly when her husband is tempted by another woman.

1922

B5. "María Concepción." *Century*, 105 (Dec. 1922), 224–39.

   Reprinted in *Flowering Judas* (A4); *Flowering Judas and Other Stories* (A7); *Selected Short Stories* (A13); and *Collected Stories* (A19).

1923

B6. "The Martyr." *Century*, 106 (July 1923), 410–13.

   Reprinted in *Collected Stories* (A19).

1924

B7. "Virgin Violeta." *Century*, 109 (Dec. 1924), 261–68.

   Reprinted in *Collected Stories* (A19) and as "Violeta" in *Redbook*, 124 (Dec. 1964).

1927

B8. "He." *New Masses*, 3 (Oct. 1927), 13–15.

Reprinted in *Flowering Judas* (A4); *Flowering Judas and Other Stories*(A7); *The Old Order* (A16); *Collected Stories* (A19); Robert Penn Warren (ed.), *A Southern Harvest* (1937, rpt. 1972); Leslie Y. Robkin (ed.), *Psychopathology and Literature* (1966); Floyd C. Watkins and Richmond Croom Beatty (eds.), *The Literature of the South*, rev. ed. (1968); Wallace Stegner and Mary Stegner (eds.), *Great American Short Stories* (1985); and Clifton Fadiman (ed.), *The World of the Short Story: A Twentieth Century Collection* (1986).

1928

B9. "Magic." *transition*, 13 (Summer 1928), 229–31.

Reprinted in *Flowering Judas*(A4); *Flowering Judas and Other Stories* (A7); *The Old Order* (A16); *Collected Stories* (A19); and Irving Howe and Ilana Wiener Howe (eds.), *Short Shorts: An Anthology of the Shortest Stories* (1982).

B10. "Rope." In *The Second American Caravan*, ed. A. Kreymborg. New York: Macaulay, 1928, pp. 362–68.

Reprinted in *Flowering Judas* (A4); *Flowering Judas and Other Stories* (A7); *Collected Stories* (A19); *Senior Scholastic*, 28 (March 1936); and James B. Hall (ed.), *The Realm of Fiction: 65 Short Stories*, 2nd ed. (1970).

1929

B11. "The Jilting of Granny Weatherall." *transition*, 15 (Feb. 1929), 139–46.

Reprinted in *Flowering Judas* (A4); *Flowering Judas and Other Stories* (A7); *The Old Order* (A16); *Collected Stories* (A19); Abraham H. Lass and Norma L. Tasman

(eds.), *"The Secret Sharer" and Other Great Stories*
(1969); Blaze O. Bonazza, Emil Roy, and Sandra Roy
(eds.), *Studies in Fiction*, enl. 3rd ed. (1982); Sandra M.
Gilbert and Susan Gubar (eds.), *The Norton Anthology of
Literature by Women* (1985); Joseph F. Trimmer and C.
Wade (eds.), *Fictions* (1985); Ben Forkner and Patrick
Samway (eds.), *A Modern Southern Reader* (1986); Sanda
Eagleton (ed.), *Women in Literature: Life Stages Through
Stories, Poems, and Plays* (1988); and Laurence Perrine
(ed.), *Literature: Structure, Sound, and Sense*, 5th ed.
(1988).

B12. "Theft." *Gyroscope*, Nov. 1929, pp. 21–25.

Reprinted in *Flowering Judas and Other Stories* (A7);
Collected Stories (A19); Edward J. O'Brien (ed.), *The
Best Short Stories of 1930* (1930); R.V. Cassill (ed.), *The
Norton Anthology of Short Fiction*, 2nd ed. (1981); Blaze
O. Bonazza, Emil Roy, and Sandra Roy (eds.), *Studies in
Fiction*, enl. 3rd ed. (1982), and Peter S. Prescott (ed.), *The
Norton Book of American Short Stories* (1988).

1930

B13. "Flowering Judas." *Hound & Horn*, 3 (Spring 1930), 316–
31.

Reprinted in *Flowering Judas*(A4); *Flowering Judas and
Other Stories* (A7); *Collected Stories* (A19); Whit
Burnett (ed.), *This Is My Best* (1942); Allen Tate and John
Peale Bishop (eds.), *American Harvest* (1942); Arthur F.
Kinney, Kenneth W. Kimper, and Lynn Z. Bloom (eds.),
Symposium (1969); Charles Kaplan (ed.), *Literature in
America: The Modern Age* (1971); A. Walton Litz (ed.),
Major American Short Stories (1980); R.V. Cassill (ed.),
The Norton Anthology of Short Fiction, 2nd ed. (1981);
Blaze O. Bonazza, Emil Roy, and Sandra Roy (eds.),
Studies in Fiction (1982); Joseph F. Trimmer and C. Wade
(eds.), *Fictions* (1985); V.S. Pritchett (ed.), *The Oxford*

Book of Short Stories (1988); and David Madden (ed.), *The World of Fiction* (1989).

1932

B14. "The Cracked Looking-Glass." *Scribner's Magazine,* 91 (May 1932), 271–76, 313–20.

Reprinted in *Flowering Judas and Other Stories* (A7); *Selected Short Stories* (A13); *Collected Stories* (A19); and Edward J. O'Brien (ed.), *The Best Short Stories of 1933* (1933).

B15. "Hacienda." *Virginia Quarterly Review,* 8 (Oct. 1932), 556–69.

Reprinted in an expanded version as a separate publication (A6) and in *Flowering Judas and Other Stories* (A7); *Selected Short Stories* (A13); and *Collected Stories* (A19).

1934

B16. "That Tree." *Virginia Quarterly Review,* 10 (July 1934), 351–61.

Reprinted in *Flowering Judas and Other Stories* (A7); *Selected Short Stories* (A13); and *Collected Stories* (A19).

1935

B17. "The Grave." *Virginia Quarterly Review,* 11 (April 1935), 177–83.

Reprinted in *The Leaning Tower* (A12); *Selected Short Stories* (A13); *The Old Order* (A16); *Collected Stories* (A19); Edward J. O'Brien (ed.), *The Best Short Stories of 1936* (1936); Thomas D. Young, Floyd C. Watkins, and Richmond Croom Beatty (eds.), *The Literature of the South,* rev. ed. (1968); Robert Gorham Davis (ed.), *Ten*

Modern Masters: An Anthology of the Short Story (1972);
Wilfred Stone, Nancy Huddleston Packer, and Robert
Hoopes (eds.), *The Short Story: An Introduction* (1976);
Louis D. Rubin, Jr. (ed.), *The Literary South* (1979);
Nancy Sullivan (ed.), *The Treasury of American Short
Stories* (1981); James H. Pickering (ed.), *Fiction 100: An
Anthology of Short Stories*(1982); and Ellen C. Wynn
(ed.), *The Short Story: 50 Masterpieces* (1983).

B18. "The Circus." *Southern Review*, 1 (July 1935), 36–41.

Reprinted in *The Leaning Tower* (A12); *The Older
Order* (A16); *Collected Stories* (A19); Jay B. Hubbell
(ed.), *American Life in Literature*, Vol. II (1949); and
William Peden (ed.), *Short Fiction: Shape and Substance*
(1971).

1936

B19. "Noon Wine." *Signatures: Work in Progress*, 1 (Spring
1936). (Only a part of the completed work. See B22.)

B20. "The Old Order." *Southern Review*, 1 (Winter 1936), 495–
509. (Title later changed to "The Journey.")

Reprinted in *The Leaning Tower* (A12); *Selected Short
Stories* (A13); *The Old Order* (A16); Edward J. O'Brien
(ed.), *The Best Short Stories of 1937* (1937); and Ben
Forkner and Patrick Samway, S.J. (eds.), *Stories of the
Old South* (1989). Reprinted as "The Journey" in
Collected Stories (A19).

1937

B21. "Old Mortality." *Southern Review*, 2 (Spring 1937), 686–
735.

Reprinted in *Pale Horse, Pale Rider* (A9); *The Old
Order* (A16); *Collected Stories* (A19); Cleanth Brooks, Jr.,
and Robert Penn Warren (eds.), *Understanding Fiction*

(1943); Cleanth Brooks and Robert Penn Warren (eds.), *An Anthology of Stories from "The Southern Review"* (1953); Caroline Gordon and Allen Tate (eds.), *The House of Fiction*, 2nd ed. (1960); Nina Baym *et al.* (eds.), *The Norton Anthology of American Literature*, 2nd ed., Vol. 2 (1985); and Donald McQuade *et al.* (eds.), *The Harper American Literature*, Vol. 2 (1987).

B22. "Noon Wine." *Story*, 10 (June 1937), 71–103. (First appearance of the complete story. See B19.)

Reprinted as a separate publication (A8); and in *Pale Horse, Pale Rider* (A9); *Selected Short Stories* (A13); *Collected Stories* (A19); Charles Clerc and Louis Leiter (eds.), *Seven Contemporary Short Novels* (1969); Martha Foley (ed.), *200 Years of the Great American Short Stories* (1975); and Cleanth Brooks and Robert Penn Warren (eds.), *Understanding Fiction*, 3rd ed. (1979).

1938

B23. "Pale Horse, Pale Rider." *Southern Review*, 3 (Winter 1938), 417–66.

Reprinted in *Pale Horse, Pale Rider* (A9); *Collected Stories* (A19); and David Thorburn (ed.), *Initiation: Stories and Short Novels on Three Themes* (1976).

1939

B24. "The Downward Path to Wisdom." *Harper's Bazaar*, Dec. 1939, pp. 72–73, 140, 142, 144–45, 147.

Reprinted in *The Leaning Tower* (A12); *Selected Short Stories* (A13); *Collected Stories* (A19); Harry Hansen (ed.), *O. Henry Memorial Award Prize Stories of 1940* (1940); Edward J. O'Brien (ed.), *The Best Short Stories of 1940* (1940); Alan A. Stone and Sue Smart Stone (eds.), *The Abnormal Personality Through Literature* (1966); William Abrahams (ed.), *Fifty Years of the Short Story:*

From the O. Henry Awards, 1919–1970 (1970); Mark Schorer (ed.), *The Literature of America: Twentieth Century* (1970); and James Malfetti and Elizabeth M. Eidlitz (eds.), *Perspectives on Sexuality* (1972).

1940

B25. "A Day's Work." *Nation,* 150 (10 Feb. 1940), 205–07, 226–34.

Reprinted in *The Leaning Tower* (A12) and *Collected Stories* (A19).

1941

B26. "The Source." *Accent* (Spring 1941), pp. 144–47.

Reprinted in *The Leaning Tower* (A12); *The Old Order* (A16); and *Collected Stories* (A19).

B27. "The Leaning Tower." *Southern Review,* 7 (Autumn 1941), 219–79.

Reprinted in *The Leaning Tower* (A12) and *Collected Stories* (A19).

1944

B28. "Kein Haus, Keine Heimat." *Sewanee Review,* 52 (Autumn 1944), 465–82.

In revised form became a part of *Ship of Fools* (A18).

1945

B29. "The High Sea." *Partisan Review,* 12 (Fall 1945), 514–29.

Said to be from a "novel in progress," *No Safe Harbor.* In revised form became a part of *Ship of Fools* (A18).

1946

B30. "The Strangers." *Accent*, 6 (Summer 1946), 211–29.

Said to be from a "novel in progress," *No Safe Harbor.* In revised form became a part of *Ship of Fools* (A18).

1947

B31. "Embarkation." *Sewanee Review*, 55 (Jan. 1947), 1–23.

Said to be from a "novel in progress." In revised form became a part of *Ship of Fools* (A18).

1950

B32. "The Prisoner." *Harper's Magazine*, 201 (Oct. 1950), 88–96.

Said to be from *No Safe Harbor.* In revised form became a part of *Ship of Fools* (A18).

B33. "Under Weigh." *Harper's Magazine*, 201 (Nov. 1950), 80–88.

Said to be from the same "novel in progress" as the excerpt in the October issue (B32). In revised form became a part of *Ship of Fools* (A18).

B34. "The Exile." *Harper's Magazine*, 201 (Dec. 1950), 70–78.

Said to be from *No Safe Harbor.* In revised form became a part of *Ship of Fools* (A18).

1953

B35. "The Seducers: A Fragment." *Harper's Magazine* 207 (Nov. 1953), 33–38.

In revised form became a part of *Ship of Fools* (A18).

1956

B36. "Ship of Fools." *Atlantic Monthly*, 197 (March 1956), 33–38.

Said to be from *No Safe Harbor*. In revised form became a part of *Ship of Fools* (A18).

B37. "Ship of Fools." *Mademoiselle*, 47 (July 1958), 26–43, 85, 89–90.

Said to be from *No Safe Harbor*. In revised form became a part of *Ship of Fools* (A18).

1959

B38. "Ship of Fools." *Texas Quarterly*, 2 (Autumn 1959), 97–151.

In revised form became a part of *Ship of Fools* (A18).

1960

B39. "The Fig Tree." *Harper's*, 220 (June 1960), 55–59.

Reprinted in *Collected Stories* (A19).

B40. "Holiday." *Atlantic Monthly*, 206 (Dec. 1960), 44–56.

Reprinted in *Collected Stories* (A19); Richard Poirier (ed.), *Prize Stories 1962: The O. Henry Awards* (1962); Harry Hansen (ed.), *First-Prize Stories from the O. Henry Awards, 1919–1963* (1963); William Abrahams (ed.), *Fifty Years of the American Short Story: From the O. Henry Awards, 1919–1970* (1970); and Ben Forkner and Patrick Samway, S.J. (eds.), *Stories of the Modern South* (1986).

1971

B41. "The Spivvleton Mystery." *Ladies' Home Journal*, 88
(Aug. 1971), 74–75, 101.

A spoof of thrillers. Ada May Spivvleton, no longer
able to endure her face-like-a-goldfish husband, murders
him. His ghost returns to exact cunning revenge.

SECTION C
ESSAYS, LETTERS, POEMS

In this section entries are in chronological order. Mention is made of significant reprints.

1912

C1. "Texas by the Gulf of Mexico." *Gulf Coast Citrus Fruit Grower and Southern Nurseryman*, 2 (Jan. 1912), 1.

A poem. Author given as "Katherine Porter Koontz." Reprinted in Joan Givner, *Katherine Anne Porter: A Life* (G65).

1914

C2. "Brother Spoiled a Romance." *Chicago Sunday Tribune*, 29 March 1914, Section 6, p. 2.

Response to question "How Did He Propose?" posed in the women's section of the *Chicago Tribune*. "K.R.P." recounts the spoiling of her first proposal by her brother.

Reprinted in Joan Givner, *Katherine Anne Porter: A Life* (G65).

1920

C3. "The Real Ray." *Motion Picture Magazine*, 20 (Oct. 1920), 36–37, 102.

Interview with movie star Charles Ray, which Porter claims to have conducted in Los Angeles. Suggests that, because Ray is dignified and reserved, the questions were restricted to his work: the roles he chose in his early career (country adolescents in *The Coward, The Egg Crate Wallop*, and *Forty-Five Minutes from Broadway*), his admiration for country people, and his new contract with First National. Contrasts the urbane, educated Ray with the characters he depicts.

1921

C4. "Striking the Lyric Note in Mexico." *New York Call*, 16 Jan. 1921, "The Call Magazine," pp. 1, 3. (Written with Roberto Haberman.)

Describes the sympathetic handling of striking workers who intruded into the Armistice Day parade in Mexico City. Porter launches into an admiring account of the Mexican republic's enlightened method of dealing with recent workers' strikes.

C5. "The New Man and the New Order." *Magazine of Mexico*, March 1921, 5–15.

Porter's examination of President Alvaro Obrégon and the Mexican political situation after his inauguration in late 1920. The piece is aimed at reassuring American businessmen, the primary audience for this publication.

C6. "Xochimilco." *Christian Science Monitor*, 31 May 1921, p. 10.

Describes a March trip with others to the village of Xochimilco and a ride through the canal there. Porter describes the place and its inhabitants. "They seem a natural and gracious part of the earth they live in such close communion with, entirely removed from contact with the artificial world."

C7. "The Mexican Trinity." *Freeman*, 3 (3 Aug. 1921), 493–95.

Letter to the editor in which Porter reports from Mexico City on the political situation in Mexico. She surveys the petty dissension, the types of enemy within the gates, the coalition government, the intellectuals, the Indians, and the prospects of peace with the U.S. She concludes that the situation is controlled by the "Mexican trinity"—"oil, land, and the Church, the powers that hold this country securely in their grip."

Reprinted in slightly revised form in *The Days Before* (A14) and *Collected Essays* (A20).

1922

C8. Letter. Quoted in G.S.L., "A Letter from Mexico and the Gleam of Montezuma's Golden Roofs." *Christian Science Monitor*, 5 June 1922, p. 22.

The letter is "from an American woman who is assembling in Mexico City the National Art Exhibit which is soon to be brought to the United States." The letter discusses the Mexican folk art being collected for the exhibition, as well as the work of Diego Rivera and Adolfo Best-Maugard.

C9. "Where Presidents Have No Friends." *Century*, 104 (July 1922), 273–84.

Recounts a story told by a young Mexican-born Spaniard about the last days of the Carranza presidency in Mexico in order to illustrate that the President of Mexico "can trust no one except his enemies," who "will be faithful in contriving for his downfall." Outlines the present

political situation in Mexico under President Obrégon: his promises, his enemies, his political theory, his actions, his supporters, and his cabinet. This government is committed to "land, liberty, for all, forever."
Reprinted in *Collected Essays* (A20).

C10. "Two Ancient Mexican Pyramids—the Core of a City Unknown Until a Few Years Ago." *Christian Science Monitor*, 19 Sept. 1922, p. 7.

Discusses Mexican mythology in connection with the archaeological excavations and research being conducted by D. Manuel Gamio at San Juan Teotihuácan. Offers some of the current speculations on the origin of the city and temples being unearthed, as well as descriptions of them.

1923

C11. "Among Our Contributors." *Century*, 106 (July 1923), unpaged [6, 8].

Porter explains that she writes about Mexico "because that is my familiar country." She originates the falsehood that she had been in Mexico during the Madero revolution and explains that she returned to Mexico in 1920 "to study the renascence of Mexican art," an art "consanguine" with her own. She asserts that her America "has been a border-land of strange tongues and conmingled races," "the familiar and beloved things" of which she writes.
Reprinted as "Why I Write about Mexico" in *The Days Before* (A14) and *Collected Essays* (A20).

C12. "Enchanted." *Literary Review, New York Evening Post*, 3 (25 Aug. 1923), 921.

A poem.
Reprinted in *Collected Essays* (A20).

1924

C13. "Two Songs from Mexico." *The Measure: A Journal of Poetry*, 35 (Jan. 1924), 9.

> Two poems: "In Tepozotlan" and "Fiesta de Santiago." Reprinted in *Collected Essays* (A20).

C14. Requiescat——." *The Measure: A Journal of Poetry*, No. 38 (April 1924), 11.

> A poem.
> Reprinted as "Little Requiem" in *Collected Essays* (A20).

C15. "To a Portrait of the Poet." *Survey Graphic*, 5 (May 1924), 182.

> A translation of a poem by the seventeenth-century Mexican writer Sister Juana Inéz de la Cruz, accompanied by Porter's notes on the poet.

C16. "Corridos." *Survey Graphic*, 5 (May 1924), 157–59.

> The *corrido* "is the primitive, indigenous song of the Mexican people," in effect, a ballad. These songs are "a genuine folk poetry . . ., "an instant record of events, a moment caught in the quick of life." The concern "death, love, acts of vengeance, the appalling malignities of Fate." The *corrido* deals with "personalities, with intimate emotions, with deeds of heroism and crime," reveals "a taste for explicit horror," and is "saturated with faith in the supernatural." Porter makes other generalizations, describes the plot of "Marbella and the Newly-born," and concludes that as the Mexicans "live and die, they sing."

C17. "The Guild Spirit in Mexican Art." *Survey Graphic*, 5 (May 1924), 174–78.

> An interview with Diego Rivera. He describes the origins and foundations of the Mexican syndicate of

painters and sculptors. Rivera also recounts his efforts to revive the old art of mural decorating in Mexico and to bring together and concentrate the diverse powers of the younger Mexican artists. Describes the syndicate's work in decorating the walls of the Preparatory School and the Ministry of Education building with a history of the Mexican people from the creation to the recent revolution.

1925

C18. "From a Mexican Painter's Notebooks." *Arts,* 7 (Jan. 1925), 21–23.

A translation of an essay by Diego Rivera that rails at the "European bad taste" and "intellectual arrogance" of the bourgeois Creoles of Mexico, who have "attempted to dominate and deform the aesthetic life of the true Mexican." The "Indian aesthetic" is "a profound and direct expression of a pure art in relation to the life which produced it, a relation not obscured by petty cults, or corrupted with theories." Rivera perceives, "as the base of all creativeness," the "architectonic or constructive sense" that comprises the "inner life: the dynamics of forces, actions and resistances striving to balance each other in harmony with the laws of the visible universe and the secret soul of man." "Classic art has always been pre-creation, not copying. It has been produced in harmony with an inner spiritual rhythm, and has never occupied itself with simply reflecting images of an exterior world." Classic art "expresses the inner world through the vibrations of the painter living in harmony with the forces surrounding him."

1926

C19. "Winter Burial." *New York Herald Tribune, Books,* 14 Nov. 1926, p. 2.

A poem.
Reprinted in *Collected Essays* (A20).

1927

C20. "Children and Art." *Nation*, 124 (2 March 1927), 233–34.

Review of international show of children's drawing, painting, and clay modeling at the Whitney Studio Club. The show "had turned out to be a joint exhibition of the Mexican and American schools only." The only important differences were "of costume, distinct preferences in subject matter, a slightly stronger feeling for design and more patience in the Mexican pictures, a certain lack of details and an ampler sweep of line in the American pictures." "The children are true primitives" who were "left free" to evoke their "own images."

C21. "Introduction." *What Price Marriage*. New York: J.H. Sears, 1927, pp. 7–13.

Porter's ruminations on marriage conclude "Reason never did and never will play any part in the consummation of a happy marriage." (See A3.)

1930

C22. Letter. Quoted in "Harcourt, Brace News." *South Dakota Clubwoman*, 12 (Sept. 1930), 7.

The letter quoted concerns the reaction of Mexican Indians to the American colony's Fourth of July celebration in Mexico City.

C23. "Music of the Jarabe and Versos—Collected in the State of Hidalgo." *Mexican Folkways*, 6 (No. 1, 1930), 24.

Translation of the verses of a version of the *jarabe*, a Mexican folk dance which originated in the state of Jalisco.

1931

C24. "Leaving the Petate." *New Republic*, 65 (4 Feb. 1931), 318–20.

Argues from specific examples that the Indian, "when he gets a chance, is leaving the *petate*," a woven straw mat used as a sort of sleeping mat. The Indian sometimes views it as "a symbol of racial and economic degradation from which there is no probable hope of rising." The specific examples are Mexican-Indian women of Porter's acquaintance who work as domestic servants; Porter details their habits.

Reprinted in *The Days Before* (A14) and *Collected Essays* (A20).

1932

C25. "Bouquet for October." *Pagany*, 3 (Winter 1932), 21–22.

A poem.

1933

C26. "Katherine Anne Porter, 1894– ." *Authors Today and Yesterday*, ed. Stanley J. Kunitz. New York: H.W. Wilson, 1933, pp. 538–39.

"Autobiographical sketch of Katherine Anne Porter, American Author." She gives her birthdate as 1894, claims to have been "brought up in Texas and Louisiana, and educated in small southern schools for girls." She asserts that writing stories "has been the basic and absorbing occupation, the intact line" of her life, a vocation she never chose and for which she was and is "willing to live and die." She also claims to be the "great-great-great-grandaughter of Daniel Boone."

1934

C27. "A Bright Particular Faith—A.D. 1700." *Hound & Horn,* 7 (Jan–March 1934), 246–57.

A chapter from never-published biography of Cotton Mather. Details Mather's actions and thoughts during his wife Abigail's illness ("he felt the rays of a particular faith, a definite belief that she would recover") through her eventual death, a period of seven months. After her death, he grew to believe "that death and Abigail had been secretly, firmly allied against him. . . . She had defeated him, had overruled his prayers with her own."
Reprinted in *Collected Essays* (A20).

1937

C28. "Readers' Forum—on 'The Wave.'" *New Masses,* 23 (18 May 1937), 22.

Refutation of negative reviews of the Mexican movie *The Wave.* Porter praises its content and form highly and excoriates the critics who assessed it negatively.

C29. Letter to Philip Horton. Quoted in his *Hart Crane.* New York: Norton, 1937, pp. 285–87.

Excerpt from a letter in which Porter recounts some of Hart Crane's exploits in Mexico in 1931.

C30. "The Olive Grove." . . . *and Spain Sings: Fifty Loyalist Ballads Adapted by American Poets,* ed. M.J. Benardete and Rolfe Humphries. New York: Vanguard, 1937, p. 10.

A translation of a poem by R. Beltram Logroño.

1938

C31. Letter to Donald Ogden Stewart. In *Writers Take Sides—Letters about the War in Spain from 418 American Authors.* New York: League of American Writers, 1938, p. 47.

Porter's reply to circular letter of 1 February 1938 from Donald Ogden Stewart, President of the League of American Writers. The questions posed included: "Are you for, or are you against Franco and Fascism?" "Are you for, or are you against the legal government and the people of Republican Spain?" Porter expresses opposition to Franco and fascism and support for the "legal government and people of Spain." She adds comments on opposition to dictatorship and propaganda and acts of war used to impose one form of government on any nation.

1939

C32. "The Situation in American Writing: Seven Questions." *Partisan Review* 6 (Summer 1939), 36–39.

Porter's response to questions posed by the editors of *Partisan Review* on American writing. The questions concern the "usable past," audience, criticism, income, political or philosophical allegiance, "literary nationalism," and the next world war. Porter comments on her material ("memory, legend, personal experience, and acquired knowledge"), Henry James, Walt Whitman, the growing audience for "serious American writing," economic and political pressures on criticism, the economic insecurity of the artist, her interest in the individual human being, American politics and subjects, and her pacifism.

Reprinted as "1939: The Situation in American Writing" in *The Days Before* (A14), *Collected Essays* (A20), and *The Partisan Reader* (1946).

C33. "Happy Land." *Vogue*, 94 (1 Nov. 1939), 48–49, 110–11, 113.

Recounts Porter's visit to seven antebellum mansions in St. Francisville, Louisiana. Also discusses the history of the parish and town as well as its association with Audubon.

Reprinted as "Audubon's Happy Land" in *The Days Before* (A14), *Collected Essays* (A20), and *Vogue's First Reader* (1944).

1940

C34. "A Goat for Azazel (A.D. 1688)." *Partisan Review*, 7 (May–June 1940), 188–99.

Chapter from never-published biography of Cotton Mather. Describes Mather's 1688 encounter with witchcraft, concerning Bridget Glover and Martha Goodwin. Porter suggests that Mather himself may have believed in sacrificing individuals to propitiate the devil (Azazel).

Reprinted in *Collected Essays* (A20).

C35. "Notes on a Criticism of Thomas Hardy." *Southern Review*, 6 (Summer 1940), 150–61.

Reaction to and refutation of T.S. Eliot's negative assessment of Hardy's work. The "intransigent, measureless force [in human nature] divided against itself, in conflict alike with its own system of laws and the unknown laws of the universe, was the real theme of Hardy's novels." Porter defends Hardy's content and style. "In the end his work was the sum of his experiences, he arrived at his particular true testimony; along the way, sometimes, many times, he wrote sublimely."

Reprinted as "On a Criticism of Thomas Hardy" in *The Days Before* (A14) and *Collected Essays* (A20).

C36. "Anniversary in a Country Cemetery." *Harper's Bazaar*, Nov. 1940, p. 139.

A poem. (See A10.)
Reprinted in *Collected Essays* (A20).

C37. "Introduction." *Flowering Judas and Other Stories*. New York: Modern Library, 1940, pp. [vii–viii].

Porter comments on the reprinting here of these "first fruits," fragments of a much larger plan which I am still engaged in carrying out, and they are what I was then able to achieve in the way of order and form and statement in a period of grotesque dislocations in a whole society when the world was heaving in the sickness of millennial change." She asserts that she has tried "to grasp the meaning of those threats [of world catastrophe], to trace them to their sources and to understand the logic of this majestic and terrible failure of the life of man in the Western World." She claims the arts "represent the substance of faith and the only reality."
Reprinted in *The Days Before* (A14) and *Collected Essays* (A20).

C38. "Notes on Writing—From the Journal of Katherine Anne Porter." *New Directions in Prose and Poetry*, ed. James Laughlin. Norfolk, Conn.: New Directions, 1940, pp. 195–204.

These excerpts from Porter's journal—from Berlin in 1931 and 1932, Basel in 1932, and Paris in 1936—range over a variety of topics concerning writing: technique, Rilke, Nietzsche, Wagner, religion, Tolstoy, an incident in Texas, a scene in Basel, sensational newspaper stories.
Reprinted with two sections omitted as "An Opinion: Notes on Writing," *Mademoiselle* 69 (Oct. 1969). Reprinted in its entirety in *Collected Essays* (A20).

1941

C39. "Now at Last a House of My Own." *Vogue*, 98 (1 Sept. 1941), 64–65, 115.

Porter recounts her long desire to own a "little house in the country," a desire which finally led to her purchase of South Hill, near Saratoga Springs, New York, in 1941. She describes the joys and tribulations of readying it for habitation. "I had become almost overnight a ton weight of moral, social, and financial responsibility."
Reprinted as "A House of My Own" in *The Days Before* (A14) and *Collected Essays* (A20).

C40. "Introduction." In Eudora Welty. *A Curtain of Green*. New York: Harcourt, Brace and World, 1941, pp. xi–xxiii.

Surveys the details of Welty's life and her growth as an artist. Porter also comments on professional teachers of writing, the artist and political systems, as well as the publication history of Welty's early stories and the individual stories in *A Curtain of Green*. "Splendid beginning that this is, it is only the beginning."
Reprinted as "Eudora Welty and 'A Curtain of Green'" in *The Days Before* (A14) and *Collected Essays* (A20).

C41. "(c. 1661–1731)—Defoe—*Moll Flanders*." In *Invitation to Learning*, ed. Huntington Cairns, Allen Tate, and Mark Van Doren. New York: Random House, 1941, pp. 135–51.

One of the transcripts from direct recordings of unrehearsed conversations broadcast by Columbia Broadcasting System on coast-to-coast radio. Porter was the guest of Huntington Cairns, Mark Van Doren, and Allen Tate in discussing Defoe's *Moll Flanders*. Porter comments on both the content and the form of the novel: its characterization, its criticism of contemporary society, its "cumulative method," its morality. Porter defines "the great art" as the ability "to look at the world and individuals and present characters that readers will recognize and will know and feel they know."

1942

C42. "Question of Royalties." *New York Times*, 8 March 1942, Section 8, p. 10.

In this letter to the *Times* Radio Editor, Porter supports the position of an earlier letter that Americans not support Germany indirectly through royalties to German musicians. "Every human being in this country should simply see to it, for himself, that not one penny of his money shall be spent for the aid and comfort of the enemy. . . . [Enemy artists] are our enemies not as artists, but as Nazis, and as Nazis they have forfeited any right to profit of this country."

C43. "Touché." *Nation*, 154 (11 April 1942), 444.

Porter responds to Polly Boyden's letter to the editor concerning her 21 March review of Boyden's *The Pink Egg* (E49). "Everything is so confused in that book the reviewer got confused too."

C44. "The Charmed Life." *Vogue*, 99 (15 April 1942), 45, 97.

Brief sketch of W.A. Nivens, an American who spent his adult life in Mexico discovering and digging up buried Indian cities. Porter was disabused of her "sentimental notion of him" over the course of their relationship. She concludes that he "bore a charmed life. Nothing would ever happen to him," despite his dangerous knowledge and position.

Reprinted in *The Days Before* (A14) and *Collected Essays* (A20).

C45. "Affectation of Praehiminincies." *Accent*, 2 (Spring 1942), 131–38; (Summer 1942), 226–32.

Chapter from never-published biography of Cotton Mather. Details the life of Cotton Mather in the years 1663–1675, including his education and the growth of his exalted self-importance. He developed his "single aspiration" to "identify publicly and unmistakably his personal interests and ambitions with the will of God." Reprinted in *Collected Essays* (A20).

C46. "No Plot, My Dear, No Story." *Writer*, 55 (June 1942), 167–68.

Tells a "fable of our times" about the rejection of a solicited short story. It had "no plot, my dear—no *story*." Contrasts the requirements for the trade of writing with those for the art or profession of writing. Asserts that it "is simply not true" that all authors aspire to publication in "the high-paying magazines." Reprinted in slightly revised form in *The Days Before* (A14) and *Collected Essays* (A20).

C47. "American Statement." *Mademoiselle*, 15 (July 1942), 21, 72–73.

Meditation on peace and liberty during World War II. Asserts admiration for those working, fighting, and dying. Refutes the assertion "that peace make spirits slothful and bodies flabby." Peace gave the time and right to "fight for our abilities as a people"; this right is now suspended because of war. Porter calls for examination of the true nature of these threatened abilities, their origins, and meanings and for decision on "what their value is and where we should be without them." Reprinted as "American Statement: 4 July 1942" in *The Days Before* (A14) and as "Act of Faith: 4 July 1942" in *Collected Essays* (A20).

C48. "Transplanted Writers: A Symposium." *Books Abroad*, 16 (July 1942): 274.

Porter's reply to a circular letter concerning the consequences of the displacement of "the ablest German authors and journalists" and "the most articulate of the Spanish intelligentsia," both to the intellectuals themselves and the countries involved. Porter feels that being "beaten and driven out of one's own place is the gravest disaster that can occur to a human being." She expresses hope that those who came to the United States will stand with Americans to help "put an end to this stampede of human beings being driven like sheep over one frontier after another." Like E.M. Forster, Porter feels that the only possibilities for real order are religion and art. The uprooted should remember "to labor at preserving the humanities and the dignity of the human spirit."
Reprinted as "1942: Transplanted Writers" in *The Days Before* (A14) and *Collected Essays* (A20).

C49. "(1707–1754)—Henry Fielding—*Tom Jones*." In *The New Invitation to Learning*, ed. Mark Van Doren. New York: Random House, 1942, pp. 192–205.

Transcript of a radio discussion of *Tom Jones* with Allen Tate and Mark Van Doren. Porter comments on Fielding and the novel, which she characterizes as "perfect in style and plot."

C50. "(1832–1898)—Lewis Carroll—*Alice in Wonderland*." In *The New Invitation to Learning*, ed. Mark Van Doren. New York: Random House, 1942, pp. 206–20.

Transcript of a radio discussion of *Alice in Wonderland* with Bertrand Russell and Mark Van Doren. Porter found it a "horror story" when she was a child, a "terrible mixture of suffering and cruelty and rudeness and false logic and traps for the innocent." Porter asserts that children should read adult literature and not just what is written for them.

C51. "(1843–1916)—Henry James—*The Turn of the Screw*." In *The New Invitation to Learning*, ed. Mark Van Doren. New York: Random House, 1942, pp. 221–33.

Transcript of a radio discussion of *The Turn of the Screw* with Allen Tate and Mark Van Doren. Porter comments on James's technique and preoccupation with evil, the character of the governess, and the theme of the conflict between good and evil in the minds of men.

Reprinted in Joan Givner (ed.), *Katherine Anne Porter: Conversations* (G66).

C52. "Introduction." In *Fiesta in November—Stories from Latin America*, ed. Angel Flores and Dudley Poore. Boston: Houghton Mifflin, 1942, pp. 1–10.

Porter asserts that this volume gives "a view of South American life and people that I have never found anywhere else." She assesses which things are and are not depicted in the stories, the themes, subjects, construction, and style. She comments on twelve of the eighteen stories.

C53. "Introduction—Notes on the Life and Death of a Hero." In *The Itching Parrot (El Periquillo Sarmiento)*, by J.J. Fernández de Lizárdi. Translated by Porter [and Eugene Pressly]. Garden City, N.Y.: Doubleday, Doran, 1942, pp. xiii–xliii.

Surveys the life and work of the Mexican writer José Joaquín Fernández de Lizárdi, whom Porter characterizes as a "humanist reformer." She briefly discusses the novel, "a true picture" of the people of Mexico. "Lizárdi was not the best of men, nor the bravest, he was only a very good man and a very faithful one." (See A11.)

Reprinted as "Notes on the Life and Death of a Hero" in *The Days Before* (A14) and *Collected Essays* (A20).

C54. "Katherine Anne Porter [Homage to Ford Madox Ford—1875–1939]." *New Directions—Number Seven—1942*, ed. James Laughlin. Norfolk, Conn.: New Directions, 1942, pp. 478–79.

One of over twenty short tributes to Ford that were printed here. Porter says that one can learn what the vocation of writing is from reading Ford's works—"You will learn from him what the effort really is, what the pains, and what the rewards, of a real writer." Reprinted in *The Days Before* (A14) and *Collected Essays* (A20).

C55. "Porter, Katherine Anne (May 15, 1894–   )." In *Twentieth Century Authors—A Biographical Dictionary of Modern Literature*, ed. Stanley J. Kunitz and Howard Haycraft. New York: H.W. Wilson, 1942, pp. 1118–19.

Revised version of sketch in an earlier edition (C26). It adds details of awards and last two marriages.

C56. "Why She Selected Flowering Judas." In *This is My Best*, ed. Whit Burnett and Burton C. Hoffman. New York: Dial, 1942, pp. 539–40.

In explaining why she chose "Flowering Judas" for inclusion in this collection, Porter explains its genesis and writing. The "central idea" of the story is "self-delusion." "I offer this story . . . because it comes very near to being what I meant for it to be, and I suppose an author's choice of his own work must always be decided by such private knowledge of the margin between intention and the accomplished fact."

1943

C57. "A Song (from the French of Clément Marot) [1496–1544]." In "Three Poets from the South." *Mademoiselle*, 16 (Feb. 1943), 180.

A translated poem.

C58. "Miss Porter Adds a Comment." *Nation*, 156 (6 March 1943), 358–59.

Letter to the editor in response to Charles Duff's defense of her translation of *The Itching Parrot* (A11), earlier reviewed by Lionel Trilling (J77). Porter details her failure to get a full version of the novel published in English. "I shall be glad to see a full translation published by someone else."
Reprinted in *Collected Essays* (A20).

C59. "The Days Before." *Kenyon Review*, 5 (Autumn 1943), 481–94.

Primarily a discussion of the family background, education, and experiences of Henry James which contributed to his growth as an artist; "there lay in the depths of his being the memory of a lost paradise; it was in the long run the standard by which he measured the world he learned so thoroughly, accepted in certain ways . . . after such infinite pains."
Reprinted in slightly revised form in *The Days Before* (A14) and *Collected Essays* (A20).

1944

C60. "Portrait: Old South." *Mademoiselle*, 18 (Feb. 1944), 89, 151–54.

Porter recalls family legends passed on to her but focuses mainly on her paternal grandmother: "her presence was singularly free from peaks and edges and the kind of color that leaves a trail of family anecdotes. She left the lingering perfume and the airy shimmer of grace about her memory."
Reprinted in *The Days Before* (A14) and *Collected Essays* (A20).

C61. "Current Comment—China's Plight." *Saratogian*, 15 Dec. 1944, p. 6.

Letter to the editor, signed by Porter, Elizabeth Ames, Agnes Smedley, Eleanor Clark, Caroline Slade, Joseph S.G. Bolton, Carl E. Smith. It solicits contributions for Chinese writers, artists, musicians, scientists, and professors who are being persecuted as a result of "internal Chinese reaction."

1946

C62. "'Public Shame to Our Intelligence as a Nation'— Katherine Anne Porter." *Westwood Hills* (Calif.) *Press* 23 Aug. 1946, pp. 1, 5.

Porter's response to the Hearst newspapers' attack on Edmund Wilson's *Memoirs of Hecate County* scourges the Hearst press, "a malignant influence in American life." The particular attack on Wilson's book is "a symptom of the whole conspiracy against human rights. . . . It is time for the American people to decide whether they are willing to submit their government, their religion, their public ethics, and their private morals—as well as their choice of what they shall read in the evenings—to the dictatorship of a pack of dreary illiterates who are, by the record, moral imbeciles as well."

C63. "A Christmas Story." *Mademoiselle*, 24 (Dec. 1946), 155, 277–79.

Recollections of niece Mary Alice Holloway. Porter recalls telling medieval legends to her niece in 1918 and their shopping together for the niece's mother. Mary Alice is "a budding diplomat" because she does not want her mother to know she doesn't believe in Santa Claus.
Reprinted as a separate publication by *Mademoiselle* (A17) and with drawings by Ben Shahn (in 1967 edition). Also reprinted in *McCalls*, 95 (Dec. 1967), and *Washington Post, Potomac*, 21 Dec. 1975.

1947

C64. "Who Will Be the Judge?" *Nation*, 164 (24 May 1947), 640.

Letter to the editor opposing legislation aimed at suppressing the subversive activities of Communists. She urges liberals to "clear their heads and look the situation in the face before they are driven underground to form a resistance movement to fascism or communism . . . in our own country."
Reprinted as A Letter to the Editor of *The Nation* in *Collected Essays* (A20).

C65. "Katherine Anne Porter Writes Views on Debate." *Westwood Hills (Calif.) Press*, 4 Sept. 1947, pp. 1, 6.

Porter's observations concerning the debate, on Communism in Hollywood, which took place on "The Town Meeting of the Air" (radio). The debate, which Porter likened to a prize fight, pitted Mrs. Lela Rogers and Senator Jack Tenney against Emmet Lavery and Albert Dekker. Porter felt that Lavery and Dekker were superior on the bases of "manners and morals in discussion, on method of argument, on personal dignity and fearlessness."
Reprinted as "On Communism in Hollywood" in *Collected Essays* (A20).

C66. "Books I Have Liked." *New York Herald Tribune, Books*, 7 Dec. 1947, p. 12.

Porter lists Henry Adams's *The Formative Years*, F.O. Matthiessen's *The James Family*, Raoul de Roussy de Sales's *The Making of Yesterday*.

C67. "Gertrude Stein: A Self Portrait." *Harper's*, 195 (Dec. 1947), 519–28.

Porter harshly characterizes Gertrude Stein's life and work. "Wise or silly or nothing at all, down everything goes on the page with the air of everything being equal, unimportant in itself, important because it happened to her and she was writing about it." Porter focuses on Stein's acquisitiveness, her "rights of possession." She wanted "success" and succeeded in becoming a celebrity. Near the end of her life she struggled "slowly, slowly, much too late to unfold."

Reprinted as "The Wooden Umbrella" in *The Days Before* (A14) and *Collected Essays* (A20).

1948

C68. "Love and Hate." *Mademoiselle*, 27 (Oct. 1948), 137, 202, 204, 206.

Hatred is "the necessary enemy and ally" of love, especially in contemporary times when chivalric "Romantic Love" has managed to get into marriage, where it was never intended to belong. We "desire to be unhappy and . . . we create our own sufferings, and out of these sufferings we salvage our fragments of happiness." Reprinted as "The Necessary Enemy" in *The Days Before* (A14) and *Collected Essays* (A20).

C69. "Books I Have Liked." *New York Herald Tribune, Books,* 5 Dec. 1948, p. 12.

Porter lists Allen Tate's *On the Limits of Poetry*, Robert Graves's *The White Goddess*, Virginia Woolf's *The Moment and Other Essays*.

1949

C70. "'The Best Books I Read This Year'—Twelve Distinguished Opinions." *New York Times, Book Review*, 4 Dec. 1949, p. 4.

Porter lists George Orwell's *Nineteen Eighty-Four*, Eudora Welty's *The Golden Apples*, Willa Cather's *Willa Cather on Writing*, Joseph Campbell's *The Hero with a Thousand Faces, The Journals of André Gide, 1928–1939, The Diaries of Franz Kafka,* Henri Michaux's *A Barbarian in Asia,* Arturo Barea's *Lorca: The Poet and His People,* Harold Nicolson's *Benjamin Constant,* and Francis R.B. Godolphin's *The Latin Poets.*

1950

C71. "The Flower of Flowers." *Flair,* 1 (May 1950), 96–106.

Porter's appreciation of the rose includes its history, legends, symbolism, perfume, and uses.
Reprinted in slightly revised form in *The Days Before* (A14) and *Collected Essays* (A20).

C72. "Measures for Song and Dance." *Harper's,* 200 (May 1950), 80–81.

A poem.
Reprinted in *Collected Essays* (A20).

C73. "Pierre Joseph Redouté." *Flair,* 1 (May 1950), 107–08.

Biographical sketch of the French artist who anatomized and engraved new roses.
Reprinted in revised form as "A Note on Pierre-Joseph Redouté" in *The Days Before* (A14), *Collected Essays* (A20), and Daniel Halpern (ed.), *Writers on Artists* (1988).

C74. "The Future Is Now." *Mademoiselle,* 32 (Nov. 1950), 75, 130–32.

Porter's contemplation of the atom bomb stresses the importance of living for each moment, notes both the advances and the failures of mankind, and sees the atom bomb as on a continuum beginning with man's discovery of fire. "I imagine that when we want something better, we may have it: at perhaps no greater price than we have already paid for the worse."

Reprinted in revised form in *The Days Before* (A14) and *Collected Essays* (A20).

1951

C75. "Marriage is Belonging." *Mademoiselle*, 33 (Oct. 1951), 79, 134–35.

Porter's observations on marriage: "love is the only excuse for marriage, if any excuse is necessary." Contemporary marriage "is holding up rather well." All successful marriages are comprised of people who "know, or are capable of learning, the nature of love." Reprinted in revised form in *The Days Before* (A14) and *Collected Essays* (A20).

1952

C76. "Allocution de Mme. Katherine Anne Porter." *L'Oeuvre de XXe Siècle-Exposition International des Arts— Conferences et Debats Littéraires Seance Inaugurale— Salle Gaveau—16 May 1952.* n.p., n.d., pp. 14–17.

Porter's opening address at this Paris conference concerns the role of the artist. "He has to speak to all of us and interpret for all of us and therefore he is very often a touchstone, or a magnet." She briefly criticizes the methods of awarding grants and prizes to artists. She asserts that artists should steer clear of politics: "If you tie yourself to any system, to any temporary, transitory thing like a political creed, you dehumanize yourself, you narrow yourself, so that you no longer can speak to every human being, to all human beings, and the artist must speak to every one without exception." Reprinted, with last paragraph omitted, as "Opening Speech at Paris Conference, 1952" in *Collected Essays* (A20).

C77. "Reflections on Willa Cather." *Mademoiselle*, 35 (July 1952), 62–65, 102–04.

Ranges over Cather's life and work and over Porter's own reading of Willa Cather and others. Cather was "a good artist" who was "provincial," "little concerned" with "aesthetics," much concerned with "morals," and "reserved." Cather is a curiously immovable shape, monumental, virtue itself in her art and a symbol of virtue—like certain churches, in fact, an exemplary woman, revered and neglected.

Reprinted in revised form in *The Days Before* (A14) and *Collected Essays* (A20).

C78. "Some Important Writers Speak for Themselves—Katherine Anne Porter." *New York Herald Tribune, Book Review*, 12 Oct. 1952, p. 8.

Porter lists among her pastimes and interests: jai alai, polo, swimming, dancing, climbing, canoeing, sailing, ballet, little theater, painting, bowling, music, photography, cooking, gardening, poker, conversation, and cats.

C79. "Books I Have Liked." *New York Herald Tribune, Books*, 7 Dec. 1952, p. 8.

Porter lists Eleanor Clark's *Rome and a Villa*, Wallace Stevens's *The Necessary Angel*, and George Orwell's *Homage to Catalonia*.

C80. "Foreword." *The Days Before*. New York: Harcourt, Brace, 1952, pp. vii–viii.

Contrasts the nonfiction here published with her fiction. "The two ways of working helped and supported each other: I needed both." (See A14.)

1954

C81. "A Defense of Circe." *Mademoiselle*, 39 (June 1954), 46, 48, 96–97.

Porter retells the story of Circe from *The Odyssey*, painting her in a favorable light. Porter warns that Greek myth should not be interpreted with moral and theological meanings: "It is our fault and our utter loss if we tarnish the bright vision with our guilt-laden breath, our nightmare phantasies."
Reprinted in slightly revised form in *Collected Essays* (A20).

C82. "Here Is My Home." *Perfect Home*, Nov. 1954, p. 3.

Porter describes her previous search for home, concluding that "home materially speaking is not a *place* for me, and I have abandoned the idea perhaps for good." Home, rather, "is a continuous, deep, sunny revery."

1955

C83. "Adventure in Living." *Mademoiselle*, 41 (July 1955), 28–34.

Exploration of the difference between adventure and experience, with illustrations from Porter's own life. "Adventure is something you seek for pleasure, or even profit. . . ; for the illusion of being more alive than ordinarily, the thing you will to occur; but experience is what really happens to you in the long run; the truth that finally overtakes you." The main illustration involves Porter's first bullfight. She, like a youth described by St. Augustine, "had been weak enough to be led into adventure but strong enough to turn it into experience."

Reprinted in slightly edited form as "St. Augustine and the Bullfight" in *Collected Essays* (A20) and Maureen Howard (ed.), *The Penguin Book of Contemporary Essays* (1984).

C84. "November in Windham." *Harper's*, 211 (Nov. 1955), 44.

A poem.
Reprinted in *Collected Essays* (A20).

C85. "Foreword." In Régine Pernoud. *The Retrial of Joan of Arc—The Evidence at the Trial for Her Rehabilitation—1450–1456.* Trans. by J.M. Cohen. New York: Harcourt, Brace, 1955, pp. v–viii.

Praises the book highly: Pernoud's "method, so direct and knowledgeable, so dedicated to the discovery and presentation of the mystical truth which inheres in the accumulated, eagerly honest, spoken and recorded testimony, simply leads the way to that truth."

C86. "No Masters or Teachers." In *New Voices #2: American Writing Today*, ed. Don M. Wolfe. New York: Hendricks House, 1955, pp. 373–74.

Porter explains how she became a writer. She had "no masters or teachers," but "write I would, it was a passion and a compulsion and a long ordeal, but I had no choice." She discusses the writing of "María Concepción" and "The Jilting of Granny Weatherall."

C87. "Porter, Katherine Anne (May 15, 1894–)." *Twentieth Century Authors—First Supplement—A Biographical Dictionary of Modern Literature*, ed. Stanley J. Kunitz and Veneta Colby. New York: H.W. Wilson, 1955, p. 785.

Supplement to earlier entry (C55). It includes Porter's comment on her work in progress: "Several things; but no more promises, no more announcements of publication. When things get finished, I shall publish, as usual."

1956

C88. "Live Memories of a Growing Season." *Village Voice*, 29 Aug. 1956, p. 4.

Letter to the editor in which Porter recalls the places she lived in Greenwich Village in the 1920's and in 1936. "I would not have missed being there just when I was there for anything."

Reprinted as A Letter to the Editor of the *Village Voice* in *Collected Essays* (A20).

C89. "'Noon Wine': The Sources." *Yale Review*, 46 (Sept. 1956), 22–39.

Porter's "meditation" on the sources from her childhood for the "short novel" "Noon Wine." Articulates the idea of "criminal collusion." Porter suggests that her childhood observation of the couple who form the basis for the Thompsons brought her "a spiritual enlightenment, some tenderness, some first wakening of charity in [her] self-centered heart."

Reprinted in *Collected Essays* (A20) and Robert Penn Warren (ed.), *Katherine Anne Porter: A Collection of Critical Essays* (H113).

C90. "The Gift of Woman." *Woman's Home Companion*, Dec. 1956, pp. 29–32, 56.

The "besetting virtue of women" is the "incontinence of giving all." The "natural genius of woman is for love and giving gladly." Contemporary, "incredibly young women who exempt themselves from nothing and yet carry everything so gracefully with lifted head and smiling face" are similar to the Virgin Mary in "the womanly genius for giving gladly, the gift for happiness and the wish to bring happiness to others."

C91. "Remarks on the Agenda by Katherine Anne Porter." *The Arts and Exchange of Persons—Report of a Conference on the Arts and Exchange of Persons Held October 4 and*

5, 1956, at the Institute of International Education. New York: Institute of International Education, 1956, pp. 70–75.

Porter answers nine questions about foreign stays for writers. She asserts that they are invaluable as education, facilitate interaction with the citizens of the foreign country, should include more exchanges, and should remain apolitical. She also discusses suggestions for facilitating broadened exchange, choosing the individuals, and obligations to sponsors.

Reprinted as "Remarks on the Agenda" in *Collected Essays* (A20).

1957

C92. "Katherine Anne Porter Remembers: Romany Marie, Joe Gould—Two Legends Come to Life." *Village Voice*, 11 Sept. 1957, pp. 3, 9.

Porter briefly gives her recollections of two Greenwich Village characters—Romany Marie, in 1926–27 and later, and Joe Gould, in 1930.

Reprinted as "Romany Marie, Joe Gould—Two Legends Come to Life" in *Collected Essays* (A20).

C93. "After a Long Journey." *Mademoiselle*, 46 (Nov. 1957), 142–43.

A poem.
Reprinted in *Collected Essays* (A20).

1958

C94. "Saturday's Child." *Newsweek*, 52 (15 Sept. 1958), 10.

Letter to the editor in which Porter corrects misquotation of an old rhyme: "It's Thursday's child who 'has far to go.'"

C95. Letter to students, Thomas A. Edison High School, Tulsa, Oklahoma. *Vignettes*, 4 (1958–59). Letter dated 24 Oct. 1958.

"Practise [sic] an art for love and the happiness of your life—you will find it outlasts about everything but breath!"

1959

C96. Letter to Paul Michael. Quoted in his Letter to the Editor. *New York Times, Book Review*, 8 March 1959, p. 36.

A response to a letter from Michael to Porter, in which he asked about her use of symbols. Porter explains her use of symbols, the silver dove in "The Grave," and her belief that "the meanings of stories" are more important than symbolic searching.

C97. "A Sprig of Mint for Allen." *Sewanee Review*, 67 (Autumn 1959), 545–46.

A tribute to Allen Tate for his sixtieth birthday. "I wish my old friend joy of his years in health and just the right degree of disturbance, upset, uproar, and controversy that he can best thrive on to write his poetry."
Reprinted in *Collected Essays* (A20).

1961

C98. Letter to the Editor. *Yale Review*, 50 (March 1961), 465–67.

Porter is one of the "American intellectuals" asked by the *Yale Review* to respond to the Nicola Chiaromonte and Ignazio Silone "Declaration of Solidarity with the French Intellectuals" who were being prosecuted for their opposition to the war in Algeria. Porter expresses sympathy for the civil disobedience of the French intellectuals but remains skeptical of the Italians' initiative, joining in, however, "with the Italian protest, with . . . rather mixed feelings." She supports *Yale Review*'s circulating the Italian Declaration, using that support as an opportunity to quote her axiom: "There is no such thing as an exact synonym and no such thing as an unmixed motive."

Reprinted as A Letter to the Editor of *The Yale Review* in *Collected Essays* (A20).

C99. "On First Meeting T.S. Eliot." *Shenandoah*, 12 (Spring 1961), 25–26.

Porter recounts her meeting T.S. Eliot in New York at a party for the opening of *The Cocktail Party*. "He was as serene and collected as if he sat easily in the void of a hurricane, where no doubt he *does* sit."

Reprinted in *Collected Essays* (A20).

C100. "Human Light." *Newsweek*, 58 (21 Aug. 1961), 6, 9.

Letter to the Editor, with which Porter enclosed a photograph (here printed). She suggests that this photograph shows her "face in a rather more human light than that little horror" which appeared with the story about *Ship of Fools* (31 July). She praises the story it accompanied, however.

C101. "Silk Purse. . . ." *Washington Post*, 10 Oct. 1961, p. A14.

Rails against scientists as "the most reckless, irresponsible, not to say suicidal, people on earth." She is responding to a "sow's ear into silk purse story." Porter suggests that the artist, in contrast to the scientist, has to deal with reality and truth and must be practical. She concludes that "it is better to acknowledge that only silkworms can make silk, only scientists can make synthetics, and only God can make a silkworm."

Reprinted as A Letter to the Editor of the *Washington Post* in *Collected Essays* (A20).

C102. "Fresh Vegetable Borscht." In *The Artists' & Writers' Cookbook*, ed. Barbara Turner Sachs and Beryl Barr. Sausalito, Calif.: Contact Editions, 1961, pp. 45–46.

Porter recalls eating in a fine Kosher restaurant in Germany years before and her passion for the food there, above all the borscht. Her recipe is "an original receipt" for a "vegetable broth."

C103. "A Note." In Willa Cather, *The Troll Garden*. New York: New American Library, 1961, pp. 150–51.

Comments briefly on Cather and *The Troll Garden*.

C104. *Recent Southern Fiction: A Panel Discussion*. Macon, Ga.: Wesleyan College, 1961.

Transcript of panel discussion, on recent Southern fiction, by Porter, Flannery O'Connor, Caroline Gordon, Madison Jones, and Louis D. Rubin, Jr. It was held at Wesleyan College on October 28, 1960. Porter comments on when she writes, her Southernness, communism, young Southern writers, William Humphrey, William Styron, symbolism, the audience for Southern writing, and John Calvin.
Reprinted in Joan Givner (ed.), *Katherine Anne Porter: Conversations* (G66).

1963

C105. "Tell Me About Adrienne. . . ." *Mercure de France*, 349 (Aug.–Sept. 1963), 154–55.

Part of an entire issue devoted to the memory of Sylvia Beach, this 6 February 1956 letter to Beach responds to her having sent Porter a copy of "The Souvenir d'Adrienne Monnier," published in *Mercure de France* in 1956. Porter comments on Monnier's death and recalls Beach and Monnier in Paris and her meeting of Hemingway in Shakespeare and Co. A translation into French by Marcelle Sibon appears on pp. 156–57.

Reprinted as "A Letter to Sylvia Beach" in *Collected Essays* (A20).

1964

C106. "Her Legend Will Live." *Ladies' Home Journal*, 81 (March 1964), 58–59.

Porter's appreciation of Jacqueline Kennedy concerns her life and her performance of duty. Porter recounts the two occasions on which she saw Mrs. Kennedy, at the Inaugural Ball and at a White House dinner.
Reprinted as "Jacqueline Kennedy" in *Collected Essays* (A20).

C107. "Paris: A Little Incident in the Rue de l'Odéon." *Ladies' Home Journal*, 81 (Aug. 1964), 54–55.

Porter recounts a 1963 visit to Shakespeare and Co. in Paris. This triggers her recollections of Sylvia Beach, "a touchstone," and of Beach's introduction of Porter and Hemingway in the 1930's.
Reprinted as "A Little Incident in the Rue de l'Odéon" in *Collected Essays* (A20).

C108. "Gracious Greatness." *Esprit*, 8 (Winter 1964), 50–59.

Porter's reminiscence of Flannery O'Connor calls her a genius, sets her in her milieu, and sketches her character. "I loved and valued her dearly, her work and her strange unworldly radiance of spirit in a human being so intelligent and so undeceived by the appearance of things."
Reprinted as "Flannery O'Connor at Home" in *Collected Essays* (A20).

C109. "Katherine Anne Porter Comments on *Good-Bye Wisconsin*." In Glenway Wescott. *Good-Bye Wisconsin*. New York: New American Library, 1964, p. 1.

"These stories by Glenway Wescott may be read with pleasure, and reread, for every reading brings out new shades of meaning and richness of feeling."

C110. "Words on Length." In *The Modern Short Story in the Making*, ed. Whit and Hallie Burnett. New York: Hawthorne Books, 1964, pp. 404–05.

Asserts that there are "four accurate classifications which cover all our needs in the matter of defining lengths of stories—short story, long story, short novel, novel." She fits some of her works into these classifications. She also describes her happy, reclusive life in August 1963 in Paris.

1965

C111. "From the Notebooks of Katherine Anne Porter—Yeats, Joyce, Eliot, Pound." *Southern Review*, 1 (n.s.) (Summer 1965), 570–73.

Porter comments on her admiration for Yeats and Joyce and compares them, discusses Joyce's genius and his personal failings, recalls T.S. Eliot reading at Shakespeare and Co., and recalls Ezra Pound as "a complete, natural phenomenon of unreason."
Reprinted as "From the Notebooks: Yeats, Joyce, Eliot, Pound" in *Collected Essays* (A20).

C112. "Book Week Symposium on Modern Fiction." *Washington Post, Book Week*, 26 Sept. 1965, pp. 7, 18.

Porter responds to questions surveying the best modern fiction. She names writers she believes will have "a long and honorable life in the story of our literature." She stresses "the importance of remembering our past and our origins, of relating our history to our customs, our arts to our lives and the things we have loved and fought for."
Reprinted as "On Modern Fiction" in *Collected Essays* (A20).

C113. "Go Little Book." *The Collected Stories of Katherine Anne Porter*. New York: Harcourt, Brace and World, 1965, pp. v–vi.

Brief introductory remarks, with specific comments on "The Fig Tree," "Holiday," "María Concepción," "Virgin Violeta," and "The Martyr." She praises the assistance and encouragement she received from Carl Van Doren, editor of *Century Magazine*. She calls again for the use of the terms "short story," "long story," "short novel," and "novel" to refer to her works. (See A19.)

1966

C114. Letter to Gerald Ashford. Quoted in his "Fowles Displays Skill in New Novel 'Magus.'" *San Antonio Express/News*, 9 Jan. 1966, p. 6–H.

Porter tells Ashford about her birthplace "on Indian Creek in Brown County near a little town named Brownwood" and about childhood homes in Kyle, Texas; San Antonio, Texas; and Louisiana.

C115. Letter to Gerald Ashford. In his "Katherine Anne Porter Tells Editor about Her Birthplace." *San Antonio Express/News*, 13 March 1966, p. 4–H.

Porter's reply to Ashford's letter asking about her exact birthplace and her recollections of and use of San Antonio. Porter recalls her birthplace and her visit to her mother's grave. She directs Ashford to "The Leaning Tower" for a reference to San Antonio.

C116. "Miss Porter Gets the Last Word." *San Antonio Express/News*, 3 April 1966, p. 8–H.

Letter to Gerald Ashford in which Porter recalls San Antonio in 1904, when she "lived over West End Lake and went to a Girls School there" and responds to Ashford's characterizing her reference to San Antonio in "The Leaning Tower" as "fallacious."

C117. "Letters to a Nephew: Observations on—Pets, Poets, Sex, Love, Hate, Fame, Treason." *Mademoiselle*, 62 (April 1966), 189, 244–50.

Two letters of Porter written to her nephew Paul Porter in June 1948 and March 1963. She discusses sex, politics, reading, melancholy, movies, literary figures, illness and dying, and drama.
Reprinted as "Letters to a Nephew" in *Collected Essays* (A20).

C118. "Ole Woman River: A Correspondence with Katherine Anne Porter." *Sewanee Review*, 74 (July–Sept. 1966): 754–67.

Porter's 1953 correspondence with Donald Sutherland concerning Gertrude Stein, as well as the role of the artist, women, criticism, and truth.
Reprinted in *Collected Essays* (A20).

C119. Letter to R., P. Blackmur. In Leonard Greenbaum. *The Hound & Horn—The History of a Literary Quarterly*. The Hague: Mouton, 1966, p. 270.

A 29 November 1929 letter Porter wrote sending "Flowering Judas" for consideration for publication in *Hound & Horn*. She says that the title is taken from T.S. Eliot's "Gerontion."

1967

C120. "Note to *A Christmas Story*." *A Christmas Story*. New York: Delacorte, 1967, pp. [33–36].

Porter explains that this piece "is not fiction but the true story of an episode in the short life of my niece, Mary Alice, a little girl who died nearly a half century ago at the age of five and one-half years." She includes a brief reminiscence of her niece. (See A17.)

1968

C121. "Acceptance by Miss Porter." *Proceedings of the American Academy of Arts and letters and the National Institute of Arts and Letters*, 18 (1968), 92–93.

Porter's speech upon accepting the Gold Medal for Fiction awarded by the National Institute of Arts and Letters. She comments briefly on her vocation, the attacks of the critics on *Ship of Fools*, and her life.

Reprinted as "Speech of Acceptance" in *Collected Essays* (A20).

C122. Letters to Robert McAlmon. Quoted in Robert McAlmon and Kay Boyle. *Being Geniuses Together—1920–1930.* Garden City, N.Y.: Doubleday, 1968, pp. 104–05.

Two letters to McAlmon, in which Porter comments on Ernest Hemingway and on McAlmon's manuscript of *Being Geniuses Together*.

1969

C123. Letter to Malcolm Cowley. Quoted in M.M. Liberman. "Some Observations on the Genesis of *Ship of Fools*: A Letter from Katherine Anne Porter." *PMLA*, 84 (Jan. 1969), 136–37.

Liberman gives some of the text of Porter's 25 September 1931 letter to Malcolm Cowley and asserts that it "seems genetic in its position between the diary [of her 1931 trip to Germany] and conscious labor" on *Ship of Fools*. The letter comments on the voyage, Berlin, her book reviewing for *New Republic*, meeting Gottfried Benn, and Peggy Baird Cowley. (See I108).

C124. Entry deleted.

C125. Letter to Philip Horton. Quoted in John Unterecker. *Voyager—A Life of Hart Crane.* New York: Farrar, Straus and Giroux, 1969, pp. 658–60, 670–71.

Quotes the same excerpt from a letter to Philip Horton that was published in Horton's *Hart Crane* (C29). Also quotes from a December 1964 interview with Porter.

1970

C126. "The Fiesta of Guadalupe." *Collected Essays and Occasional Writings of Katherine Anne Porter.* New York: Delacorte, 1970, pp. 394–98.

Meditation on the condition of the Mexican Indians ("a deathly dream") in connection with attendance at the celebration of the fiesta of Mary Guadalupe (created to commemorate her appearance to Juan Diego in 1531).
Although this essay is dated 1923, there is no evidence that it was published before 1970 (A20).

C127. "Katherine Anne Porter." In *Professional Secrets—An Autobiography of Jean Cocteau.* New York: Farrar, Straus and Giroux, 1970, p. 320.

One of the pieces in the section entitled "Glimpsed, Judged, Remembered by a Jury of His Peers." Porter recalls Cocteau in Paris in 1952 at a performance of *Oedipus Rex.*

C128. A Letter to the Editor of *The Saturday Review of Literature. Collected Essays and Occasional Writings of Katherine Anne Porter.* New York: Delacorte, 1970, pp. 209–15.

Porter responds to an editorial and articles in *The Saturday Review,* on the Ezra Pound-Bollingen Prize controversy of 1949. She defends the awarding of the prize to Pound, mainly on the basis of condemning those who attack it for their moral indignation when it is too late to be effective. The American people should "use all that fury and energy *in time,* and against the sources of our evils; to attack the real powers, the policy-makers, and finally punish the real criminals, the almost-unreachable ones." Pound's real crime seems to have been lack of mental, moral, psychic flexibility, no talent for turning with the political winds.

Although this letter is dated 1949, there is no evidence that it was published before 1970 (A20).

C129. "My First Speech." *Collected Essays and Occasional Writings of Katherine Anne Porter*. New York: Delacorte, 1970, pp. 433–41.

Although this essay is dated 1934 and a note asserts that it was composed that year, it was given as a speech at the American Women's Club in Paris in November 1935. Porter ranges over her thoughts about certain aspects of writing: the use of legend and memory, the way fiction is made, "typical" American writers, the elements of a major work of art, the writer's business, and craftsmanship.

There is no evidence that this was published before 1970 (A20).

C130. "On Writing." *Collected Essays and Occasional Writings of Katherine Anne Porter*. New York: Delacorte, 1970, pp. 464–66.

Porter provides the introduction and conclusion to remarks she made on writing at Olivet College Writers' Conference in 1936. "If you have the vocation, it is very well worth spending a lifetime at it by living in the love of your work, you cannot be wasted."

Although this is dated 1954, it was not published before 1970 (A20).

1971

C131. "And to the Living Joy." *McCall's*, 99 (Dec. 1971), 76–77.

Porter's Christmas meditation and message. "Let us warm again for this moment our very beings in this divine vision of the human possibility of man's hope, live and breathe in its grandeur while we can."

C132. "Katherine Anne Porter." In *Attacks of Taste.*, ed. Evelyn B. Byrne and Otto M. Penzler. New York: Gotham Book Mart, 1971, p. 36.

Answers "Which book or books were your favorites or influenced you most as a teenager and why? Porter's reply includes *Wuthering Heights*, Shakespeare's sonnets, *Confessions* of St. Augustine, Montaigne's *Essays*, *Adventures of Gargantua*, *Moll Flanders*, Chekhov, Henry James, and *The Odyssey*.

1973

C133. "Presentation to Eudora Welty of the Gold Medal for the Novel by Katherine Anne Porter." *Proceedings of the American Academy of Arts and Letters and the National Institute of Arts and Letters*, 23 (1973), 37.

Welty is a "breath of fresh air . . . to help purify the air of this plague of pop-porno that American literature seems to be sludging its way through." Her "splendid mind, her splendid heart living and working in perfect unison . . . know so much about human nature that it staggers me sometimes."

1974

C134. "Recollection of Rome." *Travel and Leisure*, 4 (Jan. 1974), 4, 9.

A December 1962 letter to Barbara Wescott from Rome. It recounts her attempts to rent an apartment in a fifteenth-century palace, an Italian lawyer's praise of *Ship of Fools*, her visit to the site of Keats's death, and its effect on her.

C135. "You Are What You Read." *Vogue*, 164 (Oct. 1974), 248, 250, 252.

In attempting to refute Malcolm Cowley's characterization of her as an exile, Porter gives details of her life, particularly of her reading and theater going in childhood. She asserts that she never was an exile because she discovered "The Land that is Nowhere— That is the true home."

1975

C136. "Notes on the Texas I Remember." *Atlantic Monthly*, 235 (March 1975), 102–06.

Porter recalls Kyle, Texas, in her youth, her grandmother's house, a Methodist revival from which Mexicans were expelled, early memories of places, people, and things, a train trip to Marfa and El Paso, seeing great performers in San Antonio, and bandits. "Nothing is trivial, not for a moment, if you really delve into the past."

C137. Letter to Frances Steloff. In "Katherine Anne Porter." *Journal of Modern Literature*, 4 (April 1975), 820–21.

This journal issue is devoted to Frances Steloff of the Gotham Book Mart and contains much of her correspondence from literary figures. The 27 September 1939 letter from Porter is in response to Steloff's request that Porter contribute to *We Moderns*, the Gotham Book Mart catalog distributed in 1940 to celebrate the twentieth anniversary of the book shop. Porter offers to write a paragraph about Kay Boyle and comments briefly on or mentions Josephine Herbst, Glenway Wescott, Mark Van Doren, Leonie Adams, Louise Bogan, Marianne Moore, Allen Tate, Paul Valery, and André Gide. She also notes that she is "ears deep in the last chapters" of *Ship of Fools*, "due to go to the publishers sometime this late fall."

C138. "Katherine Anne Porter Replies." *Atlantic Monthly*, 235 (May 1975), 26.

Porter replies to Amelia Falcon's letter, which pointed out errors in the Private Longoria story recounted in "Notes on the Texas I Remember" (C136). Porter asserts that the errors are not hers but rather those of a 28 October 1974 *Washington Post* article.

C139. "Extracting Blood from a Population of Turnips." *Washington Post*, 5 Aug. 1975, p. A-17.

Letter to the Editor in which Porter recounts her receiving a notice of a rent tax and later an exemption and rails against excessive taxes.

1977

C140. "The Never-Ending Wrong." *Atlantic*, 239 (June 1977), 37–48, 53–64.

Porter recalls her experiences in August 1927 during the days leading up to the execution of Sacco and Vanzetti in Boston: picketing, arrest, interaction with other protesters, rallies, the execution, trial of protesters. Sacco and Vanzetti devoted their lives "to ameliorat[ing] the anguish that human beings inflict on each other—the never-ending wrong, forever incurable."
Reprinted as a separate publication (A22).

C141. "Neglected Books of the Twentieth Century." *Antaeus*, 27 (Autumn 1977), 133.

The editors chose to print Porter's response to their request for her list of neglected twentieth-century books. She gives a few brief reasons and declines the invitation.

1982

C142. Letters to Mitzi Berger Hamovitch. In "Hunting for the *Hound & Horn*." *American Scholar*, 51 (Autumn 1982), 548.

Prints portions of Porter's 1 July and 18 July 1975 letters to Hamovitch. Porter is responding to Hamovitch's requests for information on Porter's *Hound & Horn* correspondence, which Hamovitch is editing. Porter recalls Paris in 1933, comments on *Many Redeemers*, "Adios, My Primavera," and her ballet libretto work of the 1920's and 1930's. (See C144.)

C143. Letters to Richard Blackmur, Bernard Bandler, and Lincoln Kirstein. In *The Hound & Horn Letters*, ed. Mitzi Berger Hamovitch. Athens: Univ. of Georgia Press, 1982, pp. 127–38.

Three letters, dated 29 Nov. 1929 through 12 Dec. 1929, concern the publication of "Flowering Judas"; one mentions her debt to T.S. Eliot's "Gerontion." Six letters, dated 20 March 1933 through 19 Feb. 1934, primarily concern Porter's interest in book reviewing for *Hound & Horn*, her Cotton Mather book (especially the chapter "A Bright Particular Faith, A.D. 1700," which was published by *Hound & Horn*) and the libretto for a ballet, *Doomsday*, which Porter was writing for Lincoln Kirstein. (See C144.)

1983

C144. Letters to Richard Blackmur, Bernard Bandler, Lincoln Kirstein, and Mitzi Berger Hamovitch. "Today and Yesterday: Letters from Katherine Anne Porter." *Centennial Review*, 27 (Fall 1983), 278, 280, 281, 282, 283–84, 285–87.

Hamovitch reprints the full text of one letter and parts of the texts of four others that Porter wrote between

November 1929 and February 1934 to the editors of *Hound & Horn* and which appear in Hamovitch's *The Hound & Horn Letters*. Hamovitch also prints parts of five letters she received from Porter between July and December 1975 in answer to her queries about the Porter *Hound & Horn* Correspondence. (See C142, 143.)

1989

C145. Letters to Kerker Quinn. In *Dandy & Fine: "Accent" to "Ascent" (1940–   )*. Urbana: Univ. of Illinois Public Affairs/Office of Publications, 1989, pp. 14–15.

Prints two letters to Kerker Quinn, editor of *Accent*. One, dated 15 Jan. 1942, concerns Porter's work on Cotton Mather: "Sometime towards the end of this year I hope to begin winding it up once for all for the printer." The other, dated 7 Feb. 1945, concerns her appointment as writer-in-residence at the University of Wisconsin. A third letter to Quinn, dated 29 April 1956, is briefly quoted; Porter thanks him for sending her an issue of *Accent*.

SECTION D
JOURNALISM

In this section, entries are in chronological order.

1917

D1. "Society Gossip of the Week by the Town Tatler." *Fort Worth Critic*, 2 (15 Sept. 1917), unpaged.

This two-page column, though not signed by Porter, introduces her prominently on the first page under the heading "This Is Her Page." The gossip includes discussion of war work available to women, the various activities of the War Service Board in planning music, dances, and a reading room for the soldiers at Camp Bowie, and forthcoming musical programs for all of Fort Worth. She also comments briefly on clothes for winter, Canadian aviators, a planned circus, prohibition, a man's tattoo, a sermon, and theaters rumored for Camp Bowie.

D2. "The Week at the Theaters." *Fort Worth Critic*, 2 (15 Sept. 1917), unpaged.

Porter's debut as entertainment critic consists mainly of previews of the attractions of the coming week at four local theaters. They include four movies, *The Hostage*, *Double Crossed*, *The Idolaters*, and *Ten of Diamonds*, as well as vaudeville acts.

1918

D3. "Society Gossip of the Week." *Fort Worth Critic* 3 (12 Jan. 1918), unpaged.

> Incorrectly dated 1917. Gives news of visiting and visitors of Fort Worth locals but mostly is an account of the Assembly Club ball at which Vernon Castle danced.

D4. "The Week at the Theaters." *Fort Worth Critic* 3 (12 Jan. 1918), unpaged.

> Incorrectly dated 1917. Reviews four movies to be shown in Fort Worth in the coming week: *Empty Pockets*, *Until They Get Me*, *The Judgment House*, and *The Spirit of '17*.

1919

D5. "Girls from America Out of Place in Paris, Says Society Woman." *Rocky Mountain News*, 8 Feb. 1919, p. 3.

> Mrs. Harry English, Denver society matron, advises young American girls to do war work at home rather than in France, in light of her six-month Red Cross service in France. Mrs. English also details life in France during the war and the bravery of the American soldiers.

D6. "Maxine Elliot Reviews Play in Which She Scored Success." *Rocky Mountain News*, 9 Feb. 1919, Section 2, p. 10.

> Overview of week's coming attractions at the Broadway, Orpheum, Tabor, and Denham theaters with specific comments and quotes on Maxine Elliott and *Lord and Lady Algy*, Hobart Bosworth and *The Sea Wolf*, the Courtney Sisters, Eva La Rue, Jack Gardner, May Buckley and *Spendthrift*. Also comments on New York production of *Gibour* with Yvette Guilbert and *Hobohemia*.

D7. "'Lord and Lady Algy' Delights Audience." *Rocky Mountain News*, 11 Feb. 1919, p. 10.

Praise for the "finished and skillful performance" of Maxine Elliott and William Faversham in *Lord and Lady Algy*.

D8. "Frivolities of Harmless Sort Billed to Amuse Theater Goers." *Rocky Mountain News*, 16 Feb. 1919, Section 2, p. 10.

Ironic comments on vaudeville precede discussion of the week's forthcoming attractions at the Orpheum, Tabor, Denham. Singled out for specific mention are Sarah Padden, Grace La Rue, Great Leon and Edith Packard, King and Harvey, Hathaway and McShane, Verne Dayton, and May Buckley in *Within the Law*. Also comments on "archsentimentalist" David Belasco's long analysis of his latest production in New York, *Tiger! Tiger!*

D9. "No Poodles, No Maids, Just Plain Anna Case." *Rocky Mountain News*, 18 Feb. 1919, p. 4

Interview with operatic soprano Anna Case before her Denver concert. She is depicted as an ordinary normal woman rather than a prima donna.

D10. "Singer Wins Hearts of Denver Audience." *Rocky Mountain News*, 19 Feb. 1919, p. 7.

Review of Anna Case concert. Singles out for comment "The Dawn," written by a former Denver woman. Miss Case's "songs reflect her real self to an unusual degree and that self is a wholesome, honest, emotional being of fine spiritual fiber."

D11. "Splendor and Gaiety Mark Reception Tendered Governor by People of State." *Rocky Mountain News*, 22 Feb. 1919, pp. 1, 3.

Describes the Inaugural ball and program for Governor
Shoup at the Auditorium. The festivities included
singing, veterans and servicemen's parade, and a pioneer
pageant.

D12. "Movie Actress Seen at Denver Theater." *Rocky Mountain
News*, 23 Feb. 1919, p. 9.

Reviews Dorothy Bernard and Frank Morgan in *The
Man Who Came Back* at the Broadway. "The production
is well staged and smoothly played, and will amuse
those seeking highly-colored, slightly morbid
entertainment."

D13. "Theatergoers Like to Shiver Over Sins of Stage Heroes."
Rocky Mountain News, 23 Feb. 1919, Section 2, p. 10.

Porter's Sunday column covers miscellaneous topics: the
low brow taste of audiences for such plays as *The Man
Who Came Back*, actors attending other theaters on their
days off, *What Is Your Husband Doing?* (to be performed
the next week), and personal observations on May
Buckley, Olga Cook, John Duncan Cameron, and Jobyna
Howland.

D14. "Screaming Comedy Offered at Denham." *Rocky
Mountain News*, 24 Feb. 1919, p. 3.

Review of *What Is Your Husband Doing?* performed by
the Wilkes Players at the Denham. Praises the acting
but characterizes the play as "farce of the gayest and
most inconsequential kind."

D15. "'Home Grown' Music Good, Says Hofmann." *Rocky
Mountain News*, 27 Feb. 1919, p. 7.

Interview with Josef Hofmann, Polish pianist.
Hofmann characterizes music as international and
praises American composers, commenting on the lack of
acceptance of American music by American audiences.

D16. "Hofmann's Playing Wins Music Lovers." *Rocky Mountain News*, 28 Feb. 1919, p. 3.

Josef Hofmann, the Polish pianist, "played a short program of hackneyed, frayed, old tunes in a way which restored them to one afresh."

D17. "Trouble Packed in Old Kit Bags of Two Charming Actresses." *Rocky Mountain News*, 2 March 1919, Section 2, p. 8.

Recounts various theater stories. Details the feud between touring variety performers Sarah Padden and Grace La Rue in Denver, the dying of Adelena Patti and her singing in Denver, and makes observations about Denver theater celebrities Lillian Worth, Erville Alderson, Dollie Davis Webb, and Florence Johns.

D18. "Local Amateur Actors Busily Prepare for Season of Drama." *Rocky Mountain News*, 9 March 1919, Section 2, p. 10.

Porter's Sunday column discusses the organization and plans of the Denver little theater as well as the little theater movement in the United States: its origins, important groups, repertory theaters, influence. Recounts personal stories about singers Anna Case and Maud Powell and comedienne Stella Mayhew.

D19. "Some Every-Day Fare Relegated; Hospital Attaches Are Happy." *Rocky Mountain News*, 11 March 1919, p. 3.

Reports opening of new cafeteria for nurses and doctors at the County Hospital, which supersedes an "old-fashioned boarding house style of serving meals."

D20. "Little Theater Plays Charm First Nighters." *Rocky Mountain News*, 15 March 1919, p. 2.

Praises the "smoothness and finish" of the performances in the Denver little theater's first offering, three one-act plays. Briefly recounts plot and players for Susan Glaspell's *Close the Book, The Maid of France*, and Eden Philpott's *The Point of View*.

D21. "Actress Lover of Good Books Aspires to Try Hand at Writing." *Rocky Mountain News*, 16 March 1919, section 2, p. 13.

Sunday column which features portrait of the actress May Buckley, a visit to a theater during a rehearsal, and Porter's ruminations (with illustrating anecdotes) on the practice of dramatic criticism.

D22. "San Carlo Star Singer Captures San Francisco—Opera Company to Appear Here This Week." *Rocky Mountain News*, 16 March 1919, Section 2, p. 10.

Overview of forthcoming five-day Denver opera season which includes brief sketches of three of the principals: Queena Mario, Elizabeth Amsden, and Haru Onuki.

D23. "Grand Opera Artists Please Big Audience." *Rocky Mountain News*, 19 March 1919, p. 3.

Review of the San Carlo Opera Company production of *Aida* which comments on the individual as well as ensemble performances. "Altogether, the opera more than justified the eager expectations of the hearers and received a generous due of appreciation."

D24. "Enthusiastic Audience Welcomes Haru Onuki." *Rocky Mountain News*, 20 March 1919, p. 3.

Although Puccini's *Madame Butterfly* is not a "profound opera" and comes "perilously near the 'popular' style in certain passages," the performances, especially of Haru Onuki as Butterfly, were fine in the San Carlo Opera Company's production in Denver.

D25. "Queena Mario's Voice Captivates Denver." *Rocky Mountain News*, 21 March 1919, p. 8.

Review of San Carlo Opera Company production of Donizetti's *Lucia de Lammermoor*, singles out coloratura soprano Queena Mario for particular praise.

D26. "Tenor Scores Triumph in Opera Masterpiece." *Rocky Mountain News*, 22 March 1919, p. 10.

Rave review of San Carlo Opera Company production of Leon Cavallo's *I Pagliacci*, starring Manuel Salazar. Qualified praise for performance of Wolf-Ferrari's *Secret of Suzanne* on the same bill.

D27. "Caretakers Guard Stage Genius—Mothers, Husbands, and Sisters." *Rocky Mountain News*, 23 March 1919, Section 2, p. 12.

Sunday column which discusses the caretakers of genius, most notably Haru Onuki's sister Tama, the problems of maintaining weight for performers Jaque Hays and Buster Santos, the Russian dancer Thamara Swirskaya, Denver-born movie star Rubye De Remer, and increasing censorship of movies as the implementation of Prohibition nears.

D28. "'The Boss' Is Big Hit with Denham Crowd." *Rocky Mountain News*, 24 March 1919, p. 12.

Praise for Wilkes Players' production of the melodrama *The Boss*. "The acting thruout was spirited and natural."

D29. "Girl with Personality Tops Orpheum's Card." *Rocky Mountain News*, 26 March 1919, p. 4.

Tongue in cheek review of the week's vaudeville at the Orpheum: Rae Samuels, a jazz singing comedienne; *The Groom Forgot*, a dramatic playlet; *White Coupons*, a musical allegory; a singing, dancing, piano playing duo, The Regular Vaudevillians; Charles and Madeline Dunbar, who imitate animal voices; Johannes Josefsson's company performing *Glima*, the Icelandic art of defense; and four trained elephants.

D30. "Famous Tabor Drop Curtain Dusted and Placed in Service." *Rocky Mountain News*, 30 March 1919, Section 2, p. 12.

Sunday column in which the history of the drop curtain at the Tabor theater is discussed as well as the mercenary nature of press agents and two incidents in which actor's errors provoked audience mirth.

D31. "Popular Actress Back on Stage Surpasses Former Successes." *Rocky Mountain News*, 6 April 1919, Section 2, p. 11.

Sunday column which discusses the return of Blanche Bates, wife of the former Denver police commissioner, to the Broadway stage; Booth Tarkington's *The Country Cousin*; Joseph E. Howard's return to Denver in vaudeville; and an incident involving a lady lion trainer in Chicago.

D32. "'Cameo Kirby' Wins Denham Audience." *Rocky Mountain News*, 7 April 1919, p. 8.

Review of Wilkes Players production of Booth Tarkington and Harry Leon Wilson's *Cameo Kirby* at the Denham theater.

D33. "Howard's Song Revue Wins Orpheum Crowd." *Rocky Mountain News*, 9 April 1919, p. 16.

Review of current vaudeville attractions at the Orpheum: Ethelyn Clark and Joseph E. Howard in a song review; Dane Claudius and Lillian Scarlet in a banjo sketch; the leopard trainer Delores Vallecita; *Show Me*, a playlet; a violinist dressed as a street urchin; and the Three Bennet sisters.

D34. "Noted Paris Writer to Address Alliance Francaise Saturday." *Rocky Mountain News*, 10 April 1919, p. 3.

Interview with Madame Charles Bigot, formerly a writer, who was to speak on the French Academy at the Denver Alliance Française on April 12. Daughter of an American man and an English woman, Mme. Bigot asserts the need for the study of a foreign language, particularly French.

D35. "Musical Comedy to Supplant Stock in Popular Denver House." *Rocky Mountain News*, 13 April 1919, Section 2, p. 10.

Sunday column in which Porter discusses the possibility that the Wilkes Players, a repertory company, will be replaced at the Denham theater by a traveling musical comedy company based in Los Angeles. Other topics include popular leading ladies of the stock company at the Denham, blue songs and the need for censorship of them, popular songs on prohibition, little theater locally and in New York City, and Sonya Mitchell's piano concert on April 10.

D36. "Musical Show Scores with Tabor Audiences." *Rocky Mountain News*, 13 April 1919, Section 1, p. 2.

Review of vaudeville acts at Tabor theater: *The Man Hunter*, a musical comedy; a dance act; a blackface sketch; a talking skit; a mismatched duo; and a tumbling act.

D37. "'The New Henrietta' Pleases Theatergoers." *Rocky Mountain News*, 14 April 1919, p. 7.

Review of Wilkes Players production of *The New Henrietta* at the Denham, criticizes the structure of the play but praises the actors.

D38. "Playlet Headlines Orpheum Program." *Rocky Mountain News*, 16 April 1919, p. 16.

Singles out the playlet *The Woman Intervenes*, a
Swedish violinist, and a monkey orchestra act for praise
in this review of the current vaudeville acts at the
Orpheum. The other acts include a fat barber shop
quartet, a ventriloquist act, a comic skit, and a horse act.

D39. "Vampire Idea of Actresses Dispelled by Women of
    Stage." *Rocky Mountain News*, 20 April 1919, Section 2,
    p. 8.

Porter's Sunday column features an interview with
actress Florence Roberts, who illustrates that real
actresses are "generous, kind, and loyal" rather than
vampires. Also briefly discusses creative work written
hastily and the portable stage of the Camp Lewis
Players, who will stage two Lord Dunsany plays.

D40. "'Billeted' Is Clever Comedy of England." *Rocky
    Mountain News*, 21 April 1919, p. 12.

Review of production of F. Tennyson Jesse and H.M.
Harwood's *Billeted* by the Wilkes Players at the
Denham. Primarily comments on actors' performances.

D41. "Headliner Thrills Orpheum Crowds." *Rocky Mountain
    News*, 23 April 1919, p. 11.

Review of the vaudeville bill playing at the Orpheum.
The comedy playlet *Tom Walker in Dixie* is the "topliner
on a bill not quite up to the Orpheum standard." "It's not
such a fine show, but the general atmosphere is friendly."

D42. "Tabor Bill Features Bevy of Pretty Girls." *Rocky
    Mountain News*, 27 April 1919, p. 5.

Review of the variety acts on the Tablor theater bill,
most of which are singing and dancing: "every act was
tiptop in its own fashion."

D43. "Artist and Playwright Part Over Question of Cut Doorway." *Rocky Mountain News*, 27 April 1919, Section 2, p. 8.

Porter's Sunday column reports two anecdotes about Gordon Craig gleaned from her reading, Valeska Suratt's reaction to revealing bathing costumes, a visit to Olivett Haynes backstage, the mistaken criticism by a concertgoer of the inclusion of German music on a Denver Athletic Club program, and the current employment of former Wilkes Player, Ruth Robinson.

D44. "Drama at Denham Has Many Thrills." *Rocky Mountain News*, 28 April 1919, p. 10.

Review of Wilkes Players' production of George Broadhurst's *The Woman in the Index* at the Denham, focuses on the plot and performances.

D45. "Carle's Big Comedy Scores at Broadway." *Rocky Mountain News*, 29 April 1919, p. 4.

Review of Richard Carle's musical comedy *Furs and Frills* at the Broadway. Briefly comments on the performers, plot, and songs.

D46. "'The Purple Poppy' Scores at Orpheum." *Rocky Mountain News*, 30 April 1919, p. 7.

Review of vaudeville acts at the Orpheum focuses on *The Purple Poppy*, a Russian one-act play updated as a vehicle for Valeska Suratt. Six other acts are mentioned in this "tip-top" bill.

D47. "Theaters Offer Good Bills—Playgoers Assured Treats." *Rocky Mountain News*, 1 May 1919, p. 12.

Describes programs for the coming week to be played at the Tabor, Orpheum, Denham, and Broadway theaters.

D48. "Valeska, 'Tiger Vamp,' Quite Tame Off Stage." *Rocky Mountain News*, 1 May 1919, p. 11.

Although she is promised by the manager of the Orpheum that Valeska Suratt is a real vampire, Porter finds her to be an admirer of women and a lover of the outdoors, who tints photographs as a hobby.

D49. "Beauty Unadorned Attracts When War Hero Is Passed By." *Rocky Mountain News*, 4 May 1919, Section 2, p. 11.

Porter's weekly column rails at a Denver audience which crowds in to see a pathetic singing and dancing act by chorus girls dressed in bathing suits and at the contemporary modern drama such as *The Woman on the Index*, "mostly a libel on life, on art, on . . . morals." Also reports on the forthcoming performances of the Morgan dancers and Russian dancer Theodore Kosloff, as well as the continuing success of singer Queena Mario on tour.

D50. "Tabor Bill Has Chinese Touch—Wee Oriental Sings K-K-Katie." *Rocky Mountain News*, 4 May 1919, Section 1, p. 11.

Review of vaudeville acts at the Tabor theater, the headliners, a Chinese juggling and magic act, and a Hawaiian singing and dancing troupe, as well as four other mainly singing acts.

D51. "'Unlovely' Menfolk Are Seen at Denham." *Rocky Mountain News*, 5 May 1919, p. 7.

Coyly avoiding criticizing the actors, Porter implies that *Yes or No*, produced by the Wilkes Players at the Denham, is a bad play. Decries the male characters as "short-sighted, neglectful, unlovely."

D52. "Spaghetti Didn't Suit; Opera Stars Grieved." *Rocky Mountain News*, 6 May 1919, p. 11.

Porter reports her misadventure in the attempt to interview the members of the Grand Opera Quartet who were to perform at the Auditorium on May 6.

D53. "Huge Audience Hears Grand Opera Singers Render Famous Gems." *Rocky Mountain News*, 7 May 1919, p. 8.

Review of the concert given by the Grand Opera Quartet: Martinelli (tenor), Frances Alda (soprano), Carolina (contralto), and Guiseppe De Luca (baritone). The program included solos, duets, a trio, and a quartet from various operas. The program was "the outstanding musical event of the season just closed."

D54. "Denham Presents 'Husband' Comedy." *Rocky Mountain News*, 12 May 1919, p. 2.

Review of Wilkes Players' production of *Elevating a Husband* at the Denham theater, focuses mainly on the actors.

D55. "Oriental Ballet View with Jazz at Ball of Mystic Shrine Nobles." *Rocky Mountain News*, 17 May 1919, p. 3.

Reports the acts and events of the El Jebel Shrine frolic and Oriental ball held at the Auditorium on May 16. In addition to the dancing for all in the ballroom, there were singing, dancing, and drilling by various groups and individuals.

D56. "Man Dancer Makes Costumes Even to Sewing on of Buttons." *Rocky Mountain News*, 18 May 1919, Section 2, p. 15.

Porter's Sunday column is mostly composed of an interview with Russian dancer Theodore Kosloff. Kosloff speaks of the sister arts of dancing, painting, and music; of Russian literature; and the role of art in Russia. Brief discussion of confrontation with disgruntled pantomimist and the tendency of the viewer to impose his own idea on a work of art.

D57. "'A Stitch in Time' Scores at Denham." *Rocky Mountain News*, 19 May 1919, p. 12.

The performance of May Buckley in the Wilkes Players production of *A Stitch in Time* at the Denham theater makes the production of this unextraordinary play "a charming affair." Comments briefly on performances, lighting, and sets.

D58. "Seven Foys Score Orpheum Success." *Rocky Mountain News*, 21 May 1919, p. 10.

Review of vaudeville program at the Orpheum headlined by the Foy family act composed of singing, comedy, and dancing. Also briefly mentions the other acts: a jazz skit, a personality comedian, a singing comedian, two opera singers singing popular melodies, a cellist, and an acrobatic troupe.

D59. "Skinner in Good Role as Scapegrace Hero." *Rocky Mountain News*, 23 May 1919, p. 8.

Review of *The Honor of the Family*, a play in four acts after Balzac by Emile Fabré, adapted by Paul Potter as a touring vehicle for Otis Skinner as Colonel Philippe Bridau. Comments mainly on the performers but characterizes the play as an "amazing collection of unpleasant folk . . . gathered together to do interestingly sinful things in an interesting manner."

D60. "Comedians Win Tabor Crowd—Bears Entertain Children." *Rocky Mountain News*, 25 May 1919, Section 1, p. 11.

Review of vaudeville acts on the children's matinee bill at the Tabor theater. Singles out for praise the act of black comedians, dancers, and singers McCree and Ledman. Other acts include a burlesque on a country church choir, a singing and dancing sister act, "radium models" posing as sculptures, and a little girl who sang and played musical instruments.

D61. "Lion Interviewing as Opposed to Talk with Foy Children." *Rocky Mountain News*, 25 May 1919, Section 2, p. 11.

Porter contrasts her interview with Otis Skinner, a "lion out of humor," with that with the relaxed and garrulous Foy family. This Sunday column also comments on the Art-O-Graf movie studio now operating out of Denver, the unintended humor on press sheets, and the forthcoming production of Ernest Wilkes's *Hearts Defiant*.

D62. "Good Cast Enlivens 'Cappy Ricks' Farce." *Rocky Mountain News*, 27 May 1919, p. 4

Cappy Ricks, a sentimental comedy, made from the *Saturday Evening Post* stories of Peter B. Kyne, "is a joyous romp, broad farce at times, deliciously sentimental in spots." Tom Wise as Cappy Ricks displayed "unfailing humor and ripened comic art." Other actors and their performances are discussed.

D63. "Clever Little Play Heads Orpheum Bill." *Rocky Mountain News*, 28 May 1919, p. 5.

Review of vaudeville bill at the Orpheum which singles out Paul Dickey in his one-act thriller, *The Lincoln Highwayman*, as "the best short play the Orpheum has presented this season." Other acts reviewed include a singer, acrobatic dancers, a musical magician act, a singer and piano accompanist, a skating act, and female acrobats.

D64. "Thespian Charms Party, Tho Late in Greeting Hostess." *Rocky Mountain News*, 1 June 1919, Section 2, p. 13.

Local party held for actor Tom Wise is the jumping off point for this Sunday column which focuses on playwright Ernest Wilkes and on playwright and aviator Paul Dickey. Also outlines program of forthcoming concert of violinist Maud Powell and pianist Sonya Mitchell.

D65. "Denham Presents Real Melodrama." *Rocky Mountain News*, 2 June 1919, p. 2.

Review of Ernest Wilkes's *Hearts Defiant* produced by the Wilkes Players at the Denham theater, also directed by Wilkes. The play presents divorce "with a sane, if somewhat sentimental, sympathy." The characters are praised as "rather human and likable." Comments on some of the performances at length.

D66. "Airplane Comedy Has Catchy Songs." *Rocky Mountain News*, 3 June 1919, p. 2.

Review of musical comedy drama *Going Up* at the Broadway theater. The plot, which centers around two young men's wager over an airplane race, holds the audience to the "real climax of the show," the final scene. Includes brief comments on individual performances.

D67. "Maud Powell Repeats Triumphs in Concert." *Rocky Mountain News*, 4 June 1919, p. 4.

Review of joint concert of violinist Maud Powell and pianist Sonya Mitchell. Each of Powell's numbers was "perfect in itself, done with the generous outpouring of pure golden tone that is [her] own particular gift." Mitchell is "an artist of ideals and genuine musicianly quality."

D68. "American Critics Discredit Fetish to Foreign Artists." *Rocky Mountain News*, 8 June 1919, Section 2, p. 13.

This Sunday column explores at some length American feelings of inferiority about artistic status in comparison with the art of Europe. Cites examples of extremes to which worship of foreign art forces Americans: excessive praise of American artists mistakenly thought to be

Russian, the craze for foreign folk music. Porter does extol
the beauty of indigenous folk music and explores the
current state of music, dance, literature, and theater in
the United States.

D69. "Let's Shop with Suzanne!" *Rocky Mountain News*, 8 June
1919, Section 2, p. 4.

First of a series of shopping columns Porter originated
as a means of supplementing her *Rocky Mountain News*
salary. Porter announces that "each Sunday now I shall
have such very interesting things to tell you of the
'pretties' that I find in the shops." Over sixteen
establishments are advertized here, with the theme of
the June bride as organizing principle.

D70. "Denham Saves Time by Revolving Stage." *Rocky
Mountain News*, 9 June 1919, p. 2.

Praises both the play (*A Gentleman of Leisure*, partly
by P.G. Wodehouse, performed by the Wilkes Players)
and the new revolving stage at the Denham theater.
"Both are new, interesting and decidedly out of the
ordinary."

D71. "New Songs and Gowns Feature Eltinge Show." *Rocky
Mountain News*, 10 June 1919, p. 4.

Porter praises this vaudeville bill, "The Nineteen-
Nineteen Revue," headlined by its organizer, Julian
Eltinge, whose short comedy "His Night at the Club" is
performed in drag. The rest of the acts, "brisk, snappy,
and finished," include dancers of various types,
comedians, and acrobats.

D72. "Heiress to Millions Abandons Frivolity to Handle
Tractors." *Rocky Mountain News*, 12 June 1919, p. 8.

Porter describes her conversion to "another and newer
thought" about the use of tractors in farming as a result of
her interview with Mariane Browning, the young, tall,

athletic, feminine daughter of a sugar manufacturer from Ogden, Utah, and former society girl, who was driving a Fordson tractor at the farm exhibition in Denver.

D73. "Spirited Dances by Tots and Elders Feature Benefit." *Rocky Mountain News*, 13 June 1919, p. 12.

Descriptive review of Alfrey School of Expression dance and song recital at the Broadway theater for the benefit of the Sands Home for Tubercular Girls.

D74. "High Rents in Attic Quarters Drive Artists to Mere Hotels." *Rocky Mountain News*, 15 June 1919, Section 2, p. 13.

Porter's ruminations on the problems of finding a remote and comfortable place for the working artist to reside lead into discussion of the founding of the MacDowell Colony in New Hampshire, by Edward MacDowell's widow, for young artists to find the freedom "to work out their themes in whatever medium they had chosen." Porter announces the forthcoming July benefit to be held for the MacDowell Memorial Association, a "pageant of legend and song." This Sunday column also reports on the play-writing ambitions of actress Maude Fealy as well as some local Denver show business gossip and news.

D75. "Let's Shop with Suzanne!" *Rocky Mountain News*, 15 June 1919, Section 2, p. 10.

The shopping advice in this column is centered on girl graduates.

D76. "'The Eyes of Youth' Entertaining Play." *Rocky Mountain News*, 16 June 1919, p. 5.

Porter praises the Wilkes Players production of *The Eyes of Youth* at the Denham theater as "well staged and well acted."

D77. "Ice Cream, Scenic Railway and Lakeside Joys Make Perfect Day for 100 Kiddies." *Rocky Mountain News*, 19 June 1919, p. 4.

Factual account of party held for one hundred five-year-old orphans at the Lakeside Amusement Park on June 18.

D78. "Famous Stars of Past Jokes of Today on Stage, Says Critic." *Rocky Mountain News*, 22 June 1919, Section 2, p. 13.

Porter's Sunday column comments at length on the state of the contemporary theater; "the theater was never the pillar of the fine arts it has been dubbed by enthusiasts." She asserts that the best part of the theater today is the setting and cites Gordon Craig, Joseph Urban, Maxwell Armfield, and Robert Edmond Jones as examples of artistic and successful stage designers. Praises Benelli, D'Annunzio, Ibsen, Barrie, Shaw, Dunsany, and Synge, none of whom are "the typical commercial play mechanic." Porter also comments on the conservative tastes of Denver audiences. Brief mention of the MacDowell pageant for July and the municipal band concerts.

D79. "Let's Shop with Suzanne!" *Rocky Mountain News*, 22 June 1919, Section 2, p. 8.

This shopping column takes summer and vacations as its theme.

D80. "'Better 'Ole' Pleases the Crowd at Broadway." *Rocky Mountain News*, 23 June 1919, p. 3.

Porter's review of the Coburns' production of *The Better 'Ole* at the Broadway theater singles out for praise the performance of De Wolf Hopper as Old Bill. This musical comedy/drama "is an unusual show and an immensely amusing one."

D81. "Great Omar Khayyam Pageant to Be Held in Denver
July 10." *Rocky Mountain News,* 29 June 1919, Section 2,
p. 13.

Porter reports on preparations for production of the
dramatic cantata of the *Rubiayat of Omar Khayyam* by
the MacDowell Memorial Association. Also reported are
the remarks of violinist Alexander Saslavsky on chamber
music, musical star system, classical ensemble music,
music study, and contemporary musicians. Brief mention
of forthcoming Saslavsky trio concerts in Colorado and
the million-dollar movie contract of Mary Miles Minter.

D82. "Let's Shop with Suzanne!" *Rocky Mountain News,* 29
June 1919, Section 2, p. 8.

This weekly shopping column offers advice on buying
for children.

D83. "Broadway's Last Play Merits High Praise." *Rocky
Mountain News,* 30 June 1919, p. 7.

Maytime, a musical being presented at the Broadway
theater, is "an altogether pleasant and lovely play"
filled with "charming songs and situations." Individual
performers are also singled out for praise.

D84. "'Madmen Flutter By' Latest Thing in Opera." *Rocky
Mountain News,* 2 July 1919, p. 4.

Primarily a descriptive review of a comic musical,
Madmen Flutter By by Jean Milne Gower, presented on the
Adams Hotel roof as a fund raiser for the United States
Dollar fund for disabled British Empire servicemen.

D85. "Let's Shop with Suzanne!" *Rocky Mountain News,* 6 July
1919, section 2, p. 8.

This column is organized around the idea of hot
weather and the summer weekend vacation.

D86. "Settings for Little Theaters Shown in Modern Art Display." *Rocky Mountain News*, 6 July 1919, Section 2, p. 13.

Porter uses the Denver Art Association exhibition of set designs of Maxwell Armfield, Norman Bel Geddes, John Wenger, and others as the starting point for a discussion of the real beauty and originality of contemporary stage design in contrast to the "popular sentimentality" of "present-day drama." She also suggests that the "intellectual drama" is not dying because it does not pay, that the little theaters and commercial theaters which produce it are thriving. Also mentions Deems Taylor's Denver lectures on music and the impending closing of the Wilkes Players' season at the Denham theater.

D87. "'Lottery Man' Given to Close Denham." *Rocky Mountain News*, 7 July 1919, p. 7.

Review of *The Lottery Man* by Rida Johnson Young presented at the Dedham theater by the Wilkes Players. The performances of the "oddly humorous and convincing characters" by the acting troupe are praised.

D88. "Wyoming Girl Tells of Hospital Service and Gay Paris Races." *Rocky Mountain News*, 8 July 1919, p. 12.

Recounts experiences of Mrs. Virginia Helms of Casper, Wyoming, in France since October 1918. Mrs. Helms, who entered the Red Cross in Denver in fall 1918, had sent "souvenirs" of her stay in France to Burt Wills of Denver. These diary notes and souvenirs recount her work in base hospital 61 near Beaune and her social life in Paris.

D89. "Poetry of Khayyam Depicted by Masque." *Rocky Mountain News*, 11 July 1919, p. 12.

Review of Denver little theater production of Omar Khayyam pageant for the benefit of the MacDowell artists colony. The musical cantata, written and directed by Henry Housley, was followed by five interpretive interludes of dance, pantomime, and comedy. Porter played the role of Tipsy in the comedy diversion of the potter and his pots.

D90. "It's Easy to be Mad Nowadays and M.D.'s List You as Genius." *Rocky Mountain News*, 13 July 1919, Section 2, p. 6.

Porter defends the "madness" of the creative artist under attack by doctors and the "normal" public. The "curse" of today is "excess normality that is obligating the earth, reducing the glamorous, individual minds of youth to a dead level of uniformity when each should stand starkly alone hurling fresh thoughts like thunderbolts into the world." Also comments on use of foreign and obscure vocabulary in writing, both critical and creative, and defends the use of clear simple English words. Also comments on Russian folk music and the "nauseating" ideal of prettiness for actresses insisted on by the theater-going public.

D91. "Let Suzanne Shop for You!" *Rocky Mountain News*, 13 July 1919, Section 2, p. 8.

This column also emphasizes shopping for hot summer days.

D92. "Saslavsky Concert Presents Contrast." *Rocky Mountain News*, 19 July 1919, p. 4.

The second Saslavsky trio concert at the Brown Palace was a distinctive improvement over the first in selection of the program, which included the Mozart trio in B major, the Brahms sonata in D minor, and Dvorak trio in E minor. Saslavsky, Marie Sloss (pianist), and Frederic Goerner (cellist) performed well individually and in ensemble.

D93. "Let Suzanne Shop for You!" *Rocky Mountain News*, 20 July 1919, Section 2, p. 8.

This column features items for summer days and summer pastimes.

D94. "Noted Singer Here, Appalled at America's Neglect of Music." *Rocky Mountain News*, 20 July 1919, Section 2, p. 13.

Marcia Van Dresser, opera star summering in Denver, expresses her opinions on the situation of opera in the United States; she feels that musical criticism and appreciation are at a low level in comparison with those in Europe. Porter also decries the sentimental claptrap associated with the pilgrimage to the grave of composer Edward MacDowell in Petersboro, N.H. Also comments on professional song leaders in the army and navy, former Denver resident Rubye de Remer's movie, *Dust of Desire*, and the movie attractions coming to the Rivoli, Strand, Isis, and Tabor theaters.

D95. "Let Suzanne Shop for You!" *Rocky Mountain News*, 27 July 1919, Section 2, p. 10.

This column emphasizes Suzanne's ability to shop for bargains and her knowledge of "fads and fancies."

D96. "Varied Tastes Pleased by Saslavsky Concert." *Rocky Mountain News*, 2 Aug. 1919, p. 4.

The fourth concert at the Brown Hotel ballroom "was varied enough for every taste, and of exceptional brilliance." Marie Sloss and Sonya Mitchell, pianists; Alexander Saslavsky, violinist; and Frederic Goerner, cellist, performed a program which included the Lazzari sonata in E minor, the Mendelssohn trio in C minor, and the trio in G minor by Auguste Chapius.

D97. "Let's Shop with Suzanne!" *Rocky Mountain News*, 3
Aug. 1919, Section 2, p. 10.

Once again the column emphasizes the "best values"
and "newest fads."

D98. "'Such a Life!' Says Saslavsky; 'Bullyragger,' Pupils
Retort." *Rocky Mountain News*, 3 Aug. 1919, Section 2,
p. 15.

Porter reports her visit to the music lessons of Marie
Sloss and Sonya Mitchell with Alexander Saslavsky at
the Brown Hotel ballroom. Porter asserts that she went to
discover someone whose fate was ruder and more
miserable than hers. Porter briefly comments on the
problems of Americans in pronouncing French. The column
concludes with an interview with Margaret Eletch Long
on her gardens, zoo, and theater.

D99. "Big Audience Sees Comedy at Tabor." *Rocky Mountain
News*, 4 Aug. 1919, p. 5.

Favorable review of musical comedy *Isle of Spice*
produced by the Tabor Musical Comedy company at the
Tabor theater.

D100. "Old Melodies Please at Nursery Benefit." *Rocky
Mountain News*, 8 Aug. 1919, p. 8.

Review of benefit concert for the Denver Day Nursery
Association at the Broadway theater, which included
Percy Rector Steven's chorus conducted by Deems Taylor
in some of his compositions as well as two selections by
soprano Marcia Van Dresser.

D101. "Let's Shop with Suzanne!" *Rocky Mountain News*, 10
Aug. 1919, Section 2, p. 8.

The column emphasizes early buying of winter wear
and between-seasons clothing.

D102. "Stage May Lose Best Talent to Screen Thru Actors' Union." *Rocky Mountain News*, 10 Aug. 1919, Section 2, p. 13.

Comments on the effect the impending strike of Actors' Equity might have on movies and vaudeville and on how lucrative screen writing has become. Outlines the attractions for the coming season at the Broadway, Orpheum, Tabor, and Denham theaters, as well as the proposed concert series and Little Theater plans. Concludes with praise for the Little Theater movement.

D103. "Dancers Top Bill at Orpheum Debut." *Rocky Mountain News*, 13 Aug. 1919, p. 10.

Review of opening bill at Orpheum's new vaudeville season which singles out for praise the headline act, the Marion Morgan dancers in "Attila the Hun." Other acts include dancing, singing, ventriloquism, a comedy sketch, and a dog act.

D104. "Let's Shop with Suzanne!" *Rocky Mountain News*, 17 Aug. 1919, Section 2, p. 8.

This final shopping column completed by Porter emphasizes fall items.

D105. "Why Does a 'Genius' Lose 'Pep' as Soon as Coin Rolls In?" *Rocky Mountain News*, 17 Aug. 1919, Section 2, p. 13.

Porter comments on the over use of the term "genius" for those who are not genuinely geniuses, on enjoying the coarse and vulgar in vaudeville, on demands of the Chorus Girls' union, on musicians defending the particular form of music they perform, on Jean Milne Gower's parody on the Rubaiyat pageant, and the clichés in airplane songs.

SECTION E
BOOK REVIEWS

In this section entries are in chronological order. Mention is made of significant reprints.

1924

E1. "Mexico." *New York Herald Tribune, Books,* 2 Nov. 1924, p. 9.

Review of *A Gringo in Mananaland,* by Harry L. Foster, and *Beautiful Mexico,* by Vernon Quinn. The former is "as graceless as its title"; the latter is "painstaking, blameless and uninspired," aimed at United States intervention "for Mexico's own shining good."

E2. "A Self-Made Ghost." *New York Herald Tribune, Books,* 23 Nov. 1924, pp. 3–4.

Review of *The Triumph of Gallio,* by W.L. George. "It is a pity Mr. George has mixed the elements of a hardy philosophy with the tag-ends of debased popular mysticism, hung it all upon Holyoake Tarrant [his protagonist], and called it a novel. It is really a thesis on how to rationalize an incapacity to love."

E3. "The Poet and Her Imp." *New York Herald Tribune, Books,*
28 Dec. 1924, pp. 3–4.

Review of *Distressing Dialogues,* by Nancy Boyd [Edna
St. Vincent Millay]. "I love the book. . . . It is full of low
topical humor."

1925

E4. "Maya Treasure." *New York Herald Tribune, Books,* 8 Feb.
1925, p. 9.

Review of *In an Unknown Land,* by Thomas Gann. The
work is "a valuable pioneer work of reference [on Mayan
civilization] to the amateur, a text book of suggestions for
further reading."

E5. "Shooting the Chutes." *New York Herald Tribune, Books,* 8
March 1925, p. 10.

Review of *Round the World,* by Frank Hedges Butler,
Outline of Travel, by Harman Black, and *My Trip Around
the World,* by Dorothy Dix. These travel books are
examples of the "fixed," almost "canonical" style now
current in travel writing—"being rather more explicit
than a diary, rather less entertaining than a letter home;
inflated to the bursting point, because a travel book
should be fat to be impressive; illustrated with a curious
collection of purchased stock photographs of scenery, a
few intimate camera snapshots by a member of the party
and a drawing or two if the author is lucky enough to get
hold of them."

E6. "With the Enthusiasm of a Boy Scout." *New York Herald
Tribune, Books,* 12 April 1925, p. 10.

Review of *Adventures in Peru,* by Cecil Herbert
Prodgers. The book "is a literal record of odd chores
undertaken with the enthusiasm of a Boy Scout going on
his first hike." It is delightful, but "it hasn't the
slightest importance."

E6a. "Princesses, Ladies and Adventuresses of the Reign of Louis XIV." *Equal Rights*, 12 (6 June 1925), 135–36.

Review of *Princesses, Ladies and Adventuresses of the Reign of Louis XIV*, by Therese Louis Latour, translated by Colonel Dutton Burrard. Takes up the lives of twenty women of the court of Louis XIV. Porter suggests that the irresponsible actions of these royal women were the direct result of their lack of "all human or legal rights not bound up with the family or State."

E7. "Sex and Civilization." *New York Herald Tribune, Books,* 5 July 1925, pp. 3–4.

Review of *Our Changing Morality: A Symposium*, edited by Freda Kirchwey. This is a collection of essays which originally appeared in *The Nation*. It is "a calm book, and very few of the contributors have found the subject diverting." Porter comments briefly on the essays by Bertrand Russell, Edwin Muir, Isabel Leavenworth, Charlotte Perkins Gilman, Sylvia Kepald, Alexander Goldenweiser, Beatrice M. Hinkle, Ludwig Lewisohn, Floyd Dell, and M. Vaertino.

E8. "Over Adornment." *New York Herald Tribune, Books,* 5 July 1925, p. 12.

Review of *Ducdame*, by John Cowper Powys. This novel fails because a "living book cannot be made from fragments ransacked from literature and pieced together by an effort of the will."

E9. "The Complete Letter Writer." *New Republic*, 44 (9 Sept. 1925), 77–78.

Review of *Original Letters from India (1779–1815)*, by Mrs. Eliza Fay. The letters contain the "British sense of moral obligation," Fay's "female sense of moral injury," poetry, and rhetoric. "That they should not have been suffered to drop soundlessly into oblivion is merely the final absurd accident of her absurd fate."

E10. "Dora, the Dodo, and Utopia." *New York Herald Tribune, Books*, 8 Nov. 1925, p. 14.

Review of *Lysistrata, or Woman's Future and Future Woman*, by Anthony M. Ludovici, and *Hypatia, or Woman and Knowledge*, by Mrs. Bertrand Russell. Ludovici's advocacy of a utopia in which men reign supreme over women is a "literary curiosity of genuine value and should be preserved as part of the records of our times." Dora Russell's book, in contrast, advances an argument in opposition, characterized by "abundant vigor and relevancy." Because Mrs. Russell speaks for a great number of feminists, Mr. Ludovici (whose viewpoint represents "Dodoism") may "become more and more nervous about the future he built so greatly out of dreams."

E11. "The Great Catherine." *New York Herald Tribune, Books*, 29 Nov. 1925, pp. 3–4.

Review of *Catherine the Great*, by Katharine Anthony. Primarily an admiring discussion of Catherine the Great, this review urges the reading of Anthony's two biographies, this and one on Margaret Fuller, because there are "no better modern biographies than these two."

E12. "Mr. George on the Woman Question." *New York Herald Tribune, Books*, 29 Nov. 1925, p. 11.

Review of *The Story of Women*, by W.L. George. The book is "a disconnected, rather fragmentary compilation, purposing to trace the progress of the female out of the pre-historic dark into the present filtering light of day." This "uninspired hack work" suggests that women's salvation from slavery came through men. "The woman problem has found a husband in Mr. George."

E13. "Etiquette in Action." *New York Herald Tribune, Books*, 20 Dec. 1925, p. 13.

Review of *Parade: A Novel of New York Society*, by Emily Post. Negative review, which concludes: "The moral appears to be that Literature and Etiquette make bad bed-fellows."

E14. "Ay, Que Chamaco." *New Republic*, 45 (23 Dec. 1925), 141–42.

Review of *The Prince of Wales and Other Famous Americans*, by Miguel Covarrubias. These sixty caricatures by Covarrubias evince speed, wit, lively accuracy, and genius. Covarrubias is the "latest" and "best" joke on New York.

1926

E15. "Quetzalcoatl." *New York Herald Tribune, Books*, 7 March 1926, pp. 1–2.

Review of *The Plumed Serpent*, by D.H. Lawrence. This novel "is a confession of faith, a summing up of the mystical philosophy of D.H. Lawrence," which uses Mexico, the Indians, and Quetzalcoatl as "pretexts, symbols made to the measure of his preoccupation." Although Lawrence cannot acknowledge his "blood-kin" with the Mexicans and remains a stranger, he does make "obeisance" to their beauty and their phallic god. The three main characters are merely "further variations of Lawrence's arch-type, the flayed and suffering human being in full flight from the horrors of a realistic mechanical society, and from the frustrations of sex."
Reprinted in *The Days Before* (A14) and *Collected Essays* (A20).

E16. "La Conquistadora." *New York Herald Tribune, Books*, 11 April 1926, pp. 3–4.

Review of *The Rosalie Evans Letters from Mexico*, edited by Daisy Caden Pettus. "As a personality, [Evans] is worth attention, being beautiful, daring and attractive. As a human being, she was avaricious, with an extraordinary hardness of heart and ruthlessness of will; and she died in a grotesque cause."

Reprinted (in a slightly different form) in *The Days Before* (A14) and *Collected Essays* (A20).

E17. "A Singing Woman." *New York Herald Tribune, Books*, 18 April 1926, p. 6.

Review of *Words for the Chisel*, by Genevieve Taggard. This volume of poetry "begins with feet solidly on earth, and rises through stones and trees and waters to the upper air, to a quiet, unurgent end."

E18. "History for Boy and Girl Scouts." *New Republic*, 48 (10 Nov. 1926), 353.

Review of *Daniel Boone: Wilderness Scout*, by Stewart Edward White. This children's biography of Boone is "a thrilling yarn, told with zest, and the author has resisted painting a moral until the very tag-end."

1927

E19. "'Everybody Is a Real One.'" *New York Herald Tribune, Books*, 16 Jan. 1927, pp. 1–2.

Review of *The Making of Americans: Being the History of a Family's Progress*, by Gertrude Stein. The work is "a psychological source book and the diary of an aesthetic problem worked out momently under your eyes."

Reprinted in *The Days Before* (A14) and *Collected Essays* (A20).

E20. "Enthusiast and Wildcatter." *New York Herald Tribune, Books*, 6 Feb. 1927, p. 14.

Review of *The City of the Sacred Well*, by T.A. Willard. The book recounts the adventures of "born enthusiast and wildcatter" Edward H. Thompson, archaeologist and researcher, who spent "thirty years unearthing the secrets of ancient Yucatan." Thompson is compared with another free-lance archaeologist, W.H. Nivens. "If the scientific part of this book is not of much importance, the personal story of Edward Thompson is: like Nivens, with his own hands he has brought enough mystery out of Mexico to keep the scientists busy racking their brains for twenty years."

E21. "Black, White, Red, Yellow, and the Pintos." *New Republic*, 50 (16 March 1927), 111–12.

Review of *The Ipané; Doughty Deeds, Being an Account of the Life of Robert Graham of Gartmore, 1735–1797, Poet and Politician;* and *A Brazilian Mystic, Being the Life and Miracles of Antonio Conselheiro*, by R.B. Cunninghame Graham. The first of these is a collection of short pieces on South America, Iceland, Arabia, Scotland, and Texas, "tied loosely together in a book"; "you feel that the writer was a participant, not a looker-on." In the second, "true adventurer" Graham writes of his eighteenth-century ancestor with whom he shares an "essence" as a "hard-head and poet." The last, the biography of a late nineteenth-century Brazilian mystic, Antonio Maciel, "later called the councillor," is "simply one of the best tales I have ever read."

E22. "Paternalism and the Mexican Problem." *New York Herald Tribune, Books,* 27 March 1927, p. 12.

Review of *Some Mexican Problems*, by Moises Saenz and Herbert I. Priestley, and *Aspects of Mexican Civilization*, by José Vasconcelos and Manuel Gamio. These two books are a collection of lectures given before the Chicago Annual Institute. "Four diverse, informed and civilized minds have here collaborated in presenting quite horrifying facts in an almost painless form."

E23. "A Philosopher at Court." *New York Herald Tribune, Books,* 14 Aug. 1927, p. 12.

Review of *A Lady in Waiting to Queen Victoria: Being a Memoir, Some Letters and a Journal*, edited by

Magdalen Ponsonby. Edited by her daughter, these personal papers of Mary Elizabeth Bulteel Ponsonby. Edited by her daughter, these personal papers of Mary Elizabeth Bulteel Ponsonby span the years from 1853, when she was appointed maid of honor to Queen Victoria, to 1916, the year of her death. Notable for Porter's negative comments on George Eliot.

E24. "Semiramis Was a Good Girl." *New York Herald Tribune, Books*, 16 Aug. 1927, p. 6.

Review of *Memoirs of Catherine the Great of Russia*, translated by Katharine Anthony. "Even here, in these memoirs, stripped of erotic Byzantine gold leaf fable, she remains one of the most remarkable and interesting women in history."

1928

E25. "Misplaced Emphasis." *New York Herald Tribune, Books*, 3 June 1928, p. 7.

Review of *We Are Incredible*, by Margery Latimer. "This is an impressive story of the effects a glimpse of culture . . . may have on the unformed minds of the young in a small American town."

E26. "Hand-Book of Magic." *New Republic*, 55 (25 July 1928), 257.

Review of *A Mirror for Witches*, by Esther Forbes. "This is the simple plot, but told with such candid warmth, so much sly wit and detached irony, such a lively march of episode that it make a superbly entertaining novel." The novel depicts the life of a woman who believes she is a witch in seventeenth-century Massachusetts.

E27. "Marc Lescarbot." *New Republic*, 56 (22 Aug. 1928), 24–25.

Review of *Nova Francia: A Description of Acadia, 1606*, translated by P. Erondelle. Republication of an early seventeenth-century English translation of Marc Lescarbot's 1609 French edition of his 1606–07 account of his visit to the French territory of Acadia. Originally intended to spur settlement and conversion, the book remains valuable for its style, historical truth, charming wit, and leisurely learning.

E28. "Second Wind." *New York Herald Tribune, Books*, 23 Sept. 1928, p. 6.

Review of *Useful Knowledge*, by Gertrude Stein. Porter's style is a parody of Stein's own.
Reprinted in *The Days Before* (A14) and *Collected Essays* (A20).

E29. "The Family." *New York Herald Tribune, Books*, 7 Oct. 1928, p. 2.

Review of *Nothing Is Sacred*, by Josephine Herbst. This novel about an "American family in a modest way of life" is "beautiful and full with the fullness of a perfect economy and final choice of phrase."

E30. "The Hundredth Role." *New York Herald Tribune, Books*, 7 Oct. 1928, p. 16.

Review of *The Book of Catherine Wells*, introduction by H.G. Wells. "The stories offer a strange contrast to the portrait her husband gives of a vivid, tireless, beautiful woman whose endless good sense and . . . loyalty to the man of her choice make her a model for all good women and prove that she was a writer of very slender talents."

E31. "The Dark Ages of New England—The Puritan Emerges Alive and Softened." *New York Evening Post*, 3 Nov. 1928, Section 3, p. 8.

Review of *Cotton Mather, Keeper of the Puritan Conscience*, by Ralph and Louise Boas. Critical of Mather and the society from which he sprang, Porter's review suggests that this biography "is sympathetically softened wherever possible."

1929

E32. "The Virgin and the Unicorn." *New York Herald Tribune, Books*, 17 Feb. 1929, pp. 1–2.

Review of *The True Heart*, by Sylvia Townsend Warner. Warner's "wistful, touching, somewhat tragic interpretation of this old legend of the maiden, love and fate" leaves remaining in the reader's mind two symbolic figures: the subservient, loving woman and the unconscious, irresponsible man.

E33. "Not So Lost!" *New York Herald Tribune, Books*, 3 March 1929, p. 4.

Review of *The Lost Art: Letters of Seven Famous Women*, edited by Dorothy Van Doren. Collection of selected letters by Lady Mary Wortley Montagu, Mary Wollstonecraft, Abigail Adams, Charlotte Brontë, Jane Austen, Jane Welsh Carlyle, and Margaret Fuller. The selection manages to capture the writers' "own essences; it makes an impressive showing of grand human qualities. They deserve to be remembered, to be praised."

E34. "Moral Waxworks Exposed." *New York Herald Tribune, Books*, 12 May 1929, p. 4.

Review of *The Devil Is a Woman*, by Alice Mary Kimball. Despite their New England setting and details, these narrative poems remind you "that these tales are universal, they belong to the folk-myth of all countries, they seem unreal only because much of human conduct is incredible; varying only in surface detail, they are the product of life lived at a certain level of darkness in any part of the world."

E35. "Old Gods and New Messiahs." *New York Herald Tribune, Books*, 29 Sept. 1929, pp. 1–2.

Review of *Idols Behind Altars*, by Anita Brenner. Brenner's book about Mexican art is "a stimulating record of a vital period in the history of American art told by a contemporary witness."

E36. "The Fair-Haired Man." *New York Herald Tribune, Books*, 3 Nov. 1929, pp. 1–2.

Review of *The Gothick North: A Study of Medieval Life, Art and Thought*, by Sacheverell Sitwell. Sitwell's study of medieval life, art, and thought also gives vent to his grievances and accumulated indignations with the modern world.

E37. "Bohemian Futility." *New Masses*, 5 (Nov. 1929), 17–18.

Review of *Money for Love*, by Josephine Herbst. The characters of the novel are "fascinating in a fearful way, because a good artist, perfectly in command of her method, has for her own mysterious reasons chosen to assemble them: her lack of human pity is her own business."

E38. "The Most Catholic King." *New York Herald Tribune, Books*, 1 Dec. 1929, p. 5.

Review of *King Spider: Some Aspects of Louis XI of France*, by D.B. Wyndham Lewis. This book "is a warm apology for King Louis XI of France, written by a romantically fervent Catholic who is also a devoted antiquarian, who intersperses his authentic history with hymns of praise for the church, for the blessed fifteenth century, for its music, its poetry, its customs, its laws, its spirit."

E39. "'These Pictures Must Be Seen.'" *New York Herald Tribune, Books*, 22 Dec. 1929, pp. 5–6.

Review of *The Frescoes of Diego Rivera*, introduction by Ernestine Evans. This "timely and valuable book" is the first collection of photographs of Rivera's Mexican murals which contains "an interesting introduction to the artist." "I believe he is the most important living painter."

1930

E40. "William Phips, Cotton Mather's Dear Machine." *New York Evening Post*, 1 Feb. 1930, Section 3, p. 11.

Review of *The Life of Sir William Phips*, by Cotton Mather, introduction by Mark Van Doren. A "vivid portrait of Sir William, not as he was . . . but as Cotton Mather saw him. . . . The fact that it is a defense of a loved and admired creature, a work of hatred and bitterness against his enemies, is now, in the light of time, rather in its favor than against it."

E41. "A Disinherited Cosmopolitan." *New York Herald Tribune, Books*, 16 Feb. 1930, p. 22.

Review of *Essays on American Literature*, by Lafcadio Hearn. This collection of newspaper and magazine articles, written by Hearn during his life in New Orleans from 1878 to 1887, was published to mark the twenty-fifth anniversary of his death. The judgments. "necessarily hasty, by necessity written in haste, were nonetheless in many cases true, literate and intense, and if they seem a little worn by now it is because they have become familiar by adoption."

1931

E42. "Example to the Young." *New Republic*, 66 (22 April 1931), 279–80.

Review of *Wedding Day and Other Stories* and *Plagued by the Nightingale*, by Kay Boyle. The novel "is a magnificent performance; and as the short stories left the impression of reservoirs of power hardly tapped, so this novel, complete as it is, seems only a beginning."

1936

E43. "History on the Wing." *New Republic*, 89 (18 Nov. 1936), 82.

Review of *The Stones Awake: A Novel of Mexico*, by Carleton Beals. Qualified praise which implies that the novel fails in "scenes of absolutely private lives and relationships." One character, an "Indian village girl born in peonage," is "worth knowing."

1937

E44. "Rivera's Personal Revolution in Mexico." *New York Herald Tribune, Books*, 21 March 1937, p. 7.

Review of *Portrait of Mexico*, paintings by Diego Rivera, text by Bertram D. Wolfe. This sound book gives "for the first time . . . an inclusive and coherent history of Mexico from preconquest days to the present, and a key to the work of Diego Rivera, not only as a painter but as a pictorial historian of Mexico, the land and its people."

E45. "Dulce et Decorum Est." *New Republic*, 90 (31 March 1937), 244–45.

Review of *None Shall Look Back*, by Caroline Gordon. Porter finds this novel of the Civil War set in the South a story she knows by heart, "but I have never heard it told better."

E46. "The Art of Katherine Mansfield." *Nation*, 145 (23 Oct. 1937), 435–36.

Review of *The Short Stories of Katherine Mansfield*. Porter feels that Mansfield is in danger of being "overwhelmed by her own legend," of having "her work neglected for an interest in her 'personality.'" "I judge her work to have been to a great degree a matter of intelligent use of her faculties, a conscious practice of a hard-won craftsmanship, a triumph of discipline over the unruly circumstances and confusions of her personal life and over certain destructive elements in her own nature."

Reprinted in *The Days Before* (A14) and *Collected Essays* (A20).

E47. "The First American Saint." *New York Herald Tribune, Books,* 12 Dec. 1937, p. 2.

Review of *The Life of Saint Rose,* by Marian Storm. "Miss Storm has devoted attention, sympathy, scholarship and good common sense to the superb example of sainthood that was the life of Saint Rose."

1942

E48. "Lovely Evocative Photographs." *New York Herald Tribune, Books,* 8 March 1942, p. 4.

Review of *New Orleans and Its Living Past,* photographs by Clarence John Laughlin, text by David L. Cohn. "Mr. Cohn's words fail, then, on the side of frivolity and love of the surface aspect of things, and he has fallen into the common error of putting on airs about his special knowledge, which is not so special after all, and of looking down his nose at the less privileged visitor." "Only the most beautiful and touching things are in these photographs," and "Mr. Laughlin has seen this particular reality in its true light and without once cocking a superior snoot at anyone."

E49. "The Sparrow Revolution." *Nation,* 154 (21 March 1942), 343.

Review of *The Pink Egg,* by Polly Boyden. This "fable about the downtrodden, underprivileged sparrows who make a revolution and throw all the robins and other handsomer, luckier, and more talented birds out of the orchard where they live" is neither funny nor successful.

1943

E50. "Mexico's Thirty Long Years of Revolution—A Story Told Simply and Effectively in Text and Photographs." *New York Herald Tribune, Books*, 30 May 1943, pp. 1–2.

Review of *The Wind That Swept Mexico: The History of the Mexican Revolution, 1910–1942*, text by Anita Brenner, historical photographs assembled by George R. Leighton. "The reader who knows little can find here a clear statement, a logical exposition that will serve safely as a starting point if he wishes to pursue this history further," although Brenner's work gives "too pretty and simple a picture" and needs a "few scorching lines" on certain aspects. Mr. Leighton's "distinguished, realistic" collection of pictures makes "the most convincing, most moving kind of straight narrative."

E51. "The Winged Skull." *Nation*, 157 (17 July 1943), 72–73.

Review of *This Is Lorence: A Narrative of the Reverend Laurence Sterne*, by Lodwick Hartley. "An immense amount of devoted study and trained research appears to have gone into this fairly short book, which handles with ease a baffling complexity of detail and carries the story along swiftly and with concentration on several planes at once." But "where is the real Laurence Sterne, the one who wrote 'Tristram Shandy'? That winged skull seems to have made his getaway again, taking his main secret with him."
Reprinted in *Collected Essays* (A20).

1945

E52. "They Lived with the Enemy in the House." *New York Herald Tribune, Books*, 4 March 1945, p. 1.

Review of *Apartment in Athens,* by Glenway Wescott. The novel "has exposed and anatomized that streak of Germanism in the rest of us which made possible the Germany we know today."

E53. "Pull Dick, Pull Devil." *Nation,* 161 (13 Oct. 1945), 376–78.

Review of *Saints and Strangers,* by George F. Willison. The book contains "all you need to know, now or ever, about that group of early American settlers now called the Pilgrim Fathers, their lives and hazards in the Plymouth Plantation.
Reprinted in *Collected Essays* (A20).

1949

E54. "The Calm, Pure Art of Willa Cather." *New York Times, Book Review,* 25 Sept. 1949, p. 1.

Review of *Willa Cather on Writing,* foreword by Stephen Tennant. This collection of four letters, prefaces to Cather's novels, and a number of critical essays says "the most interesting, most profound things about the art of writing, and the life of art, that have been said in our time certainly," and Cather does it "with immense grace and dignity, treating her subject, no matter who or what, with respect and the grand courtesy of true attention."

E55. "Edith Sitwell's Steady Growth to Great Poetic Art." *New York Herald Tribune, Books,* 18 Dec. 1949, pp. 1, 12.

Review of *The Canticle of the Rose, 1917–1949,* by Edith Sitwell. The poems here collected are "the true flowering branch springing fresh from the old, unkillable roots of English poetry; with the range, variety, depth, fearlessness, the passion and elegance of great art."
Reprinted as "'The Laughing Heat of the Sun'" in *The Days Before* (A14) and *Collected Essays* (A20).

1950

E56. "Orpheus in Purgatory." *New York Times, Book Review*, 1 Jan. 1950, pp. 3, 10.

Review of *Rilke and Benvenuta*, by Magda von Hattingberg. In this volume von Hattingberg "publishes some of his letters—and very interesting letters too—some of hers, passages from her diary, some very valuable transcriptions of conversations they had, and for the rest, a rhapsodical, high-flung, far-fetched romance."

Reprinted in *The Days Before* (A14) and *Collected Essays* (A20).

E57. "Virginia Woolf's Essays—A Great Art, a Sober Craft." *New York Times, Book Review*, 7 May 1950, p. 3.

Review of *The Captain's Death Bed and Other Essays*, by Virginia Woolf. This review is primarily an assessment of the achievement of Woolf. "She was full of secular intelligence primed with the profane virtues, with her love not only of the world of all the arts created by the human imagination, but a love of life itself and daily living, a spirit at once gay and severe, exacting and generous, a born artist and a sober craftsman; and she had no plan whatever for her personal salvation; or the personal salvation even of someone else; brought no doctrine, no dogma."

Reprinted as "Virginia Woolf" in *The Days Before* (A14) and *Collected Essays* (A20).

E58. "The Strange, Old World." *New York Times, Book Review*, 20 Aug. 1950, pp. 5, 17.

Review of *The Secret Game*, by François Boyer, and *The House of Breath*, by William Goyen. The first is "an interesting, honest, small work"; the second is "a sustained evocation of the past, a long search for place and identity, and the meaning of an intense personal experience."

E59. "A Quaker Who 'Had a Splendid Time of It.'" *New York Herald Tribune, Books*, 24 Sept. 1950, p. 6.

Review of *Philadelphia Quaker: The Letters of Hannah Whitall Smith*, edited by Logan Pearsall Smith, biographical preface and notes by Robert Gathorne-Hardy. "These letters glow with the utmost vitality and sincerity of feeling, the most independent powers of observation and remark, and the most gay, warm good humor."

E60. "Beerbohm Bailiwick." *New York Times, Book Review*, 22 Oct. 1950, p. 5.

Review of *And Even Now*, essays by Max Beerbohm. After thirty years, these essays "seem as sharp and even more timely" than when Porter read them in the 1920's.
Reprinted as "Max Beerbohm" in *Collected Essays* (A20).

E61. "Yours, Ezra Pound." *New York Herald Times, Book Review*, 29 Oct. 1950, pp. 4, 26.

Review of *The Letters of Ezra Pound, 1907–1941*, edited by D.D. Paige. These letters are revealing because they "contain hardly one paragraph which does not relate in one way or another to one sole theme—the arts."
Reprinted as "'It Is Hard to Stand in the Middle'" in *The Days Before* (A14) and *Collected Essays* (A20).

1951

E62. "E.M. Forster Speaks Out for the Things He Holds Dear." *New York Times, Book Review*, 4 Nov. 1951, p. 3.

Review of *Two Cheers for Democracy*, by E.M. Forster. This is "a collection of his short writings on a tremendous range of subjects, . . . an extension and enlargement of his thought, a record of the life and feelings of an artist who has been in himself an example of all he has defended from the first."

Reprinted as "E.M. Forster" in *The Days Before* (A14) and *Collected Essays* (A20).

E63. "A Most Lively Genius." *New York Times, Book Review*, 18 Nov. 1951, pp. 5, 52.

Review of *Short Novels of Colette*, introduction by Glenway Wescott. These six short novels, "for all their varying brilliancy, are not her best work." Let us just "be glad of such a gook, sound, honest artist, a hard-working one; we could do with more 'light writers' like her."

1952

E64. "The Grand and the Tragic." *New York Times, Book Review*, 13 April 1952, p. 3.

Review of *Rome and a Villa*, by Eleanor Clark. "This whole book is the distillation of a deep personal experience; it is autobiography in the truest sense, in terms of what outward impact set the inner life in motion toward its true relation to the world: the search for what is truly one's own, and the ability to recognize it when found, and to be faithful in love of it."

Reprinted as "Eleanor Clark" in *Collected Essays* (A20).

1955

E65. "His Poetry Makes the Difference." *New York Times, Book Review*, 20 Nov. 1955, p. 5.

Review of *Dylan Thomas in America*, by John Malcolm Brinnin. "This book is the story of disgrace and disaster and death that came" of Thomas's and Brinnin's hopes and plans for Thomas's transcontinental poetry reading tour in America.

Reprinted as part of "Dylan Thomas" in *Collected Essays* (A20).

1957

E66. "In the Depths of Grief, a Towering Rage. "*New York Times, Book Review*, 13 Oct. 1957, pp. 3, 32.

Review of *Leftover Life to Kill*, by Caitlin Thomas. This is Dylan Thomas's widow's story of their relationship and her life after his death. This "is not art, it is a huge loud clamor out of the depths." Reprinted as part of "Dylan Thomas" in *Collected Essays* (A20).

1958

E67. "In the Morning of the Poet." *New York Times, Book Review*, 2 Feb. 1958, p. 4.

Review of *Dylan Thomas: Letters to Vernon Watkins*, edited with an introduction by Vernon Watkins. These letters cover the period from April 1936 to 29 December 1952 and provide "a good long look at the poet in the morning of his energies and gifts." Reprinted as part of "Dylan Thomas" in *Collected Essays* (A20).

1959

E68. "A Wreath for the Gamekeeper." *Shenandoah*, 11 (Autumn 1959), 3–12.

Review of *Lady Chatterley's Lover*, by D.H. Lawrence. Porter sums up her opinions of the novel on its publication in unexpurgated form. Lawrence "was about as wrong as wrong can be on the whole subject of sex, and . . . he has written a very laboriously bad book to prove it." Porter objects to Lawrence's "misuse and perversion" of obscenity; "he makes it sickly sentimental, embarrassingly so." Reprinted in revised form in *Encounter*, 14 (Feb. 1960), 69–77, and in *Collected Essays* (A20).

1970

E69. "On Christopher Sykes." *Collected Essays and Occasional Writings of Katherine Anne Porter.* New York: Delacorte, 1970, pp. 64–67.

Review of *Character and Situation—Six Stories*, by Christopher Sykes. Sykes is an example of the contemporary "literate, careful unliterary writer who, no matter how many books he has published, still gives the impression of clinging defensively to his semi-amateur status." Furthermore, he belongs to the branch of those writers Porter characterizes as "the Romantic-Erotic-Religous . . . who have a message to convey." Porter calls for another generation of writers, who will know how to treat "the passion of love and the art of literature" with the concern and the dignity they deserve.

Although this is dated 1951, there is no evidence that it was published before 1970.

PART II

WORKS ABOUT KATHERINE ANNE PORTER

SECTION F
BIBLIOGRAPHICAL

The entries in this section are in alphabetical order.

Note: This section does not include the bibliographies that are given in the full-length books about Porter (listed in Sections G and H).

F1. Birss, John H. "American First Editions: Katherine Anne Porter." *Publisher's Weekly*, 133 (18 June 1938), 2382.

Ten entries.

F2. Bixby, George. "Katherine Anne Porter: A Bibliographical Checklist." *American Book Collector*, n.s., 1 (Nov.–Dec. 1980), 19–33.

A descriptive checklist of both primary and secondary publications.

F3. Etulain, R.W. *A Bibliographical Guide to the Study of Western American Literature.* Lincoln: Univ. of Nebraska Press, 1982, pp. 221–23.

A listing of some of the Porter scholarship.

F4. Givner, Joan, Jane DeMouy, and Ruth M. Alvarez. "Katherine Anne Porter." In *American Women Writers,*

ed. Maurice Duke, Jackson R. Bryer, and M. Thomas
Inge. Westport, Conn.: Greenwood, 1983, pp. 201–31.

A bibliographical essay. In addition to giving the
major editions of Porter's works and discussing Porter
material in libraries, the authors discuss and evaluate
the most important literature about Porter and her
writing. The Porter criticism is arranged according to
topic.

F5. Kiernan, Robert F. *Katherine Anne Porter and Carson
McCullers: A Reference Guide.* Boston: G.K. Hall, 1976.

Lists and annotates works about Porter through 1973
(with one entry for 1974). The organization is by year,
with books and shorter writings listed separately.

F6. Schwartz, Edward. "Katherine Anne Porter: A Critical
Bibliography." *Bulletin of the New York Public
Library*, 57 (May 1953), 211–47.

The first substantial Porter bibliography. Porter
herself read and corrected the manuscript. It lists both
primary and secondary works. Most entries are annotated.
Reprinted the same year, by the New York Public
Library, as a separate publication.

F7. Sylvester, William A. "Selected and Critical
Bibliography of the Uncollected Works of Katherine
Anne Porter." *Bulletin of Bibliography*, 19 (Jan.–April
1947), 36.

Eighteen entries.

F8. Waldrip, Louise, and Shirley Ann Bauer. *A Bibliography
of the Works of Katherine Anne Porter and A
Bibliography of the Criticism of Katherine Anne
Porter.* Metuchen, N.J.: Scarecrow, 1969.

A descriptive bibliography of Porter's works and an
annotated bibliography of works about Porter. The latter
is divided into five sections: Books and Section of Books,

Articles in Periodicals and Newspapers, Doctoral Dissertations and Masters' Theses, Foreign Language Material, and Book Reviews.

F9. Williams, Jerry T. *Southern Literature 1968–1975: A Checklist of Scholarship.* Boston: G.K. Hall, 1978, pp. 178–81.

An annotated checklist of Porter criticism.

F10. Woodress, James. "Katherine Anne Porter (1890–)." In *American Fiction, 1900–1950: A Guide to Information Sources.* Detroit: Gale, 1974, pp. 157–60.

A brief bibliographical essay.

SECTION G
BIOGRAPHICAL, INCLUDING
INTERVIEWS

The entries in this section are given in alphabetical order. Reprints are listed with the original entry. Reviews of books about Porter are not listed unless the reviewers make significant comments about Porter herself.

G1. Allen, Henry. "A Lioness of Literature Looks Back." *Los Angeles Times, Calendar*, 7 July 1974, pp. 1, 64–65.

Porter talks about her life, her acquaintances, and her coffin.

G2. ———. "Present at the Destruction." *Washington Post, Potomac*, 31 March 1974, pp. 12–13.

Porter's life is summarized (with one husband omitted). She speaks of the coffin she has bought, the fascinating experiences she has had, and her feelings on being old.
Reprinted as "The Vanity of Excellence" in Joan Givner (ed.), *Katherine Anne Porter: Conversations* (G66).

G3. Amory, Cleveland. "Celebrity Register." *McCall's*, 90 (April 1963), 184.

A brief passage regarding Porter's life and the reception of *Ship of Fools*.

G4. Anson, Cherrill. "Novel 30 Years in the Making." *Baltimore Sun*, 1 April 1962, Family Section, pp. 1, 3.

Katherine Anne Porter is a charming woman, and her long-awaited novel is ready for publication.

G5. Archer, Eugene. "Movie Is Planned on 'Ship of Fools.'" *New York Times*, 25 April 1962, p. 33.

Stanley Kramer plans to film the movie on "a multi-million-dollar budget."

G6. "Author Receives Medal from Libraries Group." *New York Times*, 4 April 1940, p. 24.

Porter has received the first gold medal of the Society of Libraries of New York University.

G7. "Authors Honored by National Institute." *New York Times*, 18 Jan. 1950, p. 23.

Porter and Glenway Wescott were elected vice-presidents of the National Institute of Arts and Letters.

G8. Babcock, Frederic. "Among the Authors." *Chicago Tribune, Books*, 2 Nov. 1952, p. 9.

Porter has taken part in a P.E.N. panel discussion on "The Novel as a Carrier of Ideas."

G9. Bandler, Michael. "And Then They Wrote." *Washington Star* (Sunday Magazine), 24 Oct. 1971, pp. 6–7.

Katherine Anne Porter resides in a College Park high-rise with a live-in housekeeper and is working on two books.

G10. Barnes, Bart. "Katherine A. Porter Gives Books, Grant to Md. U. Library." *Washington Post*, 16 Dec. 1966, p. C-3.

In addition to leaving her books and papers to the University of Maryland, Porter has announced that she is forming a Katherine Anne Porter foundation to aid young writers.

G11. Bart, Peter. "Filming Starts on 'Ship of Fools' After Two Years of Preparation." *New York Times*, 14 July 1964, p. 28.

> After various delays, the filming will begin.

G12. Beals, Carleton. *Glass Houses: Ten Years of Free-Lancing*. Philadelphia: Lippincott, 1938, pp. 181, 362.

> Only brief references to Porter. But interesting in the claim that at one time in Mexico she was "very ill with consumption."

G13. Benstock, Shari. *Women of the Left Bank: Paris, 1900–1940*. Austin: Univ. of Texas Press, 1986, pp. 4, 6, 120, 161–62, 187–88, 244, 248, 251, 260, 381, 444, 451, 455n, 464n, 465n.

> Several references to Porter, most of which concern her critical assertions about Gertrude Stein.

G14. Berg, Paul. "Celebrating a Celebrated Author." *St. Louis Post-Dispatch, Pictures*, 22 April 1962, pp. 4–6.

> The long-awaited publication of *Ship of Fools* has led to Porter's being honored at many receptions, teas, etc.

G15. "The Best Years." *Newsweek*, 58 (31 July 1961), 78.

> After many years in the writing, Porter's first novel will soon be published.

G16. "Biographical Sketches of the 1966 Winners of the Pulitzer Prizes." *New York Times*, 3 May 1966, p. 43.

> Brief sketch.

G17. Bode, Winston. "Miss Porter on Writers and Writing." *Texas Observer*, 31 Oct. 1958.

Porter comments upon James Agee, John Peale Bishop, Allen Tate, William Humphrey, and William Goyen. Also, she explains her means of transforming remembered experience into literature.

Reprinted in Joan Givner (ed.), *Katherine Anne Porter: Conversations* (G66).

G18. "Books Notes." *New York Herald Tribune*, 22 Dec. 1936, p. 21.

"Noon Wine" will soon be published in a limited edition of 250 copies.

G19. "Books." *Time*, 50 (4 Aug. 1947), 80, 82–83.

In an article dealing with the current activities of leading American writers, Porter is reported as having spent forty weeks working on movie scripts and to have become quite disgusted with the endeavor.

G20. Boudin, Leonard B. "A Significant Case." *Nation* 239 (22 Dec. 1984), 666.

A Letter to the Editor referring to Porter's accusation that members of the Sacco and Vanzetti Committee had wanted the two men executed. Refers also to the Elinor Langer claim that Porter had informed to the FBI on Josephine Herbst.

G21. Boutell, Clip. "Authors Are Like People." *New York Post*, 21 Sept. 1944, p. 23.

Porter announces that her novel will be published "next spring."

G22. "Brandeis Honors the Lunts, Porter." *Boston Globe*, 13 April 1972, p. 60.

Porter will be among those honored for achievement in the creative arts.

G23. Breit, Harvey. "In and Out of Books." *New York Times, Book Review*, 19 May 1957, p. 8.

Many writers, including Porter, have signed an ACLU statement condemning the National Organization for Decent Literature "for violating the principle of freedom."

G24. Brooks, Cleanth. "Katherine Anne Porter, RIP." *National Review*, 32 (31 Oct. 1980), 1311–12.

An obituary essay.

G25. Brown, John L. "Readers and Writers in Paris." *New York Times, Book Review*, 3 March 1946, p. 14.

Announces that a French translation of *Flowering Judas* has been published and is receiving "appreciative reviews."

G26. Bruno, Anne Turner. "In Her Own Words." *Saturday Review*, 7 (Dec. 1980), 11.

An excerpt from an unpublished interview of 1963. Porter is "appalled at the aimlessness of most people's lives today." She would have achieved no success at all if she had not aimed for "greatness."

G27. Buckley, Tim. "Caribbean Cruise Attempts to Seek Meaning of Apollo." *New York Times*, 12 Dec. 1972, pp. 49, 53.

Writers and other interested parties are cruising the Caribbean and participating in a seminar on the implications of the Apollo 17 shot. Among them is Katherine Anne Porter, who described her excitement at the Apollo shot "with the spontaneous enthusiasms of a child."

G28. Bufkin, E.C. (ed.). "An *Open Mind* Profile: Katherine Anne Porter Talks with Glenway Wescott and Eric F. Goldman." *Georgia Review*, 41 (Winter 1987), 769–95.

A transcript of the 13 May 1962 telecast of *The Open Mind*, in which Porter was interviewed by Glenway Wescott and Eric F. Goldman. The date was six weeks after the publication of *Ship of Fools* and two days before Porter's seventy-second birthday. Porter discusses the delays in completing her novel, the initial critical reaction to it, its themes, her attitude toward Germans, her days in Mexico, her views of good and evil, and future of the world.

G29. C., K. "Katherine Anne Porter: A's in Literature." *Christian Science Monitor*, 4 April 1966, p. 10.

Porter has had a varied life, has devoted much care to her writing, and has finally been rewarded with the success of *Ship of Fools*.

G30. Carr, Virginia Spencer. *The Lonely Hunter: A Biography of Carson McCullers*. Garden City, N.Y.: Doubleday, 1975, pp. 108, 112, 146–47, 154–57, 158, 180, 216, 234, 327, 544.

Concerns the relationship—consisting of an amount of animosity—between Porter and Carson McCullers at Yaddo.

G31. Cassini, Igor. "The New 400." *Esquire*, 39 (June 1953), 48.

This article accompanies a list—compiled by Cholly Knickerbocker—of the 400 persons (including Porter) who are "Society." (Note: In the margin of her clipping, Porter wrote "It would be nice to see us all in one zoo. I am personally acquainted with just 16 of these.")

G32. Chamberlain, John. "Books of the Times." *New York Times*, 20 Oct. 1933, p. 17.

Ford Madox Ford, in his instinctive appreciation for "unannounced genius," is currently "championing" the work of Porter.

G33. Clark, Eleanor. "The Friendships of a Lifetime." *Book World* (*Washington Post*), 11 (26 July 1981), 1–2, 9–10.

Ostensibly a review of Lopez, *Conversations with Katherine Anne Porter* (G104). But valuable for the biographical information on Porter given by Clark herself. (Also valuable for pointing out numerous errors in Lopez.)

G34. Clarke, Gerald. *Capote: A Biography*. New York: Simon and Schuster, 1988, pp. 100–02, 148–49, 375, 485, 489–90.

Touches upon the various times Capote and Porter crossed paths. In his *Answered Prayers*, Alice Lee Langman is modeled on Porter.
Reprinted in paperback by Ballantine, 1989.

G34a. Cole, Hunter, and Seetha Srinivasan. "Eudora Welty, Inquiring Photographer." *New York Times, Book Review*, 22 Oct. 1989, p. 32.

In an interview concerning her photography, Eudora Welty comments on her friendship with Porter and on the photographs she took of Porter at Yaddo.

G35. Corry, John. "Intellectuals in Bloom at Spring Gathering." *New York Times*, 18 May 1972, pp. 49, 63.

At the annual ceremonies of the American Academy of Arts and Letters and the National Institute of Arts and Letters, Porter commented on her admiration for Eudora Welty.

G36. Cowley, Malcolm. "Twenty-Five Years After." *Saturday Review*, 34 (2 June 1951), 7.

In a discussion of the lives led by American writers during the twenties, it is mentioned that Porter's "exile" was to Mexico rather than Europe.

G37. Crane, Hart. *The Letters of Hart Crane: 1916–1932*, ed. Brom Weber. New York: Hermitage House, 1952, pp. 367, 369–70, 373, 375–78, 383.

Contains notes and letters to and about Porter.

G38. Crawford, Kitty Barry. "Miss Porter Heads Clinic Campaign." *Fort Worth Record*, Sept. 1921.

Porter is to direct a fundraising drive for the establishing of a tuberculosis clinic in Fort Worth.
Reprinted in Joan Givner (ed.), *Katherine Anne Porter: Conversations* (G66).

G39. Culligan, Glendy. "Her Ship Drops Anchor." *Washington Post, Potomac*, 14 Nov. 1965, pp. 49–50, 52.

Describes Porter's twelve-room "Tudor mansion" in Washington, D.C., and her collection of elegant furniture and objets d'art.

G40. ———. "Katherine Anne Porter Returns Here After a Year's Attempt to Dodge Fame." *Washington Post*, 10 Nov. 1963, p. A-49.

Porter has returned to Washington after a year in Europe.

G41. ———. "Two from Area in Running for Book Awards." *Washington Post*, 10 March 1963, p. G-6.

Porter and Rachel Carson, two women prominent in Washington cultural life, have been nominated for National Book Awards.

G42. Cutrer, Thomas W. *Parnassus on the Mississippi: "The Southern Review" and the Baton Rouge Literary Community, 1935–1942*. Baton Rouge: Louisiana State Univ. Press, 1983, *passim*.

Concerns Porter's contributions to *The Southern Review* and her relationship with members of its staff.

G43. "Dedicated Author." *New York Times* 16 March 1966, p. 42.

Katherine Anne Porter is a fascinating woman with many interests; but her foremost identity is as a writer.

G44. Denham, Alice. "Katherine Anne Porter: Washington's Own Literary Lioness." *Washingtonian*, 1 (May 1966), 32–33, 38–39.

Porter comments upon her recent receiving of the National Book Award, upon her struggles as a writer, upon her relationships with men, and upon writers she dislikes (Bellow, Mailer, Sartre, de Beauvoir), and upon the artistic situation in the United States.

G45. "Desegregation Ruling Criticized by Author." *Richmond News Leader*, 20 Nov. 1958.

Porter comments on the Supreme Court's desegregation ruling (she disapproves) and on *Ship of Fools* (it will "appear in late spring" and will concern the "inertia good people have toward the evils of this world").
Reprinted in Joan Givner (ed.), *Katherine Anne Porter: Conversations* (G66).

G46. Dolan, Mary Anne. "Almost Since Chaucer with Miss Porter." *Washington Star*, 11 May 1975, pp. A-1, A-6.

Porter discusses her own past experiences and comments on contemporary writing.
Reprinted in Joan Givner, *Katherine Anne Porter: Conversations* (G66) and Barbara Nykoruk (ed.), *Authors in the News*, Vol. 2 (1976).

G47. Dolbier, Maurice. "'I've Had a Good Run for My Money.'" *New York Herald Tribune, Books*, 1 April 1962, pp. 3, 11.

Ship of Fools will soon be published. Porter likes Roth, dislikes Sartre, and thinks that de Beauvoir's *The Second Sex* "was a stupid performance."

Reprinted in Joan Givner (ed.), *Katherine Anne Porter: Conversations* (G66).

G48. Dorsey, John. "Katherine Anne Porter on: Truman Capote ... Edith Sitwell ... Ernest Hemingway ... And on Her Life and Writing." *Baltimore Sun Magazine*, 26 Oct. 1969, pp. 16, 18–19, 21, 23, 40–41.

Porter reminisces about her early years and about the many writers who have been her friends. She is looking back on a successful life: "I have come as near as anybody I know in the world to getting just where I wanted." Reprinted in Joan Givner (ed.), *Katherine Anne Porter: Conversations* (G66).

G49. "Ethel Merman Sings for Johnson Independents." *Washington Post*, 2 Oct. 1964, p. D-4.

Porter, Ethel Merman, Oveta Culp Hobby, Betty Friedan, and others have met with President Johnson and pledged their support for his election.

G50. "Famed Author is Abridged by One Word Only." *Washington Post*, 16 May 1968, p. E-3.

Having banished "retirement" from her vocabulary, Porter has announced the planned publication of four more books.

G51. "First Novel." *Time*, 78 (28 July 1961), 70.

Porter declares that after many years she has finally turned *Ship of Fools* over to the publisher.

G52. Ford, Hugh. *Published in Paris*. New York: Macmillan, 1975, pp. 28, 92, 225, 228, 341–44, 368.

Discusses the publication of *Hacienda* (A6) and *French Song-Book* (A5) by Harrison of Paris.

G53. "Four Authors Are Given National Book Awards." *Publishers Weekly*, 189 (21 March 1966), 47–48.

In granting the NBA for fiction to Porter, the jury praised her as "a dedicated and uncompromising literary artist, successful almost in spite of herself."

G54. "Four 'Forgotten' Books Win $2,500 Prizes." *New York Times*, 30 Jan. 1937, p. 15.

Prizes were given for works "considered to have been read insufficiently by the general public." Porter's *Flowering Judas* was one such work.

G55. Frankel, Haskel. "The Author." *Saturday Review*, 48 (25 Sept. 1965), 36.

Porter is attractive, entertaining, and fascinating.

G56. Fries, Maureen. "Miss Porter's Award Arouses Some Wrath." *Buffalo Courier Express*, 10 April 1966.

The awarding of the National Book Award to Porter for her *Collected Stories* has led to criticism because, first, most of the stories had been published before and, second, of the feeling that the Award was a consolation prize to Porter for her not receiving the NBA for *Ship of Fools*.

G57. Gannett, Lewis. "Books and Things." *New York Herald Tribune*, 30 Jan. 1937, p. 11.

Concerns Porter's getting a Book-of-the-Month Club award for insufficiently recognized writers.

G58. Gelfant, Blanche H. "Lives of Women Writers: Cather, Austin, Porter, Willa, Mary, Katherine Anne." *Novel*, 18 (Fall 1984), 64–80.

Examines recent biographies of Porter (Givner, G65), Mary Austin, and Willa Cather to determine the effects of gender upon a writer's life. On the surface the life of each woman seemed to resemble those of contemporary male writers. Each travelled widely and independently; each wrote about her travels; each was regarded as an equal by male writers; and each supported herself by her writing. All three women received honors and awards, and all participated in public life. Further, each had private dramas that served as inspiration for her art. All of these traits the three women shared with male writers. But the experience of coping with the conflict between society's expectation of the woman's role and one's own drive for literary achievement was an experience like nothing the men had encountered.

Reprinted in *Women Writing in America: Voices in Collage* (1984).

G59. Gibson, Rochelle. "The Author." *Saturday Review*, 45 (31 March 1962), 15.

In an interview, Porter says that the characters of *Ship of Fools* are "human beings with failings and prejudices or with burdens a little more than they can bear." She declares that the Germans "are just as dangerous as they were, and the moment they get back their power they are going to do it again."

G60. Gilroy, Harry. "Book Awards Go to 4 U.S. Writers." *New York Times*, 16 March 1966, p. 42.

Concerns Porter's National Book Award for *Collected Stories*.

G61. Givner, Joan. "A Fine Day of Homage to Porter." *Dallas Morning News*, 23 May 1976, p. G-5.

Howard Payne University honored Porter on her eighty-sixth birthday with a party, an honorary degree, and a Katherine Anne Porter Symposium. The events were held in Brownwood, Texas, near her birthplace. And, as she read "Anniversary in a Country Cemetery" (C36), there was a feeling "that something had come full circle for Katherine Anne Porter on this day."

Reprinted in *Katherine Anne Porter: Conversations* (G66).

G62. ———. "Introduction." In *Katherine Anne Porter: Conversations*. Jackson: Univ. Press of Mississippi, 1987, pp. ix–xix.

Although the Porter interviews are not reliable as sources of biographical fact, they do give a sense of her spirit. "She lives in these interviews as the brilliant raconteur and wit that she was." (See G66.)

G63. ———. "Katherine Anne Porter (15 May 1890–)." In *American Writers in Paris, 1920–1939*, ed. Karen Lane Rood. Detroit: Gale, 1980, pp. 311–14.

Concerns Porter's residence in Paris and her feelings about the city. She lived there the greater part of four years in the early 1930's. It was a productive period, during which she completed several of her best stories and apparently was planning the three works published in *Pale Horse, Pale Rider*. Also, she was surrounded by a good many friends, and her marriage to Eugene Pressly, although not perfect, seems to have been conducive to creativity. And the fact Paris was so "antithetical to Texas" allowed her to revaluate her early years.

G64. ———. "Katherine Anne Porter (1890–)." In *Southern Writers: A Biographical Dictionary*, ed. Robert Bain, Joseph M. Flora, and Louis D. Rubin, Jr. Baton Rouge: Louisiana State Univ. Press, 1979, pp. 360–62.

A biographical sketch. (Apparently, the first work on Porter to mention her second marriage.)

G65. ———. *Katherine Anne Porter: A Life*. New York: Simon and Schuster, 1982.

The only book-length Porter biography, by the scholar whom Porter herself chose for the task. It is grounded in thorough research, including the use of the large Porter Collection at the University of Maryland and correspondence and interviews with persons connected with Porter at each step of her life. Many of the myths that Porter created about her family background, her relationships with men, and her literary career are replaced with facts.

Reprinted by Jonathan Cape (1983) and Touchstone (1984). Givner is currently working on a revision.

G66.   ———. *Katherine Anne Porter: Conversations*. Jackson: Univ. Press of Mississippi, 1987.

A collection of Porter interviews spanning a sixty-year period. Contents: Joan Givner, "Introduction" (G62); Gordon K. Shearer, "What One Woman Is Doing to Help Children" (G153); Kitty Barry Crawford, "Miss Porter Heads Clinic Campaign" (G38); Archer Winsten, "Presenting the Portrait of an Artist" (G181); Robert Van Gelder, "Katherine Anne Porter at Work" (G169); "The New Invitation to Learning: 'The Turn of the Screw'" (C51); Mary McGrory, "Reading and Writing" (G108); Winston Bode, "Miss Porter on Writers and Writing" (G17); "Desegregation Ruling Criticized by Author" (G45); "Recent Southern Fiction: A Panel Discussion" (C104); James Ruoff, "Katherine Anne Porter Comes to Kansas" (G149); Elizabeth Janeway, "For Katherine Anne Porter *Ship of Fools* Was a Lively Twenty-Two Year Voyage" (G82); Maurice Dolbier, "'I've Had a Good Run for My Money'" (G47); Barbara Thompson, "Katherine Anne Porter: An Interview" (G163); Roy Newquist, "An Interview with Katherine Anne Porter" (G124); Hank Lopez, "A Country and Some People I Love" (G105); Josephine Novak, "Katherine Anne Porter Makes a Feast of Life" (G128); John Dorsey, "Katherine Anne Porter on . . . . ." (G48); Josephine Novak and Elise Chisholm, "Don't Scare the Horses, Miss Porter Tells Liberation Women" (G129); Mildred Whiteaker, "Glimpses of San Antonio at Turn of the Century" (G178); Henry Allen, "Katherine Anne Porter: The Vanity of Excellence" (G2); Carl Schoettler, "Katherine Anne Porter Reigns for Students" (G150); Mary Anne Dolan, "Almost Since Chaucer with Miss Porter" (G46); Doris Grumbach, "The Katherine Anne Porter Watch: After

Sacco and Vanzetti, What? 'The Devil and Cotton Mather'?" (G73); Joan Givner, "A Fine Day of Homage to Porter" (G61).

G67. ———. "Katherine Anne Porter: Queen of Texas Letters?" *Texas Libraries*, 45 (Winter 1984), 119–23.

Porter's personal life should not prevent her being recognized as a major writer, especially (in this case) a major Texas writer. Her probable informing on Josephine Herbst was a treacherous betrayal of a friend, even if it can be explained by her personal problems and her mental state at the time. Still, her "moral delinquencies" should not "undercut her recognition as a writer." Perhaps the problem would not have arisen if Porter had been a man: "I believe that moral flaws are allowed to detract much more from the reputations of women writers than from men." Close attention to Porter's life "surely reveals much to her credit," in spite of her frequent mishandling of facts. However, "her place in American literature is firmly established because of her work and because of her influence on a host of important writers." Also, "her reputation extends beyond the United States."

G68. ———. "Katherine Anne Porter's Texas." *Vision: The Magazine of the Public Communications Foundation for North Texas*, 2 (Sept. 1979), 18–22.

In spite of the ambivalence in Porter's relationship with Texas, "no one had deeper roots in Texas" than she. "Her personal history intersected the state's history at various points, she had blood knowledge of nearly every region of the state and a deep affection for most of it." She was born in a small settlement near Brownwood and spent most of her childhood near Austin and part of her adolescence in San Antonio. As a young woman, she lived in Houston, Dallas, and Fort Worth. Although she spent relatively little of her adult life in Texas, "her material and her speech were nurtured by the soil of Texas." The language of Texas became "'my native speech.'" In the

1980's she believed that the Univ. of Texas in Austin was to name a library after her. This was a misunderstanding that was "bitterly disappointing." Consequently, she gave her "papers, books and personal mementoes" to the University of Maryland, not to the University of Texas as she had intended.

G69. ———. "The Lady from Indian Creek." *Texas Observer*, 7 May 1982.

Not examined by compiler.

G70. ———. "'The Plantation of This Isle': Katherine Anne Porter's Bermuda Base." *Southwest Review*, 63 (Autumn 1978), 339–51.

Porter claimed that the Old South of magnolias and white columns was the environment of her childhood. But, even though she credibly portrays such a background in the Miranda stories, she herself grew up dirt poor in tiny houses. It is likely that the inspiration for Miranda's environment was actually Bermuda, where Porter spent five months in 1929. Helgrove, the mansion in which she stayed, seems a replica of the Gays' town house, while a house across the street from it is named Cedar Grove—the name Porter gave to the grandmother's farm in "The Fig Tree." This part of Bermuda is known for tree frogs, also included in that story. Amy Clendenen and her uncle of Bermuda may have been the sources of Aunt Amy and Uncle Gabriel in "Old Mortality."

G71. ———. "Porter's Subsidiary Art." *Southwest Review*, 59 (Summer 1974), 265–76.

Porter's correspondence is a revealing aid to understanding her temperament and her writing. For her a personal letter "assumes a special form, poised somewhere between fact and fiction." The letters she wrote to Glenway Wescott and Monroe Wheeler, perhaps intended for eventual publication, are especially interesting. In them we read of her problems with the publication of some of her stories (e.g., "The Leaning Tower"), of the progress of her critical writing, and of the hopes and frustrations involved in the long gestation of *Ship of Fools*.

G72. Green, Martin. "Of Lies, Luxuries, & Literature." *Commonweal*, 110 (25 March 1983), 187–88.

Ostensibly a review of Givner's *Katherine Anne Porter: A Life* (G65). But interesting for its speculation on the implications of Porter's need to transform the truth about herself into something more fascinating. Likens her to Truman Capote's Holly Golightly, and to the protagonist in D.H. Lawrence's "The Lovely Lady."

G73. Grumbach, Doris. "The Katherine Anne Porter Watch: After Sacco and Vanzetti, What? 'The Devil and Cotton Mather'?" *Village Voice*, 26 Jan. 1976, pp. 43–44.

Porter reminisces about the many years during which she worked from time to time on the projected Cotton Mather book. She also recalls Sacco and Vanzetti and explains her reasons for giving her papers and library to the University of Maryland.
Reprinted in Joan Givner (ed.), *Katherine Anne Porter: Conversations* (G66).

G74. Gunn, Drewey Wayne. "'Second Country': Katherine Anne Porter." In *American and British Writers in Mexico, 1556–1973*. Austin: Univ. of Texas Press, 1974, pp. 102–22.

A discussion of Porter's residence in Mexico, of her involvement with revolutionaries and artists, and of her essays, poems, and stories connected with Mexico. Although D.H. Lawrence might have focused literary attention on Mexico, it is Porter who "seems to dominate this period in her use of Mexican materials."

G75. Gustaitis, Rosa. "Top Authors Leave Mark at University." *Washington Post*, 22 April 1962, p. 3.

People at the University of Virginia are proud to have had William Faulkner, Katherine Anne Porter, and Stephen Spender as Writers-in-Residence.

G76. Hamovitch, Mitzi Berger. "Hunting for the *Hound & Horn.*" *American Scholar*, 51 (Autumn 1982), 543–49.

Concerns Porter's relationship with *Hound & Horn* and correspondence she had with Hamovitch, who was compiling *The Hound & Horn Letters.* (See C142, 143.)

G77. ⸺. "Today and Yesterday: Letters from Katherine Anne Porter." *Centennial Review*, 27 (Fall 1983), 278–87.

Concerns correspondence between Hamovitch and Porter, written while Hamovitch was compiling *The Hound & Horn Letters.* (See C143, 144.)

G78. Hoffman, Frederick J., Charles Allen, and Carolyn F. Ulrich. *The Little Magazine: A History and a Bibliography.* Princeton: Princeton Univ. Press, 1947, pp. 135, 208, 285, 291, 325, 336, 350, 398.

Concerns Porter's contributions to the little magazines of the 1920's and 1930's.
Reprinted by Kraus (1967).

G79. Hogan, William. "The Porter Novel Will Create News." *San Francisco Chronicle*, 23 March 1962, p. E-3.

"A first novel by the legendary Katherine Anne Porter cannot help but be an event."

G80. Horton, Philip. *Hart Crane: The Life of an American Poet.* New York: Norton, 1937, pp. 283–87.

Concerns the period during which Hart Crane stayed in Mexico, first at Porter's house and then in the house next to hers.

G81. Humphrey, William. "Can Write Anywhere if not Distracted." *New York Herald Tribune, Book Review*, 17 Aug. 1958, p. 2.

Among the early influences on Humphrey were Porter's stories. "They taught me, first of all that it was possible to be a Texan and a Writer."

G82. Janeway, Elizabeth. "For Katherine Anne Porter, 'Ship of Fools' Was a Lively Twenty-Two Year Voyage." *New York Times, Book Review*, 1 April 1962, pp. 4–5.

Porter is a lively, gracious woman. She has explained that all of her characters "are drawn from life."
Reprinted in Joan Givner (ed.), *Katherine Anne Porter: Conversations* (G66).

G83. Jason , Phillip K. "The University as Patron of Literature: The Balch Program at Virginia." *Journal of General Education*, 35 (no. 3, 1983), 174–88.

Concerns the University of Virginia's Balch Program for writers-in-residence. Porter's residence was during the semester lasting from September 1958 to January 1959.

G84. Jefferson, Margo. "Self Made: Katherine Anne Porter." *Grand Street*, 2 (Summer 1983), 152–71.

A discussion of Porter's life. Focuses on her attempts to re-create her background and to mould herself into a character fitting her image of "perfection."

G85. Johnston, Laurie. "Katherine Anne Porter Dies at 90; Won a Pulitzer for Short Stories." *New York Times*, 19 Sept. 1980, pp. A-1, D-15.

An obituary noting Porter's critical acclaim and the honors granted her.

G86. Josephson, Matthew. *Life Among the Surrealists*. New York: Holt, Rinehart, and Winston, 1962 , pp. 352–54.

In 1928 and 1929 Josephson encouraged Porter in her writing and in her publishing efforts.

G87. Kamata, Nobuko. "Katherine Anne Porter—Her Life and Literature." *Kyushu American Literature*, No. 25 (July 1984), 68–70.

A synopsis of a report given at the thirty-sixth Annual Convention of the English Literary Society of syushu in 1983. Summarizes Porter's life and work under three headings: "Influence of Her Environment," "On Human Relations," and "On Social Consciousness."

G88. "70: Katherine Anne Porter." *In A Creative Century—An Exhibition—Selections from the Twentieth Century Collections at the University of Texas*. Austin: Univ. of Texas Press, 1964, pp. 48–50.

An exhibition catalog entry describing the Porter materials displayed. These included the first draft of "Old Mortality," a first edition of *Pale Horse, Pale Rider*, and a typed letter to Tennessee Williams of 30 June 1943 (an excerpt from which appears in the catalog).

G89. "Katherine Anne Porter." *Life*, 53 (9 Nov. 1962), 66.

The publication of *Ship of Fools* was "the literary event of 1962."

G90. "Katherine Anne Porter." *Publishers Weekly*, 203 (12 Feb. 1973), 36–37.

"Even as she approaches her 83rd birthday . . ., she is still energetically at her writer's task."

G91. "Katherine Anne Porter Wins Medal." *Publishers Weekly*, 137 (13 April 1940), 1490.

For *Pale Horse, Pale Rider*, Porter has been awarded the gold medal of the New York Society for the Libraries.

G92. "Katherine Anne Porter Cited for Writings." *New York Times,* 11 Oct. 1962, p. 45.

Porter received the Emerson-Thoreau Medal of the American Academy of Arts and Sciences for her contributions to prose fiction.

G93. Kernan, Michael. "'It's Just Fine to Be 83.'" *Washington Post,* 30 March 1974, p. D-3.

At Trader Vic's, Porter's eye surgeon gave a party for her, at which she reminisced about past experiences.

G94. "'Keyhole Literature' Knocked by Author." *Tuscaloosa News,* 12 Feb. 1964, p. 22.

Katherine Anne Porter tells University of Alabama students that a writer should not merely "peep" at life; "you must receive it through your pores, absorb it."

G95. Langer, Elinor. "Below 14th Street (Josephine Herbst in the 1920s)." *Grand Street,* 2 (Winter 1983), 76–88.

Concerns Josephine Herbst's experiences in Greenwich Village and her growing friendship with Porter.
Reprinted as part of *Josephine Herbst* (G96).

G96. ———. *Josephine Herbst.* Little, Brown, 1984, *passim.*

A sizable part of the biography concerns the relationship between Herbst and Porter. The friendship flourished in the Greenwich Village of the 1920's. For many years thereafter the two maintained a steady correspondence. When Herbst visited Porter in Paris in 1935, she was troubled by what she saw as a lack of true political commitment from Porter. There is credible evidence that Porter "informed" the FBI of Herbst's radical political connections. In fact, she seems to have informed creatively, accusing Herbst of ties with Stalinist Russia that would not have been possible. When *Ship of Fools* was published, Herbst was very critical and read a condemnatory letter over New York radio station WBAI.

Reprinted in paperback as *Josephine Herbst: The Story She Could Never Tell*. New York: Warner, 1985.

G97. ———. "The Measuring Stick." *Grand Street*, 3 (Summer 1984), 108–39.

Focuses on evidence that Porter informed (with some fictitious details) to the FBI on her friend Josephine Herbst.

Reprinted as part of *Josephine Herbst* (G96).

G98. Lasswell, Mary. "Katherine Anne Porter Takes Jones Award." *Houston Chronicle*, 17 Feb. 1963.

For *Ship of Fools*, Porter was awarded the Texas Institute of Letters Jesse H. Jones Award.

G99. Ledbetter, Nan. "Finally Comes the Novel." *American-Statesman*, 8 April 1962, p. E-7.

The long-awaited novel of this accomplished writer should be of special interest to Texans.

G100. Lefkowitz, Bernard. "Author Finds Luxury too Costly." *New York Post*, 5 March 1962, p. 34.

Interview with Porter. She makes various political comments: The 1954 Supreme Court decision to integrate public schools was "irresponsible"; the Congressional investigations of Communism in Hollywood were justified; "Facism constitutes the most serious threat to personal liberty."

G101. "Letters by Writers Are Given to N.Y.U. by Frances Steloff." *New York Times*, 21 June 1965, p. 26.

Miss Steloff, owner of the Gotham Book Mart, has donated letters written by Katherine Anne Porter, James Joyce, and Henry Miller to New York University.

G102. Levitas, Gloria. "'I Wrote the Book I Meant To.'" *New York Herald Tribune, Books*, 11 Nov. 1962, pp. 4, 15.

In a lecture at the YMHA in New York City, Porter feels that she has had a good life and insists that she hasn't let negative criticism of *Ship of Fools* bother her.

G103. Liberman, M.M. "Meeting Miss Porter." *Georgia Review*, 41 (Summer 1987), 299–303.

In 1973, Porter summoned Liberman to College Park, announcing that she wanted him to be her literary executor. He stayed for a weekend, during which he was bored by Porter's chattery reminiscences. Months later he was notified that he was not to be the executor after all.

G104. Lopez, Enrique Hank. *Conversations with Katherine Anne Porter: Refugee from Indian Creek*. Boston: Little, Brown, 1981.

The author and Porter had a series of "conversations" that were to be "an autobiographical recollection that would have to stand for her life." The result is "the revelation of the life perceived by the subject, not always the life that was led."

G105. ———. "A Country and Some People I Love." *Harper's* 231 (Sept. 1965), 58–68.

Porter comments upon her experiences with Mexican revolutionaries, her role in organizing an exhibition of Mexican art, the years spent in composing *Ship of Fools*, and contemporary writers.

Reprinted in Robert Penn Warren (ed.), *Katherine Anne Porter: A Collection of Critical Essays* (H113) and Joan Givner (ed.), *Katherine Anne Porter: Conversations* (G66).

G106. Martin, Judith. "Porter at 80." *Washington Post*, 15 May 1970, pp. C1–C2.

Concerning her fiction, Porter declares, "Everything I've written from 'Flowering Judas' to 'Pale Horse, Pale Rider' through 'Ship of Fools,' is one continuous line." The basic idea of her literature is "illusion, delusion, and self-deception."

G107. McDowell, Edwin. "Publishing: Was Katherine Anne Porter an Informer?" *New York Times*, 13 July 1984, p. C-23.

Elinor Langer's forthcoming biography of Josephine Herbst (G96) will present the researched possibilities that Porter informed to the FBI on her "friend" Herbst.

G108. McGrory, Mary. "Reading and Writing." *Washington Star*, 12 April 1953, p. E-9.

Porter protests the congressional inquiries into Communism on campuses. The investigators are "not only perfectly ignorant but perfectly malignant. . . . We will pay a big price for this kind of foolishness."
Reprinted in Joan Givner (ed.), *Katherine Anne Porter: Conversations* (G66).

G109. Mercer, Charles. "The Local Angle—Tragic Story of Denver Writer on 'Climax.'" *Denver Post*, 22 March 1956, p. 29.

A dramatization of *Pale Horse, Pale Rider* is to be televised. Concerning the events used in the story, Porter told the interviewer: "It seems to me that I died then. I died once, and I never have feared death since."

G110. "Middle Man Represents Death to Art, Katherine Anne Porter Says at UR." *Richmond Times-Dispatch*, 19 Nov. 1958, p. 5.

In a lecture Porter insists that schools or anything else that places a "middle man between the artist and the public, teaching writing—it's death to art."

G111. Millett, Fred B. "Porter, Katherine Anne." In *Contemporary American Authors*. New York: Harcourt, Brace, 1940, pp. 96, 528.

Brief sketch.

G112. "Miss Porter and Schlesinger Cited." *New York Times*, 16 March 1967, p. 54.

Porter and Arthur M. Schlesinger, Jr., will be awarded Gold Medals by the National Institute of Arts and Letters.

G113. "Miss Porter Sees Book in Hospital." *Baltimore Evening Sun*, 6 Dec. 1967, p. B-8.

In the hospital for a back ailment, Porter has seen the first copy (as a book) of *A Christmas Story*.

G114. Mitgang, Herbert. "Publishing: For Sacco and Vanzetti." *New York Times*, 5 Aug. 1977, p. C-19.

Porter's *The Never-Ending Wrong* will be published on the fiftieth anniversary of the executions of Sacco and Vanzetti. In it "she deplores not only the prejudice of the trial but also the self-serving interests of some of the radical defenders of the two convicted anarchists."

G115. Mizener, Arthur. *The Saddest Story: A Biography of Ford Madox Ford*. New York: World, 1971, pp. 359, 405, 415–16, 434, 438, 522.

Ford's friendship with Porter and Eugene Pressly is recounted.

G116. Molz, Kathleen. "Presenting a Fellow Passenger— Katherine Anne Porter." *Pennsylvania Library Bulletin*, 18 (Summer 1962), 9.

Not examined by compiler.

G117. Mort, John. "Novelist Porter Irked at UT." *Fort Worth Star-Telegram*, 18 Dec. 1966.

Porter has announced that she is giving her papers, books, and manuscripts to the University of Maryland because the University of Texas has not carried out a promise to set aside a room in its library and name it after her.

G118. Mortimer, Gail. "Katherine Anne Porter." In *American Women Writers: A Critical Reference Guide from Colonial Times to the Present*, Vol. 3, ed. Lina Mainiero and Lynne Langdon. New York: Ungar, 1981, pp. 402–06.

A biographical sketch with a bibliography. Porter "severely limited the number of stories she would allow to be published, yet her choices seem to have been wise ones, for they offer us a surprisingly consistent vitality in their revelation of human truth."
Reprinted in slightly briefer form in the one-volume edition (1988).

G119. Entry deleted.

G120. Nance, William L. "Katherine Anne Porter and Mexico." *Southwest Review*, 55 (Spring 1970), 143–53.

Porter's involvement with Mexico was a productive one. For one thing, it provided her with settings and themes for many of her stories. For another, it served as the scene of her "lost generation" exile. Also, it allowed her to have a sense of independence. And its thriving artistic community of the 20's stimulated her. The revolutionary political circumstances of Mexico paralleled the revolutionary urge within Porter's soul.

G121. Nathan, Paul S. "Rights and Permissions." *Publishers Weekly*, 162 (22 Nov. 1952), 2098.

If MGM proceeds with plans to film *Young Bess*, some of Porter's Hollywood script writing will finally reach the screen.

G121a. Naylor, Pauline. "Katherine Anne Porter's Fort Worth Days Recalled." *Fort Worth Star-Telegram*, 10 April 1966, Section 5, p. 16.

Concerns the private Katherine Anne Porter collection of Beniti McElwee, a friend of Porter when the latter wrote for the *Fort Worth Critic*. Valuable for the quotations from Porter's journalism.

G122. "NBA Ceremony: The Mayor and the Winning Authors." *Publishers Weekly*, 189 (28 March 1966), 34–35.

In accepting her National Book Award, Porter insisted that she is a "disappointed idealist" rather than a misanthrope.

G123. "NBA 1966." *Newsweek*, 67 (28 March 1966), 106.

Concerning the NBA fiction award, many persons think that Flannery O'Connor was more deserving than Porter.

G124. Newquist, Roy. "An Interview with Katherine Anne Porter." *McCall's*, 92 (Aug. 1965), 87–89, 137–42.

Porter tells interviewer about her life experiences. She thinks that the younger writers and artists lack "respect for excellence." She reminisces about the twenties in Mexico. And she declares that the critics who disliked *Ship of Fools* the most "were really protesting the glimpses they caught of themselves."
Reprinted in Joan Givner (ed.), *Katherine Anne Porter: Conversations* (G66).

G125. Nichols, Lewis. "In and Out of Books." *New York Times, Book Review*, 22 April 1962, p. 8.

Porter announces that, having published *Ship of Fools*, she is turning her attention to a book on Cotton Mather and donating her manuscripts and papers to the University of Texas at Austin.

G126. "1966 NBA Award." *Publishers Weekly*, 189 (28 March 1966), 28–35.

Deals with the presentation of the *National Book Award* to Porter for *Collected Stories*.

G127. Nordell, Rod. "Women Who Write: In Person, 'I Can't Retreat....'" *Christian Science Monitor*, 8 March 1962, p. 6.

Porter discusses her soon-to-be published *Ship of Fools* and announces that she will soon return to her book on Cotton Mather.

G128. Novak, Josephine. "Katherine Anne Porter Makes a Feast of Life." *Baltimore Evening Sun*, 26 Feb. 1969.

Porter looks back over her life and feels that it has been a good one.
Reprinted in Joan Givner (ed.), *Katherine Anne Porter: Conversations* (G66).

G129. ———, and Elise Chisholm. "Don't Scare the Horses, Miss Porter Tells Liberation Women." *Baltimore Evening Sun*, 25 March 1970.

At a champagne party given to celebrate the publication of her *Collected Stories*, Porter gave her opinion of the Women's Liberation Movement: "I don't agree with them." She commented that "Any man who ever did wrong to me got back better than he gave."
Reprinted in Joan Givner (ed.), *Katherine Anne Porter: Conversations* (G66).

G130. "A Novelist in Mexico." *Boston Evening Transcript*, 19 Nov. 1930, Part 4, p. 5.

Report that Porter is living in Mexico, finishing the novel "Thieves' Market" and planning to go to Europe.

G131. "Novelist Gives Papers, Grants." *Baltimore Evening Sun*, 16 Dec. 1966, p. B-6.

Porter is leaving her professional and personal papers to the University of Maryland.

G132. O'Connor, Flannery. *The Habit of Being: Letters*, ed. Sally Fitzgerald. New York: Farrar, Straus & Giroux, 1979, *passim*.

Numerous references to Porter's character and to her work.

G133. Olsen, Tillie. *Silences*. New York: Delacorte, 1978.

Porter's life and comments exemplify the difficulties inherent in being a woman writer.

G134. "People." *Time*, 100 (25 Dec. 1972), 29.

The cruising seminar on board the *SS Statendam*, attended by Porter, Norman Mailer, and about 38 other paying participants, had an estimated loss of $250,000.

G135. Phillips, McCandlish. "Brandeis Awards Given in Four Fields." *New York Times*, 1 May 1972, p. 39.

For their achievement in the creative arts, Porter, Louis I. Kahn, Merce Cunningham, and Alfred Lunt were awarded medals by Brandeis University.

G136. "Poetry of Our Times." *Variety*, 29 April 1953, p. 39.

Porter will read American poetry over the radio Sunday mornings.

G137. "Porter, Katherine Anne." In *Celebrity Register*, ed. Earl Blackwell. New York: Simon and Schuster, 1973, p. 35.

This short biographical sketch of Porter quotes her brief remarks on a "man's world," the writing of *Ship of Fools*, Mexico, romantic love, and friends.

G138. "Porter, Katherine Anne (May 15, 1894– , Author). In *Current Biography 1940*, ed. Maxine Block. New York: H.W. Wilson, 1940, pp. 657–58.

A biographical sketch (with the factual errors common to such early sketches of Porter). Superseded in 1963 (G139).

G139. "Porter, Katherine Anne, May 15 1890– , Writer." In *Current Biography 1963*, ed. Charles Moritz. New York: H.W. Wilson, 1963, pp. 337–40.

Supersedes a 1940 biographical sketch (G138). Summarizes her life and comments critically on her writing. (Corrects some of the factual errors made in the earlier piece, but adds others.)

G140. Porter, Paul. Letter to the Editor. *Village Voice*, 26 (7–13 Oct. 1981), 3, 27.

Points out many errors in Lopez, *Conversations with Katherine Anne Porter* (G104) and casts doubts on Lopez's reliability as a "biographer" of Porter.

G141. Prescott, Peter S. "Crafting Truth in Elegant Fiction." *Newsweek*, 96 (29 Sept. 1980), 88.

An obituary.

G142. "Principal at the White House." *Washington Daily News*, 28 April 1964, p. 40.

Porter and other "women doers" will be the guests of Mrs. Lyndon Johnson at a White House luncheon.

G143. Entry deleted.

G144. "Pulitzer Drama Prize Omitted. Schlesinger's *1,000 Days* Wins." New York Times, 3 May 1966, pp. 1, 42.

Porter has been awarded the Pulitzer Prize for her *Collected Stories*.

G145. "Pulitzer Prize Goes to Texan." *San Antonio Express*, 3 May 1966, p. A-18.

Points out that Porter was born in Indian Creek, Texas, and is a former resident of San Antonio.

G146. Ramsdell, Charles. "Some Texas Writers: Katherine Anne Porter." *Texas Spectator*, 21 July 1947, pp. 4–5.

Although Porter might not think of herself as a Texas writer, her years there have influenced many of her stories.

G147. Rockwell, Jeanne. "The Magic Cloak." *Michigan Quarterly Review*, 5 (Fall 1966), 283–84.

The author once ran into Porter at a lunch counter in Michigan, and Porter (attired in a purple velveteen coat) encouraged her in her writing attempts.

G148. Rosson, John. "D.C. Audience Cheers Porter Short Stories." *Washington Evening Star*, 23 Oct. 1956, p. B-6.

Porter read "Rope" and "That Tree" to an enthusiastic audience.

G149. Ruoff, James. "Katherine Anne Porter Comes to Kansas." *Midwest Quarterly*, 4 (July 1963), 305–14.

Speaking at a college in Pittsburgh, Kansas, Porter answers questions on her own writing and offers comments on the writing of others.

Reprinted in Joan Givner (ed.), *Katherine Anne Porter: Conversations* (G66).

G150. Schoettler, Carl. "Katherine Anne Porter Reigns for Students." *Baltimore Evening Sun*, 15 April 1974.

A description of Porter's receiving two teachers and a group of students from Baltimore's College of Notre Dame. They brought her the honorary Doctor of Human

Letters degree that the college had conferred on her the previous spring.

Reprinted in Joan Givner (ed.), *Katherine Anne Porter: Conversations* (G66).

G151. Secrest, Meryle. "Freedom Was the Cargo When Her Ship Came In." *Washington Post*, 1 April 1962, pp. F8-F9.

Deals with Porter's financial freedom that has come with the publication of *Ship of Fools*. Also, she voices disappointment that the reviews of the novel seem to have missed its point—"that evil is always done with the collusion of good."

G152. "Seminar at Sea Studies Space Impact." *Boston Evening Globe*, 5 Dec. 1972, p. 28.

On board the *SS Statendam* Porter, Norman Mailer, and others will be attending a seminar on space and on the he "relationship between civilization and science." Porter announces her plans to cover the Apollo 17 shot for *Playboy*.

G153. Shearer, Gordon K. "What One Woman is Doing to Help Children." *Dallas Morning News*, 16 Dec. 1916.

Porter has organized a school for twelve children who are patients at the Woodlawn Sanitorium.

Reprinted in Joan Givner (ed.), *Katherine Anne Porter: Conversations* (G66).

G154. Shenker, Israel. "Katherine Anne Porter Reaches Peak Where Enduring Wisdom is Cherished." *New Orleans States-Item*, 17 April 1970.

Porter comments on her relationships with her "three" husbands and on getting old.

G155. Shi, David E. *Matthew Josephson, Bourgeois Bohemian.* New Haven: Yale Univ. Press, 1981, pp. 124–27, 278.

Concerns the 1928 love affair between Josephson and Porter.

G156. Smith, Harrison. "Writers as Readers." *Saturday Review*, 36 (28 Nov. 1953), 64.

Of American writers who have been recently recorded (by Columbia) reading their own works, Porter is the most successful.

G157. Stallman, Robert Wooster. "Collecting Katherine Anne Porter." *Four Quarters*, 12 (Nov. 1962), 56.

A brief anecdote concerning Porter's speaking at the University of Connecticut.

G158. Steloff, Frances. "In Touch with Genius." *Journal of Modern Literature*, 4 (April 1975), 820–22.

The founder of New York's Gotham Book Bart reminisces about her relationship with Porter.

G159. Stephen, C. Ralph (ed.). *The Correspondence of Flannery O'Connor and the Brainerd Cheneys*. Jackson: Univ. Press of Mississippi, 1986, pp. 84, 122, 123, 143, 144.

Previously uncollected letters, a few of which allude to Porter and to her work.

G160. Stroud, Kandy. "Sick Transit." *Women's Wear Daily*, 120 (18 March 1970), 4–5.

Porter could not have a personal interview because of illness. But by phone she discussed clothes, food, cooking, illness, and her *Collected Essays*.

G161. Thayer, Mary V.R. "Two Lady Literati to Brighten Local Winter Scene." *Washington Post*, 11 Oct. 1959, p. F-5.

Porter and Caresse Crosby are both "settling down in conversation-piece" Washington houses.

G162. "This Is Her Page." *Fort Worth Critic*, 2 (15 Sept. 1917), unpaged.

Under a picture of Porter is a description, part of which reads: "The exuberant young person pictured above is Miss Katherine Anne Porter, late of the staff of several prominent newspapers. She has come to Fort Worth to devote her life to *The Critic*."

G163. Thompson, Barbara. "Katherine Anne Porter: An Interview." *Paris Review*, 8 (Winter-Spring 1963), 87–114.

Porter discusses the genesis of some of her work and gives her views on the creative act of writing. Although existence might seem to "be almost pure chaos," the artist must "take these handfuls of confusion and desperate things, things that seem to be irreconcilable, and put them together in a frame to give them some kind of shape and meaning." All of her stories have had "a very firm foundation in actual human experience, even if it were another person's experience."
Reprinted in *Writers at Work: The Paris Review Interviews*, Second Series (1963), Lodwick Hartley and George Core (eds.), *Katherine Anne Porter: A Critical Symposium* (H51), and Joan Givner (ed.), *Katherine Anne Porter: Conversations* (G66).

G164. Thompson, Ralph. "Books of the Times." *New York Times*, 30 Jan. 1937, p. 15.

Porter received and deserved the Book-of-the-Month Club Fellowship Award, given to writers who have not been sufficiently recognized by readers.

G165. Tinkle, Lon. "New Texas Loss: KAP Collection." *Dallas Morning News*, 1 Jan. 1967, p. C-8.

The loss, to the University of Maryland, of Porter's manuscripts and papers is a "stunning" blow to Texas.

G166. "Top U.S. Scientists Dine at White House." *Boston Herald*, 30 April 1962, pp. 1, 6.

President and Mrs. Kennedy honored forty-nine Novel laureates; among other guests was Katherine Anne Porter.

G167. "University Names 10 to Receive Honorary Degrees." *Ann Arbor News*, 12 June 1954, p. 9.

Porter will receive a Doctor of Human Letters Honorary Degree from the University of Michigan.

G168. Unterecker, John. *Voyager: A Life of Hart Crane.* New York: Farrar, Straus and Giroux, 1969, pp. 651, 658–62, 666, 668, 670–73, 681–83, 696.

Concerns the friendship and the hostility between Porter and Crane, focusing on his escapades in Mexico and her reaction.

G169. Van Gelder, Robert. "Katherine Anne Porter at Work." *New York Times, Book Review*, 14 April 1940, p. 20.

Porter has lived many places, goes about her writing very carefully, and "expects to have a novel finished by June."
Reprinted in *Writers and Writing* (1946) and Joan Givner (ed.), *Katherine Anne Porter: Conversations* (G66).

G170. "Voices of Authors: Noted Writers Record Their Own Work." *Life*, 35 (12 Oct. 1953), 129–30, 132, 134.

Porter has recorded "Flowering Judas."

G170a. Waldron, Ann. *Close Connections: Caroline Gordon and the Southern Renaissance.* New York: G.P. Putnam's Sons, 1987, *passim.*

Numerous references to Porter's friendship with Caroline Gordon and Allen Tate. Many of Gordon's letters to Porter are quoted.

G171. Warren, Robert Penn. "Genius of Katherine Anne Porter." *Saturday Review*, 7 (Dec. 1980), 10–11.

A tribute written soon after Porter's death. Porter has left us "a body of work ... that bears the stamp of a personality distinctive, delicately perceptive, keenly aware of the depth and darkness of human experience, delighted by the beauty of the world and the triumphs of human kindness and warmth, and thoroughly committed to a quest for meaning in the midst of the ironic complexities of man's lot."

G172. Watkins, Floyd C., and John T. Hiers. *Robert Penn Warren Talking: Interviews 1950–1978*. New York: Random House, 1980, pp. 72, 118, 132, 133–34, 154, 218, 249, 255.

Various comments on Warren's friendship with Porter and on her work.

G173. Webber, Alan C. "American Literature at Low Ebb, Maintains Woodbury Writer of Successful Short Stories." *Waterbury Sunday Republican*, 2 Oct. 1955.

Porter has declared that American literature is "about as low as it can get." Wouk is "a poor, cheap writer"; Bellow is "vile, cheap, nasty"; Hemingway is a "sentimentalist." The problem with modern writers is that "they think to be strong they have to be hoodlums."

G174. Weil, Fran. "Katherine Anne Porter at a Spry 82, Not About to Throw in the Towel." *Boston Herald Traveller and Advertiser*, 16 July 1972, section 5, p. 9.

Porter discusses her satisfaction with her writing.

G175. Weiner, Rex. "Happenings." *Penthouse,* 4 (April 1973), 32.

> Concerning the shipboard seminar on the Apollo flight, Porter remarked that the undertaking was "Ship of Fools II."

G176. Wescott, Glenway. "Katherine Anne Porter." *Book-of-the-Month Club News,* March 1962, pp. 5–7.

> Mostly a biographical essay. "No youthful or even middle-aged person could have written *Ship of Fools.* It has required an entire lifetime of unshrinking endeavor, of hardheadedness and heat of heart and almost fanaticism."
>
> Reprinted in expanded, revised form as "Katherine Anne Porter: The Making of a Novel," *Atlantic Monthly,* 209 (April 1962). Reprinted with further revisions as "Katherine Anne Porter Personally" in *Images of Truth: Remembrances and Criticism* (1963); Lodwick Hartley and George Core (eds.), *Katherine Anne Porter: A Critical Symposium* (H51); and Robert Penn Warren (ed.), *Katherine Anne Porter: A Collection of Critical Essays* (H113).

G177. White, Jean. "White House to Honor High School Scholars." *Washington Post,* 17 April 1964, p. 1.

> President Johnson has announced a new program to benefit outstanding high school graduates. Porter is a member of the selection commission.

G178. Whiteaker, Mildred. "Glimpses of San Antonio at Turn of the Century." *San Antonio Express and News,* 21 Jan. 1973, pp. A-2, A-4.

> Porter reminisces about San Antonio, New Orleans, and "that narrow-minded family" of her first husband.
>
> Reprinted in Joan Givner (ed.), *Katherine Anne Porter: Conversations* (G66).

G179. "Winners' Press Conference." *Publishers Weekly*, 189 (28 March 1966), 30–34.

At the press conference for winners of the National Book Awards, Porter commented on her feelings for stories.

G180. Winslow, Marcella Comes (as told to Teresa Moore). "A Washington Life." *Washington Post Magazine*, 9 July 1989, pp. 24–27.

Winslow reminisces about writers she knew in Washington, D.C., during the 1940's, among them Porter. References are made to Porter's affair with "a young military man named Shannon," to her socializing, to her visiting Ezra Pound at St. Elizabeths, and to her habit of embroidering reality.

G181. Winsten, Archer. "Presenting the Portrait of an Artist." *New York Post*, 6 May 1937, p. 17.

Porter is a perfectionist, having burned "four complete novels and four short stories" that she wrote but then decided she did not like. From childhood, she has been determined to write.

Reprinted in Joan Givner (ed.), *Katherine Anne Porter: Conversations* (G66).

G182. "Women 'Doers' Meet Men Who Did All Right." *Washington Post*, 29 April 1964, p. D-1.

At Mrs. Lyndon Johnson's luncheon for "women doers," Porter was among the guests.

G183. Young, Thomas Daniel, and Elizabeth Sarcone (eds.). *The Lytle-Tate Letters*. Jackson: Univ. Press of Mississippi, 1987, *passim*.

Scattered references are made to Porter in this collection of the correspondence of Andrew Lytle and Allen Tate.

G184. Young, Thomas, and John J. Hindle (eds.). *The Republic of Letters in America: The Correspondence of John Peale Bishop and Allen Tate*. Lexington: Univ. Press of Kentucky, 1981; pp. 168, 170–73, 178–80, 220.

References to the work and character of Porter.

SECTION H
GENERAL CRITICISM

Entries in this section are given in alphabetical order. Each concerns at least two works by Porter. Reprints are listed with the original entry. Reviews of books about Porter are not listed unless the reviewers comment significantly on her works.

H1. Allen, Charles A. "Katherine Anne Porter: Psychology as Art." *Southwest Review*, 41 (Summer 1956), 223–30.

Usually Porter's theme is "the betrayal of life though the hostility that develops if physical and social needs are repeatedly and consistently frustrated." This theme is seen clearly in "The Downward Path to Wisdom," "The Cracked Looking-Glass," "The Jilting of Granny Weatherall," "Flowering Judas," and "Hacienda."

H2. ———. "The Nouvelles of Katherine Anne Porter." *University of Kansas City Review*, 29 (Winter 1962), 87–93.

Although there is "a somewhat oppressive pessimism" in "Noon Wine," "Old Mortality," "Pale Horse, Pale Rider," and "The Leaning Tower," "they remain bright and memorable: there is a vividness of character, a buoyancy of language, a display of atmospheric effect, and a subtle though skeptical tone."

H3. ———. "Southwestern Chronicle." *Arizona Quarterly*, 2
(Summer 1946), 90–95.

Uses "María Concepción," "Flowering Judas,"
"Hacienda," and "Noon Wine" to show Porter's talents.
In her stories we have themes "of weighty dignity,"
which "are given their extraordinary power through a
rich and complex characterization." With a few strokes,
she can show the contradictions and nuances that make up
a person. Further, her power of characterization is given
impact by her recognition of "the well of the unconscious
and its dark power over our action." Also, she presents
characters in terms of "their cultural conditioning."
Finally, her "depth and keenness of vision" is matched
by her "flexible and precise language."

H4. "American Fiction: The Postwar Years, 1945–65." *New
York Herald Tribune, Book Week*, 26 Sept. 1965, pp. 1–
3.

200 prominent members of the literati were asked,
"Which authors have written the most distinguished
fiction during the period 1945–65?" Porter was the
nineteenth most frequently mentioned.

H5. "The Art of the Short Story: Principles and Practice in the
United States." *Times Literary Supplement*, 17 Sept.
1954, pp. xl, xlii.

Because of differences in culture and history, the short
story has flourished more in the United States than in
Great Britain. At present, there are many Americans
writing superb short stories, among them the "highly
intelligent and highly polished" Porter.

H6. Auchincloss, Louis. "Katherine Anne Porter." In *Pioneers
and Caretakers: A Study of Nine American Women
Novelists*. Minneapolis: Univ. of Minnesota Press, 1965,
pp. 136–51.

An overview of Porter's work. "At least to some of us ... Miss Porter is the American Flaubert." The Miranda stories "say the essential with a minimum of incident." Some of her other short stories and *Ship of Fools* show her grasp of "the unself-consciousness of the Latin American." And in *Ship of Fools*, she "has reproduced the very stuff of life ... and her novel sparkles with vitality and humor."

H7. Baker, Howard. "The Contemporary Short Story." *Southern Review*, 3 (Winter 1938), 595–96.

Porter is peerless in her understanding of "the impoverishment of spirit and mind" that accompanies physical impoverishment.

H7a. ———. "The Upward Path: Notes on the Work of Katherine Anne Porter." *Southern Review*, 4 n.s. (Winter 1968), 1–19.

For Porter the path to wisdom is, paradoxically, both downward and upward. In interpreting Porter's work, two "propositions" must be acknowledged: (1) she is a "Modern, a beneficiary of a discipline which has been known as Modernism," and (2) she lived for a "span of some ten formative years in the bosom of a civilization much different from our own, Mexico." These have affected her technique and her themes. Her "healthy, corrosive point of view" does not deserve the attacks made by imperceptive critics.

Reprinted in *Sense and Sensibility in 20th Century Writing: A Gathering in Memory of William Van O'Connor* (1970).

H8. Baldeshwiler, Eileen. "Structural Patterns in Katherine Anne Porter's Fiction." *South Dakota Review*, 11 (Summer 1973), 45–53.

Porter's stories can be classed according to three "modes," each of which Porter practiced throughout her literary career. The first mode is the traditional "syllogistic" form—in which two or more characters are in conflict and in which the plot moves through fixed stages to the concluding resolution. Examples of such stories are "He," "Noon Wine," and "The Downward Path to Wisdom." The second mode is that of memory—sketches taking the form of remembered events. "The Old Order" stories fall into this group. The third mode is "the 'new' form associated with the post-Chekhovian story" in which "an emotion or a complex of emotions is meticulously traced though moments of partial revelation to total knowledge, vision, or insight." Among Porter's stories in this group are "Theft," "Flowering Judas," "Old Mortality," and "The Leaning Tower."

H9. Barrett, Phyllis W. "More American Adams: Women Heroes in American Fiction." *Markham Review*, 10 (Spring 1981), 39–41.

Critics often discuss American literature in terms of certain of its male protagonists—innocent, untamed Adams. They ignore the Adamic traits of certain female characters—Hawthorne's Hester Prynne, James's Isabel Archer, Kate Chopin's Edna Pontellier, and Porter's Miranda. These women are "androgynous"—scorning traditional femininity and exhibiting an adventurousness and boldness usually attributed to men. "Old Mortality" is an initiation story comparable to Hemingway's Nick Adams stories. The Miranda of "Pale Horse, Pale Rider" is recognizable as a member of the Lost Generation.

H10. Bates, H.E. *The Modern Short Story: A Critical Survey.* Boston: Writers, Inc., 1941 (rpt. 1965), 185–87.

Porter is included in the chapter "American Renaissance." This chapter concerns American writers who look at their country and their art with a freshness not seen in this century before Sherwood Anderson. Porter is the "most accomplished" of contemporary American short story writers. Her great strength is her versatility.

"For Miss Porter there are no fences, either territorial or social, technical or psychological."

H11. Bloom, Harold, ed. *Katherine Anne Porter*. New York: Chelsea, 1986.

A collection of critical essays on Porter. Contents: "Introduction" (I4); Robert Penn Warren, "Irony with a Center" (H114); Robert B. Heilman, *"Ship of Fools:* Notes on Style" (I99); Howard Moss, "No Safe Harbor" (J212); Eudora Welty, "The Eye of the Story" (H116), M.M. Liberman, "Symbolism, the Short Story and 'Flowering Judas'" (excerpted from H68); Constance Rooke and Bruce Wallis, "Myth and Epiphany in Porter's 'The Grave'" (I29); Joan Givner, "Katherine Anne Porter, Journalist" (H37); Thomas F. Walsh, "The Dream Self in 'Pale Horse, Pale Rider'" (I87); Joanne P. Cobb, "Pascal's Wager and Two Modern Losers" (I46); Bruce W. Jorgensen, "'The Other Side of Silence': 'He' as Tragedy" (I35); Debra A. Moddelmog, "Narrative Irony and Hidden Motivations in Katherine Anne Porter's 'He'" (I37); Jane Krause DeMouy, "Face to Face, 'Old Mortality'" (excerpted from H25).

H12. Bode, Elroy. "On Katherine Anne Porter." In *Alone in the World Looking*. El Paso: Texas Western Press, 1973, pp. 25–26.

"There seems to be a curious lack of breath and air in much of her work—a dry feeling as if her words were too lacking in 'juices.'"

H13. Bolsterli, Margaret. "'Bound' Characters in Porter, Welty, McCullers: The Prerevolutionary Status of Women in American Fiction." *Bucknell Review*, 24 (Spring 1978), 95–105.

The stories of Porter, Welty, and McCullers portray women in a "prerevolutionary" state. They are trapped by society's determination of a woman's role, and the authors do not allow them to escape. Miranda in "Old

Mortality" is a rebel against social expectations, but when we see her again in "Pale Horse, Pale Rider" she is trapped in the "routine female job" of theater reviewer.

H14. Bradbury, John M. *Renaissance in the South: A Critical History of the Literature, 1920–1960*. Chapel Hill: Univ. of North Carolina Press, 1963, pp. 70–74.

In Porter "the symbolic naturalist tradition reached a new sort of perfection." In subject matter she has been concerned with her contemporary social and political problems.

H15. Bradford, M.E. "The Passion of Craft." In *The History of Southern Literature*, ed. Louis Rubin *et. al*. Baton Rouge: Louisiana State Univ. Press, 1985, pp. 375–78.

Porter—like Caroline Gordon and Andrew Lytle—is a writer who invites "readers into the invented universe of imaginative experience by way of a dramatic representation of consciousness." Her Mexican stories and the Miranda stories are successful because she is writing of persons and events close to her. *Ship of Fools*, on the other hand, is unsuccessful.

H16. Brannan, Dana. "Andre Maurois States His Views." *New York Times, Book Review*, 3 Feb. 1946, p. 6.

Review of Maurois's *Etudes Americaines*. Maurois has compared Porter to Katherine Mansfield and to Proust.

H17. Brinkmeyer, Robert H., Jr. "'Endless Remembering': The Artistic Vision of Katherine Anne Porter." *Mississippi Quarterly*, 40 (Winter 1986–87), 5–19.

Porter sees "engaging one's memory as essential for discovering meaning and initiating growth." Preventing oneself from remembering is to deny one's inner self. Granny Weatherall's life serves as an example of such a denial. On the other hand, to be "ruled" by memories without a conscious adaptation of them to the present day's needs is equally dangerous. The Grandmother of "The Old Order" is an example of one whose "life is out of balance" because she lives only according to "memory's interior self."

H18. Camati, Anna Stegh. "Violence and Death: Their Interpretation by Katherine Anne Porter and Eudora Welty." *Revista Letras* (Brazil), 32 (1983), 39–59.

An examination of the stories of Porter and Eudora Welty might explain "the reasons for the prevalence of violence in Southern fiction." Through the violent plot of "María Concepción," Porter acknowledges her hope in a primitive world with its own order, morality, and ethic. In "Hacienda" she "expresses her aversion towards the encroachment of Western society and religion." (Note: Though this author claims to be dealing with Porter's stories of the American South, only a few sentences refer to these. The analyses are of two of Porter's Mexican stories.)

H19. Carson, Barbara Harrell. "Winning: Katherine Anne Porter's Women." In *The Authority of Experience: Essays in Feminist Criticism*, ed. Arlyn Diamond and Lee R. Edwards. Amherst: Univ. of Massachusetts, 1977, pp. 239–56.

An examination of the Miranda stories shows that the women characters all "seek the same prize"—"the creation of an essence for oneself through self-initiated actions, rather than the passive acceptance of a role assigned by others." Nannie, Cousin Amy, and Eva are all slaves to invisible bonds—family, tradition, custom, and their own psychological reluctance to seize independence. The grandmother and Miranda also must fight against these restraints, but they are more successful in overcoming them. Unfortunately, the grandmother does ultimately accept the restraints and thus never achieves true liberation. Only Miranda—at the end of "Pale Horse, Pale Rider"—has broken through successfully.

She has found her selfhood and will express it through art.

Reprinted in Winifred F. Bevilacqua (ed.), *Fiction by American Women: Recent Voices* (1983).

H19a. Cheatham, George. "Death and Repetition in Porter's Miranda Stories." *American Literature*, 61 (Dec. 1989), 610–24.

Not examined by compiler.

H20. ———. "Literary Criticism, Katherine Anne Porter's Consciousness, and the Silver Dove." *Studies in Short Fiction*, 25 (Spring 1988), 109–15.

Critics who insist that, because Porter was generally an atheist, there can be no suggestion of Christian concepts in her work have too narrow a view of human consciousness. Very likely, the epiphany of "The Grave" and Miranda's vision of a beatific afterlife in "Pale Horse, Pale Rider" can be interpreted as suggestions of redemption.

H21. Core, George. "The *Best* Residuum of Truth." *Georgia Review*, 20 (Fall 1966), 278–91.

A discussion of Porter's *Collected Stories* and of some of the criticism written about her. Porter is "the greatest living writer of short fiction." Her fiction is characterized by "what Henry James calls 'the *best* residuum of truth': it is truth which is earned through the strenuous discipline and the artistic integrity of tight rhetorical control and ironic vision—the truth of a 'deep-breathing economy and an organic form.'"

A brief discussion of "Holiday" included in this essay was expanded and printed as "'Holiday': A Version of the Pastoral" (I 38).

H22. Cory, Jim. "'Ship of Fools': Katherine Anne Porter in Decline." *Four Quarters*, 34 (Spring-Summer 1985), 16–25.

That Porter's short stories are successful and *Ship of Fools* is not can be explained by the differences between the Porter of the 1920's and 30's and the Porter of the 50's and early 60's. "The author of the stories was a somewhat less grand, less worldly, less cynical person than the novelist. There's a quality of humility and sympathy in the stories that just isn't in the novel.... The young, aimless, pragmatic bohemian was more capable of hitting on human truths than the self-styled *grande dame* struggling to convey deep philosophical insights in a form uncongenial to her."

H23. Cruttwell, Patrick. "Swift, Miss Porter, and 'The Dialect of the Tribe.'" *Shenandoah*, 17 (Summer 1966), 27–38.

Porter resembles Jonathan Swift in her reverence for "pure English" and in her fear that this purity is disappearing. As did he, she sees a moral connection between language and social behavior. And, as did he, she sees the influence of "foreign tongues" as partly to blame.

H24. Curley, Daniel. "Katherine Anne Porter: The Larger Plan." *Kenyon Review*, 25 (Autumn 1963), 671–95.

Ship of Fools is "a bad book." In most of her stories Porter treats "a human being simply as a human being"; this she does superbly. But in "The Leaning Tower" and *Ship of Fools*, "when she tries to work in a broader context," she fails. The Miranda stories and "Flowering Judas" are successful. But in *Ship of Fools* the three (older) counterparts of Miranda—Jenny Brown, Mrs. Treadwell, and La Condesa—are discouraging reflections of Porter's spirit. Jenny is unable to love; Mrs. Treadwell—in her inability to respond to others, in her attack on Denny and her later "merriment" over the incident—is terrifying; La Condesa is "going into forced political exile, the deepest exile this side of death."

H24a. DeMouy, Jane. "Katherine Anne Porter 1890–1980." In
       Heath Anthology of American Literature, Vol. 2, ed.
       Paul Lauter, *et al.* Lexington, Mass.: D.C. Heath, 1990,
       pp. 1349–51.

   An overview of Porter's life and work, concluding with
   an analysis of her significance. Porter should be
   considered an "important" writer for three reasons. First,
   she "is a master of the American short story." Then, she
   offers a "feminine perspective" of the psychological
   conflicts within women; much of her literature is focused
   on a woman's "innate dilemma: great personal strength
   linked to a longing for love." Also, she is significant for
   having created "feminine examples of the lone American
   Adam."

H25. ———. *Katherine Anne Porter's Women: The Eye of Her
       Fiction.* Austin: Univ. of Texas Press, 1983.

   Regarding Porter's work from "the view point of
   feminine psychology" gives, first, a unity to her fiction
   that many critics have missed, and, second, "a sensitive
   prophecy for contemporary femininity." Most of Porter's
   stories concern the conflict within women between, on the
   one hand, the need for love and the desire to play the
   traditional role of wife and mother and, on the other
   hand, the desire for independent self-fulfillment, a
   desire intensified by a changing society. The desire for
   love and motherhood leads to a loss of identity and,
   possibly, death. The desire for independence leads to
   loneliness and repression. In *Ship of Fools* this conflict
   has been universalized to apply to both men and women.
   An excerpt concerning "Old Mortality" reprinted in
   Harold Bloom (ed.), *Katherine Anne Porter* (H11).

H26. Elliott, Emory, *et al.*, ed. *Columbia Literary History of
       the United States.* New York: Columbia Univ. Press,
       1988, pp. 740, 745, 781–83, 822, 834, 851, 853, 871.

   References to Porter in the sections entitled: "Literary
   Scenes and Literary Movements," "Regionalism,"

"Women Writers Between the Wars," "The Diversity of American Fiction."

H27. Emmons, Winfred S. *Katherine Anne Porter: The Regional Stories.* Southwest Writers Series, no. 6. Austin: Steck-Vaughn, 1967.

Porter wrote several stories that can be termed regional, even though a few of these stories and most of the characters in the others could be easily transplanted to another part of the United States. In "The Old Order" stories and in "Old Mortality," Porter has most closely approximated the environment of her own childhood. Of these "Old Mortality," "The Source," "The Journey," and "The Last Leaf" provide the background from which Miranda developed. "The Circus," "The Fig Tree," and "The Grave" each present a crisis in this development. Also, "The Grave" is effective in giving a strong sense of place. Two further regional stories, "He" and "Noon Wine," succeed in giving a sympathetic view of "plain people." "Noon Wine" and "Holiday" both successfully convey a sense of place.

H28. "Expressive Voices: The Emergence of a National Style." *Times Literary Supplement,* 17 Sept. 1954, pp. xii, xiv.

Passages from Mark Twain, Ambrose Bierce, Stephen Crane, Gertrude Stein, Ernest Hemingway, and Porter are used to show that a truly American style does exist. This style has "a basis of scepticism" and avoids "imported or unnatural mannerism." It reflects "a standard of human sincerity and community."

H29. Fetterley, Judith. "The Struggle for Authenticity: Growing Up Female in *The Old Order." Kate Chopin Newsletter,* 2 (1976), 11–19.

Not examined by compiler.

H30. Flanders, Jane. "Katherine Anne Porter and the Ordeal of
      Southern Womanhood." *Southern Literary Journal,* 9
      (Fall 1976), 47–60.

As a Southern woman writer, "Porter takes as her
subject the rigidly circumscribed experience and sexual
repression of the white Southern woman—kept like the
blacks in submission and fear by the doctrines, taboos, and
social realities of a paternalistic culture." Miranda grows
up without any satisfactory female role models. Through
her grandmother, she learns that for a woman to survive
and acquire independence she "has to repudiate men and
the attitudes of a male society." Amy's desire for freedom
has no socially satisfactory outlet; she dies. Eva has
given up into bitterness. But it is through listening to her
that Miranda decides to repudiate family ties and the
love of men. "Miranda will never know the 'truth about
herself' because she cannot reconcile her need to express
her own identity with any acceptable model of mature
womanhood; she has never known one."

H31. ———. "Katherine Anne Porter's Feminist Criticism:
      Book Reviews from the 1920's." *Frontiers,* 4 (Summer
      1979), 44–48.

The book reviews Porter wrote before publishing her
short stories show not only her "forthrightness, her
liberal spirit, and her witty mastery of English"; they
also provide evidence of her "strong feminist beliefs."

H32. Gaston, Edwin W., Jr. "The Mythic South of Katherine
      Anne Porter." *Southwestern American Literature,* 3
      (1973), 81–85.

The fiction of Porter, like that of Faulkner, shows both
the positive and negative sides of the vast body of
Southern mythology. The positive side is seen in "The
Journey" and "The Last Leaf"—stories showing a strong
bond between a mistress and her slave and showing
characters who "demonstrate courage and pride and
compassion to rival the best of Faulkner's characters."

But "The Last Leaf" also shows the maltreatment of blacks, as does "The Witness." "Old Mortality" deflates the myth of the pure Southern belle. In this story Miranda learns to see through the myth, but at the price of alienation.

H33. Gessel, Michael. "Katherine Anne Porter: The Low Comedy of Sex." In *American Humor: Essays Presented to John C. Gerber*, ed., O.M. Brack, Jr. Scottsdale, Ariz.: Arete, 1977, pp. 139–52.

Porter is a "comic writer. The purest form of love is, in her comic sense, a good honest, lusty fuck, whose attachment is real because it is physical, chemical, and hormonal, and honest only if it is not binding beyond the orgasm." That love which is usually regarded as being loftier than mere sex is "seen, in Porter's comic exposures, as displaying various degrees of vulgarity and varying degrees of perverted obscenity (such as tenderness and special attentions)."

H34. Gibbons, Kaye. "Planes of Language and Time; The Surfaces of the Miranda Stories." *Kenyon Review*, 10 (Winter 1988), 74–79.

"Porter's language, for all its superficial simplicity, pulls the reader vertically towards submerged meanings and horizontally backward through time and memories." In reading the Miranda stories, one must accept that an adult Miranda is the narrator: "Her maturity and her distance from her early community are necessary as she views the past with the objectivity of a theater critic."

H35. Givner, Joan. "Katherine Anne Porter and the Art of Caricature." *Genre*, 5 (March 1972), 51–60.

Explores Porter's use of the technique of caricature to expound her moral philosophy (the collusion of apparently innocent people with those who are evil) in "Theft," "Flowering Judas," "Virgin Violeta," "The Leaning Tower," and *Ship of Fools*.

H36. ———. "Katherine Anne Porter and the Southwest." In *A Literary History of the American West*. Fort Worth: Texas Christian Univ., 1987, pp. 559–66.

Porter personally was ambivalent toward her native state and misleading about her upbringing. The Texas stories in which she best captures the dirt farm environment of her childhood have no fictional counterpart to herself; but those stories with the fancied plantation environment have as a protagonist (Miranda) a character based on Porter herself. However, the influence of her native region is seen throughout her work in the language: "the strength of Porter's distinctive idiom in all her work derives from her combining and harmonizing of the qualities of the speech of both the South and the Southwest." Her conversation, her correspondence, and her fiction were distinctive for her mingling of the poetic and the "colloquial and racy expressions of her local dialect."

H37. ———. "Katherine Anne Porter, Journalist." *Southwest Review*, 64 (Autumn 1979), 309–22.

Although Porter suppressed information regarding her work as a journalist, her newspaper pieces are valuable for the insights they yield into her philosophy of evil. In her drama criticism of 1919, she asserts that an outright villain is not as despicable as the supposedly innocent individual who collaborates with him by passively accepting evil. This theme is conveyed throughout Porter's work, probably most noticeably in "Flowering Judas" and *Ship of Fools*. We see it even in the final work, *The Never-Ending Wrong*.
Reprinted in Harold Bloom (ed.), *Katherine Anne Porter* (H11).

H38. ———. "Katherine Anne Porter: The Old Order and the New." In *The Texas Literary Tradition: Fiction, Folklore, History*, ed. Don Graham, James W. Lee, and William T. Pilkington. Austin: The College of Liberal

Arts, The Univ. of Texas at Austin and The Texas State Historical Association, 1983, pp. 58–68.

Porter's relationship with Texas was "a notoriously strained one." Much of the strain can be traced back to 1939, when J. Frank Dobie was given the Texas Institute of Letters award for the best book by a Texan, even though *Pale Horse, Pale Rider* had appeared the same year. After her death, Larry McMurtry claimed in *The Texas Observer* (H74) that she could not be seen as a major writer. The problem may be that the Institute and McMurtry could not fit Porter to their image of the masculine Texas. They probably felt a "sexual bias, a dislike for Porter's markedly feminine style and sensibility." However, Porter has been a major influence on the writing of two Texas males—William Humphrey and William Goyen. Humphrey credited her with making him realize the worth of birthplace and native speech. Goyen was drawn to her use of "allusive, lyrical, sensuous prose and to the imagery and symbolic poetic mode." Porter's significance as a writer "was that she extended the practise of literature (dare I say rescued it?) and extended it beyond a domain that was exclusively masculine."

H39. "A Good Anthology." *New York Times, Book Review*, 21 May 1933, p. 7.

A review of *Twentieth Century Short Stories* (ed. Sylvia Chatfield Bates). Criticizes the editor for omitting "some of our newest and most promising" American writers, among them Katherine Anne Porter.

H40. Gordon, Caroline. "Katherine Anne Porter and the ICM." *Harper's*, 229 (Nov. 1964), pp.146–48.

Although correct in seeing all of Porter's protagonists as one person in various forms, William Nance (H77) errs in seeing a theme of rejection running throughout her work. Miranda's never accepting a present condition is not a mark of mere rejection. Rather, she is a "pilgrim"; her rejections are necessary so that she can reach the "holy land."

H41. Gray, Richard. *The Literature of Memory: Modern Writers of the American South.* Baltimore: Johns Hopkins Univ. Press, 1977, pp. 150–52, 185–96, 203.

Porter is discussed, along with Caroline Gordon and Eudora Welty, in the chapter "Back to the Old Plantation: The Recovery and Reexamination of a Dream." Porter sees the myth of the Old South as something that must be rejected (or escaped from). One's consciousness must then "evolve a subjective world that represents a reconciliation of rule and freedom, value and raw experience."

H42. Greene, George. "Brimstone and Roses: Notes on Katherine Anne Porter." *Thought*, 36 (Autumn 1961), 421–40.

In such stories as "María Concepción," "He," "The Cracked Looking-Glass," and "The Jilting of Granny Weatherall," there is a note of "distillation," which "verifies the premise that even drab, subliterary settings conceal a world throbbing with contradictions." Another group of stories, such as "Theft" and "Hacienda," concerns young persons in an artistic environment. "Her fictions all constitute a challenge hurled against the uncertainties which have become one of the grim constants of our epoch."

H43. Gretlund, Jan Nordby. "Katherine Anne Porter and the South: A Corrective." *Mississippi Quarterly*, 34 (Fall 1981), 435–44.

Written to correct details from Lopez's "inaccurate and unreliable book" book (G104). Uses Porter's marginalia in a copy of Hendrick's *Katherine Anne Porter* (H53) as a basis for "the corrective." Regarding Porter's involvement with the south, concludes that "in the best of her fiction, she did manage to create a dialogue between the past and the new order of the present. It is a dialogue of a universal significance."

H44. ———. "The Wild Old Green Man of the Woods: Katherine Anne Porter's Faulkner." *Notes on Mississippi Writers*, 12 (Winter 1980), 67–79.

Among Porter's unpublished work—"marginalia, letters, lecture notes, and interviews"—can be found evidence of her mostly admiring view of Faulkner's literature. These notes, letters, and jottings reveal her thoughts on *The Sound and the Fury*, "Spotted Horses," "Raid," "A Rose for Emily," "That Evening Sun," and "The Bear."

H45. Gwin, Minrose. "Mentioning the Tamales: Food and Drink in Katherine Anne Porter's *Flowering Judas and Other Stories*." *Mississippi Quarterly*, 38 (Winter 1984–85), 49–57.

Porter's success depends to a great extent upon her piling up of realistic details; in the *Flowering Judas* stories, these details often concern food and drink. References to eating and drinking reinforce theme, help create an atmosphere, and aid in characterization.

H46. Hagopian, John V. "Katherine Anne Porter: Feeling, Form, and Truth." *Four Quarters*, 12 (Nov. 1962), 1–10.

Some generalizations can be made about Porter's art. It is sensitive and subtle; the characters are complex; the symbolism is not obvious but "embedded" skillfully in the story. Also, Porter's "narrative method is usually that of indirect dialogue or monologue. . . . The purpose of this technique is to control the sequence of perceptions and misperceptions while at the same time maintaining a certain distance from the narrative events." Also, the "basic experience" is "the process of self-discovery (or the failure of self-discovery)." Porter is not utterly pessimistic about the human condition. Like Camus, she feels that life is essentially meaningless but that man can impose a meaning of his own upon it.

H47. Hankins, Leslie K. "Ritual: Representation and Reversal in Katherine Anne Porter's 'The Old Order.'" In *Ritual in the United States: Acts and Representations*, ed. Don Harkness. Tampa, Fla.: American Studies Press, 1985, pp. 20–23.

With "The Old Order" stories, Porter has written "a highly ritualized work on the levels of theme, language, and imagery." But she uses these not, in the expected way, to validate tradition, but to attack it, to challenge "traditional racial hierarchies."

H48. Hardy, John Edward. *Katherine Anne Porter*. New York: Ungar, 1973.

Begins with a chapter detailing the problems concerned with gathering biographical data about Porter. The discussion of her literature begins with an analysis of those stories dealing with the family. Although Porter shows the family to be stifling and corrupting, she does not hate it as an institution: "In her treatment of evil in the family, just as in her treatment of corruption in politics and religion, she always holds an implicit vision of an ideal that has been vitiated, betrayed, or perverted." Her views of the family—in both its good and its malevolent aspects—can be seen in "The Fig Tree," "The Grave," "Old Mortality," and "He." Usually in Porter's stories, black characters exist mainly to cast light upon the white characters' lives and motivations. "Only in 'Magic' . . . does Miss Porter distinctly identify with the black woman." Married couples in Porter are miserable, bitter, and usually childless. And in only one story focused on marriage—"The Cracked Looking-Glass"—can we find a character "for whom full human sympathy is possible."

In the stories that have usually been considered Miss Porter's finest work, the central figures are people whose desperate preoccupation with themselves cuts them off from effective communication with all other human beings." In this group of stories are "Theft," "Flowering Judas," "Pale Horse, Pale Rider," "The Jilting of Granny Weatherall," and "Noon Wine."

Of all Porter's stories, only "The Leaning Tower" and "Hacienda" are "recognizable as definite foreshadowing of *Ship of Fools*." The former story resembles the novel in terms of its use of near-allegory to present Fascism. "Hacienda" resembles *Ship of Fools* in its "all but total objectivity and disengagement." *Ship of Fools* is a much better novel than many critics have realized. "Caricature is Miss Porter's dominant method in the book. . . . But the caricature of *Ship of Fools* is caricature raised finally to the level of tragic myth and mystery."

H49. Hartley, Lodwick. "Katherine Anne Porter." *Sewanee Review*, 48 (April–June 1940), 206–16.

Regarding genre, Porter's works are hard to classify; some of her short stories (e.g., "The Cracked Looking-Glass" and "Pale Horse, Pale Rider") have an "expansiveness" that suggests a novel in which "all but essential matter' has been omitted. Although Porter can sometimes use a subjective approach effectively, she "achieves her greatest success when she is most objective (e.g., "He" and "Noon Wine"). The endings of some of her stories are flawed by a near-sentimental subjectivity (as in "Theft" and "Flowering Judas"). But, "whatever may be her structural or emotional limitations, she has the uncanny power of evoking richness from minutiae." This gift can be found everywhere in her work.

H50. ———, and George Core. "Introduction." In *Katherine Anne Porter: A Critical Symposium*. Athens: Univ. of Georgia Press, 1969, pp. xi–xxi.

A discussion of Porter's life and art. "In any list of the best Southern and even American writers of the twentieth century, Miss Porter deserves a place of the highest rank."

H51.   ———, eds. *Katherine Anne Porter: A Critical Symposium*. Athens: Univ. of Georgia Press, 1969.

A selection of essays. Contents: "Introduction" (H50); John Aldridge, "Art and Passion in Katherine Anne Porter" (J245); Eudora Welty, "The Eye of the Story" (H116); Cleanth Brooks, "On 'The Grave'" (I23); Ray B. West, Jr., "Symbol and Theme in 'Flowering Judas'" (I18); Sarah Youngblood, "Structure and Imagery in 'Pale Horse, Pale Rider'" (I89); Joseph Wiesenfarth, "Reflections in 'The Cracked Looking-Glass'" (I1); George Core, "'Holiday': A Version of Pastoral" (I38); Lodwick Hartley, "The Lady and the Temple" (J125); Edward Schwartz, "The Way of Dissent" (H91); M.M. Liberman, "Responsibility of the Novelist' (I106); Robert B. Heilman, "*Ship of Fools*: Notes on Style" (I99); Lodwick Hartley, "Dark Voyagers" (I98).

H52.   Heilman, Robert B. "The Southern Temper." *Hopkins Review*, 6 (Fall 1952), 5–15.

Porter's work fits into the context of Southern literature by having certain representative qualities: "a sense of the concrete, a sense of the elemental, a sense of the ornamental, a sense of the representative, and a sense of totality."
Reprinted in Louis D. Rubin and Robert D. Jacobs (eds.), *South: Modern Southern Literature in Its Cultural Setting* (1961).

H53.   Hendrick, George. *Katherine Anne Porter*. New York: Twayne, 1965.

Begins with an attempt at a biographical sketch— made difficult by the hazy and contradictory accounts given by Porter. In the discussion of the stories, emphasis

is given to "settings, themes, and literary indebtedness."
Concerning Porter's Mexican stories, her relationship
with the country changes "from seeing Mexican culture
from the inside in 'María Concepción' to the later stories
of alienation." (e.g., "Hacienda" and "That Tree"). The
Miranda stories are fictionalized autobiography with
the grandmother and Miranda as central characters."
Miranda, born into a decaying order, learns of the glories
of the cruel illusions of that culture. After taking herself
into the outer world, she goes beyond other illusions,
eventually to find "in the midst of death that death
could no longer frighten her." The maturation of Miranda
is completed at the end of "The Grave" when she sees "at
that moment a vision of her initiation into some of the
mysteries of the world."

The remaining Porter stories can be grouped into four
sections: (1) Southern, Southwestern, Autobiographic
("He," "Noon Wine," "The Jilting of Granny
Weatherall," and "Magic"); (2) Universalized ("Rope,"
"The Downward Path to Wisdom," and "Theft"); (3) The
Irish ("The Cracked Looking-Glass" and "A Day's
Work"); (4) Germans ("Holiday" and "The Leaning
Tower"). Each of the stories in these four groups "is an
investigation into what Miss Porter has rightly called
'the terrible failure of the life of man in the Western
world.'" In style and effect "they are as subtle and
perceptive as the best works of Joyce or James." In *Ship of
Fools*, Porter has explored attitudes toward life and
death, love and sex, religion and religiosity, love and
hate, racism and politics; she has presented the deadly
sins in old forms and in new guises." It is unfair to criticize
the work for its pessimism; a work emphasizing human
nobility would not have given "a true picture of the 1930's
or of much of man's experience in the twentieth century."
Porter's nonfiction is difficult to evaluate because of its
nature and its variety. It can be divided into five sections:
"Critical," "Personal and Particular," "Mexican," "Two
Uncollected Essays," and Cotton Mather."

A revised edition, with Willene Hendrick as co-author, was published in 1988. The chapter on Porter's life has been rewritten, with corrections and additions. The discussion of the nonfiction has five additional sections: "On Writing," "The Poetry," "A Christmas Story," "Sacco and Vanzetti," and "Mexican Arts and Crafts."

H54. Hennessy, Rosemary. "Katherine Anne Porter's Model for Heroines." *Colorado Quarterly*, 25 (Winter 1977), 301–15.

The Miranda stories, taken together, serve as a *Bildungsroman*, portraying "a young girl's development toward adulthood n terms of a genuine search for identity and self-fulfillment." "The Source," "The Journey," "The Last Leaf," and "Old Mortality" show "the past and Miranda's evaluation of it." Also, they present four possible role models—two with positive codes (Sophia and Nannie) and two with negative codes (Amy and Eva). "The Fig Tree," "The Circus," and part of "The Grave" present the next stage of development—"her childhood epiphanies contrasted with the standards of her social environment." With the final scene of "The Grave" and "Pale Horse, Pale Rider," Miranda is initiated into adulthood. She faces death and despair. And she "realizes that forfeiting romantic love is the price of self-knowledge." She discovers "an art of living based on her own vision of meaning and personhood"; thus she can serve as a role model tor today's woman.

H55. Hernandez, Frances. "Katherine Anne Porter and Julio Cortázar: The Craft of Fiction." In *Proceedings of the Comparative Literature Symposium; Vol. 5: Modern American Fiction: Insights and Foreign Lights*, ed. Wolodymyr T. Zyla and Wendell M. Aycock. Lubbock: Texas Tech Univ., 1972, pp. 55–66.

A comparison and contrast of Porter and Julio Cortázar, concluding that "In the craft of fiction, particularly in the short story, we have two masters at work in our time." They are similar in the control of their materials, means of presenting characters, expert use of language, and "the cool and canny structure of their plots." But "while Miss Porter sums up in many ways the classic achievements of the first half of the century, Cortázar continues to launch new experiments in technical virtuosity."

H56. Hoffman, Frederick J. *The Art of Southern Fiction: A Study of Some Modern Novelists.* Carbondale: Southern Illinois Univ. Press, 1967, pp. 39–50.

Porter is concerned with the Southern past and its influence on the present, but she cannot be termed "regionalist." The Miranda stories, especially, show her linking of the past and present. These stories, "Noon Wine," and *Ship of Fools* are noteworthy works of fiction.

H57. Howell, Elmo. "Katherine Anne Porter as a Southern Writer." *South Carolina Review*, 4 (Dec. 1971), 5–15.

Porter is not a Southern writer in the tradition of Faulkner and Welty—writers who would have been quite different if they had not been Southerners. But she is also unlike writers, such as Poe, "for whom regional classification is gratuitous." Her Southern stories depend greatly on setting, yet her detachment prevents setting and plot being successfully interwoven with theme. This problem is seen clearly in "Old Mortality," where Miranda as a character is not vivid and where her rejection of her past seems imposed upon the story. What is most successful in the story—"the rich panoply of a family' corporate life in a particular place and time"— overshadows the development of Miranda. The short sketches set in the South are more successful, but even here Porter's detachment, her willed objectivity prevents the scenes and the characters from eliciting "a deep response from the reader."

H58. Hubbell, Jay B. *Who Are the Major American Writers.* Durham: Duke Univ. Press, 1972, pp. 72, 132, 155, 194, 228, 229, 259, 279, 280, 283. 297, 299.

Porter is mentioned occasionally to support the point that there is a lack of consensus as to who the great American writers are.

H59. Ibieta, Gabriella. "The North American Exile's Vision of Mexico According to Katherine Anne Porter." In *Proceedings of the Xth Congress of the International Comparative Literature Association.* New York: Garland, 1985, III, pp. 233–38.

Not examined by compiler.

H60. Johnson, James William. "Another Look at Katherine Anne Porter." *Virginia Quarterly Review,* 36 (Autumn 1960), 598–613.

Although Porter's publications have been few, she is—and should be—regarded as a major writer. "A few basic themes, an adroit use of symbols, a limpid prose style—these combine in Miss Porter's stories to the propagation of a fictional point of view which is amazingly consistent and complete." This point of view is a bleak one—human beings live in isolation and life is frustrating, cruel and meaningless.

H61. Johnson, Shirley E. "Love Attitudes in the Fiction of Katherine Anne Porter." *West Virginia Philological Papers,* 13 (Dec. 1961), 82–93.

Porter is consistently a nonromantic in her view of marriage; she sees it as a condition of dullness, drudgery, and bondage. "Her married characters finally accept their marital state with an attitude—not of reconciliation—but of resignation."

H62. Jones, Anne Goodwyn. "Gender and the Great War: The Case of Faulkner and Porter." *Women's Studies*, 13 (nos. 1–2, 1986), 135–48.

"Wars shake up traditional structures but only temporarily. Deeply disturbed by the wasteland of and after World War I, both Faulkner and Porter connect its horrors with the gender system, which rewards men who exploit hierarchy, conflict and force, and suppresses the power of the female in both men and women." However, both writers fail to fully explore this destructive system. "Faulkner turns away because of his apparent anxiety over the power of the autonomous female." And Porter "turns away because of her apparent conviction that female autonomy is in fact impossible in a patriarchally gendered world." A look at "Xochimilco," "Flowering Judas," "Hacienda," and "Pale Horse, Pale Rider" brings forth Porter's concerns.

H63. Jones, Llewelyn. "Contemporary Fiction." In *American Writers on American Literature*, ed. John Macy. New York: Horace Liveright, 1931, p. 502.

Believes that Porter will be to the 1930's what Willa Cather was to the 1920's.

H64. Joselyn, Sister M., O.S.B. "Animal Imagery in Katherine Anne Porter's Fiction." In *Myth and Symbol: Critical Approaches and Applications*, ed. Bernice Slote. Lincoln: Univ. of Nebraska Press, 1963, pp. 101–15.

Porter uses animal imagery "to describe character and to define structural elements of her stories." This imagery also serves to convey value judgments.

H65. Kaplan, Charles. "True Witness: Katherine Anne Porter." *Colorado Quarterly*, 7 (Winter 1959), 319–27.

An examination of the six "Old Order" stories and "Old Mortality" reminds the reader of Porter's "lasting artistry." These stories reflect Porter's own rebellion and search for truth.

H66. Kiely, Robert. "The Craft of Despondency—The Traditional Novelists." *Daedalus*, 92 (Spring 1963), 220–37.

Graham Greene, Evelyn Waugh, and Porter can be compared as post-World War II novelists writing in a traditional mode. Also, each has moral concerns and conveys a sense of hopelessness. And there are many individual similarities among their created characters.

H67. Krishnamurthi, M.G. *Katherine Anne Porter: A Study.* Mysore: Rao and Raghavan, 1971.

Porter's works are here examined according to her treatment of certain themes. "The child's growing awareness of the world around him" is the theme of "The Circus," "The Fig Tree," "The Grave," "The Witness," and "The Downward Path to Wisdom." They concern children thrust into the world, the complexity of which they find bewildering. Another group of stories deals with "the failure of adults to assist children in their growth into experience." This group consists of "The Journey" (here called "The Old Order"), "The Source," "The Last Leaf," and "Old Mortality." Three other stories—"Pale Horse, Pale Rider," "The Leaning Tower," and "Flowering Judas"—concern a search for "new experience," once the order represented by the family has been found wanting. The three protagonists find their desire for personal fulfillment thwarted by "impersonal forces . . .; and all three gradually realize their impotence in the face of catastrophe." The relativity of appearance and reality, and the difficulty of accepting the real are the concerns of another group of stories: "The Cracked Looking-Glass," "Noon Wine," "Holiday," "Hacienda," and "María Concepción." Concerning *Ship of Fools*, "the way in which corruption on the instinctive levels of life is seen as identical with strains in and the failure of a social order gives the novel's exploration of the theme of moral order the force it has."

H68. Liberman, M.M. *Katherine Anne Porter's Fiction.* Detroit: Wayne State Univ. Press, 1971.

It is valuable to examine Porter's work through "its formal properties, verbal and rhetorical. Those make clear an impressive talent for showing forth a first-rate and peculiarly feminine intelligence in a compositional mode precisely appropriate to its singular feeling." Those who have attacked *Ship of Fools* do not realize that it was not intended as a conventional novel. Rather, it is "a kind of modern apologue, a work organized as a fictional example of the truth of a formulable statement or a series of such statements." We should expect caricatures rather than rounded characters, many characters rather than a few, "fragmented" narration rather than a focused, linear plot. And we should expect the theme to be developed through repetitive exemplification.

An examination of the first draft of "Old Mortality" and of the few changes Porter made in it yields an understanding of the work itself. In spite of Porter's insistence to the contrary, "Noon Wine" should be considered a novella, since in the story Porter gives "a sense of the passage of time without the drama of an extended action." "María Concepción" gives a more effective portrayal of female sexual vitality than anything in D.H. Lawrence. Critics who read "Flowering Judas" only in terms of the religious symbolism are missing the story's greatest significance. Laura's most important role is not as a betrayer of others but as a betrayer of herself.

"Holiday," "He," and "Noon Wine" are similar in the use of an inarticulate person (Ottilie, the retarded boy, Olaf Helton) to induce "a more articulate character" (the narrator of "Holiday," the neighbor driving Mrs. Whipple and her son to the institution, Mr. Thompson) with whom the reader can identify, to experience a revision of life. As with "Flowering Judas," critics often miss the meaning of "The Leaning Tower" because they can't get beyond the obvious symbolism. The success of the story lies in Porter's use of Charles's consciousness as focal. The perceptions are, at times, "inadequate," but "inadequate only enough to permit the reader to participate in the experience at Charles's side without losing patience with his limitations."

Discussion of *Ship of Fools* is a revised form of "Responsibility of the Novelist: The Critical Reception of *Ship of Fools*" (I106) and "The Short Story as Chapter in *Ship of Fools*" (I107). Discussion of "Flowering Judas" reprinted in Harold Bloom (ed.), *Katherine Anne Porter* (H11).

H69. Malik, Meera. "Love and Marriage in Katherine Anne Porter." *Panjab University Research Bulletin (Arts)*, 17 (April 1986), 51–59.

Porter's fiction reveals "smouldering hatreds, bitter marital quarrelling and hate, suppressed resentments, inability to love, brutal beatings, violent murder, and yet intimately connected with this violence is man's need to live in peace and harmony with one another, to 'love.'"

H70. ———. "Use of Animal Imagery in the Work of Katherine Anne Porter." *Panjab University Research Bulletin (Arts)*, 16 (April 1985), 31–38.

Not examined by compiler.

H71. Marsden, Malcolm M. "Love as Threat in Katherine Anne Porter's Fiction." *Twentieth Century Literature*, 13 (April 1967), 29–38.

Underneath the quarreling, hatred, and violence of Porter's fiction lies the assumption that man needs love. But her characters (with the exception of the shadowy honeymoon couple in *Ship of Fools*) fail to achieve a consistently loving relationship. The failure is of three types. Some of the characters have an intermittent relationship that is broken and then revived from time to time by tumultuous quarrels. Others are not able, even temporarily, to purge themselves of hatred for their partners. A third type of character withdraws completely from human contact.

H72. Marshall, Margaret. "Writers in the Wilderness: Katherine Anne Porter." *Nation,* 150 (13 April 1940), 473–75.

Highly complimentary, summary view of Porter.

H73. May, Charles E. "Chekhov and the Modern Short Story." In *A Chekhov Companion,* ed. Toby W. Clyman. Westport, Conn.: Greenwood, 1985, pp. 149, 153–54, 161.

The hallucinatory effects of "The Jilting of Granny Weather all" and of parts of "Pale Horse, Pale Rider" show the influence of Chekhov upon Porter.

H74. McMurtry, Larry. "Ever a Bridegroom: Reflections on the Failure of Texas Literature." *Texas Observer,* 23 Oct. 1981, pp. 8–9.

Not examined by compiler.

H75. Mooney, Harry J., Jr. *The Fiction and Criticism of Katherine Anne Porter.* Critical Essays in English and American Literature, No. 2. Pittsburgh: Univ. of Pittsburgh Press, 1957.

The Miranda stories are Porter's "finest achievement." Taken together, they have a unity of plot and theme. With the exception of "The Cracked Looking-Glass," Porter's novelettes successfully portray "the all-important little human world senselessly sundered from without, its private harmony destroyed by the hostility of blind, incomprehensible forces." The other stories continue her theme of "the terrible predicament of the individual in the modern world." In all of her shorter works, the characters, although battered and disillusioned by their experiences, maintain a spirit of

hope that makes them "important to all of us who wish
to continue believing and struggling and surviving."
Reprinted in revised and expanded form in 1962.

H76. Murphy, Edward F. "'Endless Relations'—Henry James
and Katherine Anne Porter." *Saint Michael's Review*, 2
(Spring 1962), 14–15.

Not examined by compiler.

H77. Nance, William L., S.M. *Katherine Anne Porter and the
Art of Rejection.* Chapel Hill: Univ. of North Carolina
Press, 1964.

All of Porter's characters—whether assertive or
passive—conform to a "life-pattern" of rejection. This
motif of rejection can be examined in detail by dividing
her work into five sections: (1) the early stories; (2)
"Noon Wine," "The Downward Path to Wisdom," "A
Day's Work," "The Leaning Tower" ; (3) the Miranda
stories; (4) *Ship of Fools*; (5) the nonfiction. Her
protagonists   can   be   divided   into   "alpha"
(autobiographical) and "beta" (not closely modeled on
Porter herself). The autobiographical connection between
Porter and her art provides intensity. "The principle of
rejection which impelled Katherine Anne Porter into
art . . . enabled her to give form to a limited area of
human experience in such a way that she has provided
for her contemporaries a penetrating insight into the
dark reality that faces them."

H78. ———. "Variations on a Dream: Katherine Anne Porter
and Truman Capote." *Southern Humanities Review*, 3
(Fall 1969), 338–45.

Whereas Capote's fiction has been characterized by
"deliberate change," Porter's has been marked by "a sort
of deliberate fixity." For her, the American dream is
"engulfed in a nightmare chilling in its finality." This
vision pervades her work but is most obvious in "Pale
Horse, Pale Rider."

H79. O'Connor, William Van. "The Novel of Experience." *Critique*, 1 (Winter 1956), 37–44.

Porter belongs to the group of modern novelists writing in the tradition of Henry James. These writers create the "novels of experience." Characters in these works cope with the moral problems inherent in mere existence. Broader or more violent concerns are not dealt with.

H80. Orvis, Mary Burchard. *The Art of Writing Fiction.* New York: Prentice-Hall, 1948, pp. 27–29, 54, 66, 97, 105–07, 123–25, 167–68.

Uses brief passages from Porter's stories to illustrate various literary techniques.

H81. Partridge, Colin. "'My Familiar Country': An Image of Mexico in the Work of Katherine Anne Porter." *Studies in Short Fiction,* 7 (Fall 1970), 597–614.

There is a pattern of individual response to a betrayal followed by the "reversal of values in the individual who undergoes the betrayal" in some of Porter's fiction. A brief discussion of some of her nonfiction (primarily on Mexico) precedes a discussion of the pattern of the "moment of discovery" followed by the "culminating moments of experience" in "María Concepción," "The Martyr," "Virgin Violeta," "Flowering Judas," and "Hacienda."

H82. Pinkerton, Jan. "Katherine Anne Porter's Portrayal of Black Resentment." *University Review,* 36 (Summer 1970), 315–17.

In "The Old Order" stories, underneath the surface portrayal of a smoothly functioning relationship between blacks and whites, Porter "gives glimpses of the apparently docile black's recognition of his long-standing injustices and of his desire for compensation." But this "compensation" has to come within the bounds of the socially acceptable. Uncle Jimbilly ("The Witness") works out his bitterness through he horrifying stories of slavery that he tells children, making them feel guilty. The adults know nothing of these. Nannie manages to "chasten" and "rebuke" the whites by retiring to her own cabin rather than stay at the main house.

H83. "Place and Time—The Southern Writer's Inheritance." *Times Literary Supplement*, 17 Sept. 1954, p. xlviii.

A brief assessment of Porter's work. "Miss Porter has perhaps the greatest purity and elegance of style of all living American writers." Her prose has "the moral masculine power of mental and moral strength. She deals with states of mind, moral journeying, with good and evil."

H84. Poss, S.H. "Variations on a Theme in Four Stories of Katherine Anne Porter." *Twentieth Century Literature*, 4 (April–July 1958), 21–29.

Taken together, "The Circus," "Old Mortality," "Pale Horse, Pale Rider," and "The Grave" are a "quasi-*bildungsroman*." The first three deal with the failure of myth; the ending of "The Grave" "provides a static suspension of irreconcilables," bringing a temporary peace.

H85. Powers, James F. "She Stands Alone." *Four Quarters*, 12 (Nov. 1962), 56.

Porter has given us "the nearest thing to reality in American fiction."

H86. Robinson, Cecil. *Mexico and the Hispanic Southwest in American Literature*. Tucson: Univ. of Arizona Press, 1977, pp. 153, 218–20, 240–41, 258–59.

Porter shares three traits with other Americans setting stories in Mexico. In "That Tree" she satirizes the romantic view of Mexico. In "María Concepción" she shows admiration for the elemental nature of Mexicans.

In "Flowering Judas" she contrasts passionate, amoral Mexicans with inhibited, guilt-ridden Americans.

A revised edition of *With the Ears of Strangers; The Mexican in American Literature* (1963).

H87. Ryan, Marjorie. "*Dubliners* and the Stories of Katherine Anne Porter." *American Literature,* 31 (Jan. 1960), 464–73.

Although the short stories of Joyce and the better known stories of Porter share few surface traits, they do share the dominant theme of "moral paralysis." Also, "A Day's Work," "The Downward Path to Wisdom," and "The Cracked Looking-Glass" are similar to Joycean stories in technique. "Theft," "That Tree," and "Rope" have some striking similarities to *Dubliners* also. And even some of the longer Porter stories have similarities if closely examined.

H88. ———. "Katherine Anne Porter: *Ship of Fools* and the Short Stories." *Bucknell Review,* 12 (March 1964), 51–63.

Although *Ship of Fools* must be considered on its own terms, comparing it with Porter's short stories will add to an understanding of her intentions. The novel has the same basic types of characters as the stories, and the attitudes toward life are the same.

H89. Schorer, Mark. "Katherine Anne Porter." Afterword to *Pale Horse, Pale Rider.* New York: New American Library, 1962, pp. 167–75.

Porter's central concerns can be given as "three enormous questions": "From where did we come? Where are we at this moment? Where are we going?" In her fiction one troubled stage gives way to another. "What Miss Porter makes me know, finally, is that with every present creation the artist dies into his past in order to bring forth another creation."

Reprinted in *The World We Imagine* (1968).

H90. Schwartz, Edward G. "The Fictions of Memory."
     Southwest Review, 45 (Summer 1960), 204–15.

     The Miranda stories are "a profoundly moving drama,"
     a progress of "initiation, conflict, and survival." In "The
     Circus," Miranda first comprehends, though emotionally,
     the horrors of human existence. By the end of "Old
     Mortality," she has learned that she must search for her
     own truth beyond legend and clichés. Then, at the end of
     "Pale Horse, Pale Rider," Miranda is brought back to life
     from death, but her faith is in "a deluding dream
     concocted by the instinct of self-preservation." A more
     valid rebirth and acceptance is seen in "The Grave,"
     when Miranda in Mexico suddenly remember the
     childhood experience of twenty years earlier.
     Reprinted in Lodwick Hartley and George Core (eds.),
     Katherine Anne Porter: A Critical Symposium (H51).

H91. ———. "The Way of Dissent: Katherine Anne Porter's
     Critical Position." *Western Humanities Review*, 8
     (Spring 1954), 119–30.

     Porter has rebelled against religious orthodoxy and has
     refused to align herself with political ideologies. She
     has, like Henry James, transformed her social, moral, and
     political concerns into art. She is in "the tradition of
     dissent and inquiry, of selfless devotion to the search for
     meaning and order in the world of fiction."
     Reprinted in Lodwick Hartley and George Core (eds.),
     Katherine Anne Porter: A Critical Symposium (H51) and
     Robert Penn Warren (ed.), *Katherine Anne Porter: A
     Collection of Critical Essays* (H113).

H92. Scott, Shirley Clay. "The Mind of Katherine Anne
     Porter." *Nimrod*, 25 (Fall/Winter 1981), 7–19.

     Although sometimes overlooked, the formative
     imagination is most significant in the best Porter stories.
     Although an observer does not seem to intrude into the
     stories, the reader is aware "of someone who sees and for
     whom sight is a form of sensibility, of unified emotional

and intellectual apprehension." The means of communicating insight is quite apparent in "Noon Wine," "The Jilting of Granny Weatherall," "Flowering Judas," "Old Mortality," and "Pale Horse, Pale Rider."

H93. ———. "Origins of Power in the Fiction of Katherine Anne Porter." *Journal of Evolutionary Psychology*, 7 (March 1986), 46–56.

With Porter, "consciousness and art were, almost literally, mothered by death." The early death of her mother and her own near death in 1918 gave birth to her preoccupation with mortality. She had "from earliest childhood a powerful intuition of death, and her creative power (as distinct from her artistic skills) and her most urgent theme have an inherent relationship to that intuition."

H94. Slocum, Kathleen. "Katherine Anne Porter: A Fiercely Burning Particle." *Censor*, 4 (Fall 1961), 5–15.

Not examined by compiler.

H95. Smith, Rebecca W. "The Southwest in Fiction." *Saturday Review of Literature*, 25 (16 May 1942), 12–13, 37.

Eleven writers, among them Porter, are evidence of the noteworthy literature of the American Southwest. Porter's stories portray the region with "quiet, penetrating truthfulness."

H96. Snell, George. *The Shapers of American Fiction: 1798–1947*. New York: Dutton, 1947 (rpt. 1961), p. 301.

Porter "seems still on the threshold of great achievement."

H97. Spiller, Robert E., *et al. Literary History of the United States*, 4th and rev. ed. New York: Macmillan, 1974, I, pp. 1297, 1314, 1387.

Brief, general comments.

H98. Stallman, Robert W. "Life, Art, and the Secret Sharer." In *Forms of Modern Fiction*, ed. William Van O'Connor. Minneapolis: Univ. of Minn. Press, 1948, pp. 229–42.

Unlike the fiction of Conrad, Porter's stories "take their origin in remembered experiences." This essay was omitted from the 1959 ed. "at author's request."

H99. Stanford, Donald E. "Katherine Anne Porter." *Southern Review*, 17 (Jan. 1981), 1–2.

Porter "may be, in fact, the greatest stylist in prose fiction in English of this century."

H100. Stout, Janis P. "Miranda's Guarded Speech: Porter and the Problem of Truth-Telling." *Philological Quarterly*, 66 (Spring 1987), 259–78.

Throughout the Miranda stories and those stories with Miranda surrogates ("Flowering Judas" and "Hacienda"), the protagonist is characterized by a reserve, a withholding of her true feelings. In "The Circus" and "The Fig Tree," she does not express her bewilderment because she is unable to articulate it. In "The Grave," she purposely conceals her "agitation." In "Flowering Judas," Laura's reticence stems from her "trying to reconcile involvement with detachment, to be in the world and yet not of it." In "Old Mortality," Miranda's "habit of keeping her own counsel" has been "affirmed as the story's positive center." In "Pale Horse, Pale Rider," her "stoical reserve" is brought "to fullness."

H101. Straumann, Heinrich. *American Literature in the Twentieth Century*. London: Hutchinson, 1951, pp. 91–93.

Porter's stories are marked by "an element of genteel irony peculiar to herself and a preference for motives and moods that are in some hidden correlation to an impending catastrophe."

H102. Suzue, Akiko. "Katherine Anne Porter: The Abyss Beneath the Smooth Surface." In *American Literature in the 1940's*. Tokyo: Tokyo Chapter, American Literature Society of Japan, 1976, pp. 92–100.

"The clairvoyant eyes of Katherine Anne Porter see the abyss underlying the smooth surface of daily life." Some of her characters fail to recognize the abyss. But Porter "plunges deep into those who recognize it, adheres to their point of view, understands them, sympathizes with them, and most powerfully presents them." Such characters are Miranda Gay, Laura in "Flowering Judas," and the protagonist of "Theft."

H103. Teixeira, Cristina Maria. "Fiction as an Outlet for Problems of Identity: Analysis of Some of Katherine Anne Porter's Stories." *Estudos Anglo-Americanos* (Brazil), 7–8 (1983–84), 43–58.

Not examined by compiler.

H104. Titus, Mary. "'Mingled Sweetness and Corruption': Katherine Anne Porter's 'The Fig Tree' and 'The Grave.'" *South Atlantic Review*, 53 (May 1988), 111–25.

"The Grave" and "The Fig Tree"—when read in conjunction with certain other Porter pieces—"are revealed as explorations of the sexual terror and guilt originating in her most painful childhood experience: her mother's death after childbirth when Porter was almost two years old." The sense of horror, corruption, and death in "The Grave' is more powerful than any other emotion. In the other story, Porter uses the symbol of the fig tree as a rich, fertile balance to the terror and decay represented by the grave. But, throughout her life it was the corruption of the grave that haunted her.

H105. Unrue, Darlene Harbour. *Truth and Vision in Katherine Anne Porter's Fiction.* Athens: Univ. of Georgia Press, 1985.

Porter's fiction has unity when we consider it in terms of her concern with *truth*. For her, "truth can be both subjective and elusive"; the search for it is difficult and "filled with illusion." Part of that search must consist of "confronting all parts of elemental self, including darkness." Art and religion can provide the "order" that reflects truth, but we must beware of "unnatural art and perverted religion." All of Porter's fiction concerns "confronting and accepting the totality of life, including one's own nature and the unknowable, or the bewilderment and suffering that come from failing to do so; or about the deception of system and the illusion of ideals which we embrace as we attempt to find truth."

Several of Porter's stories reflect the journey into "the inner darkness," the primitive, terrifying instincts beneath the veneer of civilization. These "corners of darkness . . . must be penetrated in our perpetual groping toward truth." The stories focusing on this journey are "María Concepción," "Hacienda," "The Circus," "The Fig Tree," "The Grave," "Flowering Judas," "He," "Holiday," "The Downward Path to Wisdom," and "Noon Wine." Two Porter stories—"The Jilting of Granny Weatherall" and "Noon Wine"—show the ineffectiveness of organized (i.e., perverted) religion as a life guide. Other "faiths" are also found to be inadequate (in "Magic" and "Theft"). "Flowering Judas" and "Hacienda" show the disappointments inherent in political revolution. "Visible patterns" such as class consciousness (in "He" and "Noon Wine") or an obsession with orderliness (in "The Jilting of Granny Weatherall" and "Holiday") are also merely means of obscuring truth. Another false existence is based on "the human tendency to idealize persons or places, making them seem the embodiment of truth and perfection. "The Martyr," "The Cracked Looking-Glass," "Old Mortality," and "The Leaning Tower" are among the stories conveying this theme. In only a few of Porter's stories are there characters who gain even a glimmer of insight. In only three stories—"Holiday," "The Grave," and "Pale

Horse, Pale Rider"—does the protagonist reach "true reconciliation."

Ship of Fools is the thematic culmination of Porter's work. Here, as in the stories, the characters must confront darkness. And, here too, we see that there are certain contrived systems or frameworks of belief—class consciousness, nationalism, anti-semitism, organized religion, etc.—that obscure truth. Also, the novel presents the evils stemming from the idealizing tendency. And, as is the case in the stories, most of the characters gain no insight. Only Jenny and Dr. Schumann "make significant gains toward truth."

H106. ———. *Understanding Katherine Anne Porter.* Columbia Univ. of South Carolina Press, 1988.

Part of the *Understanding Contemporary American Literature* series for "students as well as good nonacademic readers." Discusses Porter's life and her fiction, with a concluding chapter concerning her nonfiction.

H107. Van Zyl, John. "Surface Elegance, Grotesque Content: A Note on the Short Stories of Katherine Anne Porter." *English Studies in Africa*, 9 (Sept. 1966), 168–75.

In Porter's fiction "untidy, grotesque reality meets the organized, elegant experience."

H108. Voss, Arthur. "Symbolism and Sensibility." In *The American Short Story*. Norman: Univ. of Oklahoma Press, 1973, pp. 288–301.

A general discussion of Porter's short fiction. Asserts that she is one of the great modern masters of the short story.

H109. Walsh, Thomas. "Xochitl: Katherine Anne Porter's Changing Goddess." *American Literature*, 52 (May 1980), 183–93.

By examining the contrasting uses of Xochitl and of
pulque in "The Children of Xochitl" (a typescript sketch
among Porter's papers) and in "Hacienda," we can trace
Porter's loss of "hope for happiness in this life." In the
sketch (which reflects the early stage of Porter's Mexican
period), the Indians of Xochimilco are innocent, happy,
self-assured. They still revere the Aztec goddess as a
nurturing lifegiver; the pulque (with which she is
associated) is refreshing and nourishing. This sketch is
"the positive of hope out of which 'Hacienda' developed
as the despairing negative." In "Hacienda" the bountiful
goddess—as seen in a faded fresco—and the nurturing
pulque have been transformed into purveyors of doom,
death, corruption.

H110. Wanning, Andrews. "The Literary Situation in
America." In *The Novelist as Thinker*, ed. B. Rajan.
London: Dennis Dobson, 1947, pp. 156–57.

Brief mention. Porter and Faulkner "appear to continue
as the divergent models for younger writers."

H111. Warren, Robert Penn. "Introduction." In *Katherine Anne
Porter: A Collection of Critical Essays*. Englewood
Cliffs, N.J.: Prentice-Hall, 1979, pp. 1–19.

A summary of the known biographical data on Porter
and a discussion of her work. Like other modern writers,
Porter is concerned with ambiguity of motive. But she is
different from them in important respects. First, the
ambiguity she attributes to her characters' thoughts and
acts does not lead to a "vagueness of structure in the
fiction itself." Also, she—unlike many other writers—
believes in the existence of evil. And "she presumably
believes in the sanctity of what used to be called the
individual soul." A careful examination of the body of
Porter's work allows one to perceive "the inner
coherence—the work as a deeply imaginative
confrontation of a sensibility of genius with the

chiaroscuro of modern civilization, in which it is often hard to tell light from dark."

H112. ———. Introduction to "Katherine Anne Porter: A Critical Bibliography" by Edward Schwartz. *Bulletin of the New York Public Library*, 57 (May 1953), 211–16.

Porter's writing "has been peculiarly outside of fashion. It has always been peculiarly itself and, in that identity, peculiarly appealing to our imaginations." Concerning the ideas of her story, there seem to be two central points: "the necessity for moral definition, and the difficulty of moral definition." (See F6.)

H113. ———, ed. *Katherine Anne Porter: A Collection of Critical Essays*. Englewood Cliffs, N.J.: Prentice-Hall, 1979.

Essays (written during the 40's, 50's, and 60's) on Porter and her work. Contents: "Introduction" (H111); Hank Lopez, "A Country and Some People That I Love" (G105); Glenway Wescott, "Katherine Anne Porter Personally" (G176); "'Noon Wine': The Sources" (C89); Eudora Welty, "The Eye of the Story" (H116); Edward G. Schwartz, "The Way of Dissent" (H91); Robert Penn Warren, "Irony with a Center" (H114); V.S. Pritchett, "The Collected Stories of Katherine Anne Porter" (J272); Cleanth Brooks, "On 'The Grave'" (I23); George Core, "'Holiday': A Version of Pastoral" (I38); Edmund Wilson, "Katherine Anne Porter" (J110); Mark Schorer, "We're All on the Passenger List" (J228); Theodore Solotaroff, "*Ship of Fools* and the Critics" (I115); Sybille Bedford, "Voyage to Everywhere" (J161); Howard Moss, "No Safe Harbor" (J212); Louis Auchincloss, "Bound for Bremerhaven—and Eternity" (J159); Smith Kirkpatirck, "*Ship of Fools*" (I105); M.M. Liberman, "The Responsibility of the Novelist" (I106).

H114. ———. "Katherine Anne Porter (Irony with a Center)." *Kenyon Review*, 4 (Winter 1942), 29–42.

Discusses passages from "Flowering Judas," "Old Mortality," and "The Cracked Looking-Glass" to show the thoroughness and complexity of Porter's irony. This irony, moreover, "is an irony with a center." The irony reflects a refusal to accept readymade codes of morality and the necessity of facing reality with discrimination and an awareness of paradox. Her style reinforces the irony. For Porter, "a story must test its thematic line at every point against total circumstantiality; the thematic consideration must, as it were, be validated in terms of circumstance and experience, and never be resolved in the poverty of statement."

Reprinted in *Contrasts* (1951); *Selected Essays* (1958); Lodwick Hartley and George Core (eds.), *Katherine Anne Porter: A Critical Symposium* (H51); Robert Penn Warren (ed.), *Katherine Anne Porter: A Collection of Critical Essays* (H113); Harold Bloom (ed.), *Katherine Anne Porter* (H11); and Heather McClave (ed.), *Women Writers of the Short Story* (1980).

H115. ———. "Uncorrupted Consciousness: The Stories of Katherine Anne Porter." *Yale Review*, 55 (Winter 1966), 280–90.

On the surface Porter's stories might not show her to be an especially "modern" writer. But, below the surface these stories have a "root modernism" that, paradoxically, allows them to have implications beyond the moment. Her stories show the necessity of an "existential commitment" in a world of ambiguity and flux. Porter is superb at showing "the dark pit [of the mind] where motives twine and twist." With this very modern concern, she goes beyond most of her contemporary writers by believing strongly in the existence of evil and in the sanctity of the human soul. The tension between the intellect and the emotions also shows her to be a modern writer.

H116. Welty, Eudora. "The Eye of the Story." *Yale Review*, 55 (Winter 1966), 265–74.

Generally, Porter's stories are not "visible"; they do not move through scenes. They take place in the "interior of our lives" and "show surface only at her choosing." Her imagery is often that of the past being "distilled, reformed" by memory. The point of view is actually "the dispassionate eye of time."

Reprinted in Lodwick Hartley and George Core (eds.), *Katherine Anne Porter: A Critical Symposium* (H51); Robert Penn Warren (ed.), *Katherine Anne Porter: A Collection of Critical Essays* (H113); and Harold Bloom (ed.), *Katherine Anne Porter* (H11).

H117. West, Ray B., Jr. *Katherine Anne Porter*. University of Minnesota Pamphlets on American Writers, no. 28. Minneapolis: Univ. of Minnesota Press, 1963.

"As a non-practicing Catholic and a liberal Southerner," Porter has focused on the tensions of a changing moral and social order. "Her fiction portrays a small but inclusive, grotesque but convincing, world, rendered as at times absurd, always pathetic, but rendered, finally, with compassion." Porter's protagonists are almost always based upon herself. They are usually southern; often they are either Roman Catholic or politically liberal. Her creative approach consists of "remembering" an experience from her past and molding that experience into a story. *Ship of Fools* resembles her stories in that it is consistently skeptical but permeated by a sense of compassion.

Excerpt concerning *Ship of Fools* reprinted in Robert Penn Warren (ed.), *Katherine Anne Porter: A Collection of Critical Essays* (H113).

H118. ———. "Katherine Anne Porter." In *American Writers*, Vol. 3, ed. Leonard Unger. New York: Scribner's, 1974, pp. 433–55.

"There is probably no other writer of fiction in America who has maintained so consistently high a level." Her fiction begins with a remembered incident from her past which creativity develops into a story. She is "a major figure in what has become a literary revival in American letters in the twentieth century."

H119. ———. "Katherine Anne Porter and 'Historic Memory.'" *Hopkins Review*, 6 (Fall 1952), 16–27.

Porter's Southern, Roman Catholic upbringing has had a determining effect on her stories. From the inherent myths and from her own experiences, she has—with the creative agent of memory—constructed her art and new myths.
Reprinted in Louis D. Rubin and Robert O. Jacobs (eds.), *Southern Renaissance: The Literature of the Modern South* (1953); Louis D. Rubin and Robert D. Jacobs (eds.), *South: Modern Southern Literature in Its Cultural Setting* (1961); and in expanded and revised form in *Katherine Anne Porter* (H117).

H120. ———. *The Short Story in America, 1900–1950*. Chicago: Henry Regnery, 1952, pp. 72–76.

Although Porter has not been prolific, "there is probably no writer of short stories in America who has maintained so consistently high a level." With the exception of "The Leaning Tower," her stories are masterpieces of implication; she does not spell out her themes.

H121. Whicher, George. "The Resurgent South." In *The Literature of the American People: An Historical and Critical Survey*, ed. Arthur H. Quinn. New York: Appleton-Century-Crofts, 1951, p. 925.

Porter "has created an instrument of marvelous precision to register highly sensitive and intense awareness of life, both of people and of backgrounds."

H122. Wiesenfarth, Joseph. "Negatives of Hope: A Reading of Katherine Anne Porter." *Renascence*, 25 (Winter 1973), 85–94.

Porter's "stories project a disordered world in which conflict is generated in lives where self-knowledge and love have failed to find their place." "The Downward Path to Wisdom," with "martyr" Stephen, is "an account of civilized disorder." Granny Weatherall realizes at her death that she has failed to love. "Noon Wine" is "the story of a man making every attempt to live an orderly life without ever learning that order must emanate from within." In "Theft" and "Magic," life without love . . . is revealed mainly as endurance." "He" and "A Day's Work" show "the inadequacy of endurance divorced" from life. *Ship of Fools* is a more thorough treatment of "the restless and frustrating search of human beings for the order of human love." The solution to such a barren, unfulfilling condition is to seek self-knowledge, to create order "from within," and to "learn" to love.

Reprinted in Harold Bloom (ed.), *American Fiction: 1914–1945* (1987).

H123. Wykes, Alan. *A Concise Survey of American Literature.* London: Arthur Barber, 1955, p. 175.

Porter belongs to that group of Southern writers whose stories have "a multiplicity of psychological detail."

H124. Young, Vernon A. "The Art of Katherine Anne Porter." *New Mexico Quarterly Review*, 15 (Autumn 1945), 326–41.

Porter's style is not distinctive in the sense of the styles of Hemingway or Virginia Woolf. It is effective because it varies to fit the character being portrayed. Concerning her characters, only Miranda in "Old Mortality" has both an insight into a situation and the will to act upon it. The stories from *The Leaning Tower*, although worthy, are not as successful as those of Porter's earlier collections.

Reprinted in *American Thought 1947* (1947).

SECTION I
Criticism of Individual Works

In this section, Porter's works are given in alphabetical order; the entries concerning each work are also alphabetical. Reprints are listed with the original entry.

"The Cracked Looking-Glass"

I1. Wiesenfarth, Br. Joseph, F.S.C. "Illusion and Allusion: Reflections in 'The Cracked Looking-Glass.'" *Four Quarters*, 12 (Nov. 1962), 30–37.

In the story there is a "diachronic movement" showing the interrelationship of reality and illusion and culminating with the acceptance of reality. There is also a "centripetal and centrifugal" movement centering on the central symbol of the cracked mirror. Porter has allusions to "Beast in the Jungle," "In the Cage," *Ulysses*, "Lady of Shalott," and *I Corinthians*.

Reprinted in Lodwick Hartley and George Core (eds.), *Katherine Anne Porter: A Critical Symposium* (H51).

"The Downward Path to Wisdom"

12. Hartley, Lodwick. "Stephen's Lost World: The Background
    of Katherine Anne Porter's 'The Downward Path to
    Wisdom.'" *Studies in Short Fiction*, 6 (Fall 1969), 574–
    79.

    There are many parallels between the childhood of
    Hart Crane and that of the protagonist in the story.
    Porter and Crane had, of course, been good friends.

"The Fig Tree"

13. Hughes, Linda K. "Katherine Anne Porter's 'The Fig Tree':
    The Tree of Knowing." *Publications of the Arkansas
    Philological Association*, 3 (Summer 1977), 54–58.

    "The symbols of 'The Fig Tree' imbue the story with a
    mythic pattern which reinforces the work's
    epistemological theme." In the story "Miranda moves
    from a naive epistemology . . ., to a direct exposure to the
    chaos underlying human experience . . ., to a repudiation
    of her simplistic basis of knowing and the adoption of a
    more rigorous mature epistemology."

"Flowering Judas"

14. Bloom, Harold. "Introduction." *Katherine Anne Porter.*
    New York: Chelsea, 1986, pp. 1–5.

    Ostensibly an introduction to a collection of essays, but
    deals almost entirely with "Flowering Judas." This story
    does not deal with betrayal, loss of faith, or wasteland
    sterility. Rather, Laura is a representative of necessary,
    womanly narcissism, as defined by Freud.

15. Bluefarb, Sam. "Loss of Innocence in 'Flowering Judas.'"
    College Language Association Journal, 7 (March 1964),
    256–62.

Laura's loss of innocence occurs when she becomes aware of the reality of the cynical Braggioni. In certain other fictional characters, such a loss is followed by a temporary withdrawal from action and, finally, positive action. But in Laura the loss does not affect her actions. She continues to serve the revolution, but "as a kind of somnambulant victim, a zombie."

16. Bride, Sister Mary, O.P. "Laura and the Unlit Lamp." *Studies in Short Fiction*, 1 (Fall 1963), 61–63.

"Flowering Judas" may be compared to Browning's "The Statue and the Bust" in that its theme "is a condemnation not of chastity but of that peculiar spiritual deadness so much feared and decried in medieval treatises under the title of 'accedia.'"

17. Flood, Ethelbert, O.F.M. "Christian Language in Modern Literature." *Culture*, 22 n.s. (March 1961), 28–42.

Not examined by compiler. (According to Kiernan, F5, it deals with "Flowering Judas.")

18. Gerlach, John. *Toward the End: Closure and Structure in the American Short Story*. University, Ala.: Univ. of Alabama Press, 1985, pp. 92, 100–07, 140, 161.

The structure of "Flowering Judas" is nonlinear. At times a "resolution" seems promised, but then the story opens up again. This helps to create the tension and ambiguity of the work. That Laura's unconscious awakens her at the end shows that, even if she is "fixed in her attitude," the reader can see "the process of change potentially at work."

19. Gottfried, Leon. "Death's Other Kingdom: Dantesque and Theological Symbolism in 'Flowering Judas.'" *PMLA*, 84 (Jan. 1969), 112–24.

The world of "Flowering Judas" is very much the world of T.S. Eliot's poems of spiritual death. Laura's evil is not

an active sort, as is that of Braggioni (who can be
compared with Eliot's "lost violent souls"). Instead, she
is simply not good. She feels nothing, has no faith in any
system, is incapable of meaningful action. Porter, in
presenting this very modern condition, has chosen to use
the symbolism of the Catholic Church and of Dante.

I10. Gross, Beverly. "The Poetic Narrative: A Reading of
    'Flowering Judas.'" Style, 2 (Spring 1968), 129–39.

In "Flowering Judas" Porter has made great use of poetic
devices. "The poetic language deepens our apprehension
of Laura, the atmosphere of her mind, her perceptions,
her very life. And the story's moral and dramatic
consequence comes from the subordination of its narrative
energy in favor of this poetic evocation of a state of
mind."

I11. Madden, David. "The Charged Image in Katherine Anne
    Porter's "Flowering Judas.'" Studies in Short Fiction, 7
    (Spring 1970), 277–89.

"Flowering Judas" has as its "hub" the beginning image
of Braggioni singing to Laura. "All other images spoke out
from it, and the author's meditating voice is the rim,
and . . . the reader's active participation is the energy
that makes the wheel turn." Further, "the contrast
between the static quality of the images and the
immediacy of the historical present tense generates a
tension that enhances the effect of Miss Porter's basic
image technique."

I12. Redden, Dorothy S. "'Flowering Judas': Two Voices."
    Studies in Short Fiction, 6 (Winter 1969), 194–204.

It is misleading to believe that Porter has a "unitary"
view of life. "Flowering Judas" is evidence that Porter's
"outlook is essentially and irrevocably dual." Laura is
immobilized by the tension between her fear of death and
her fear of life. She can reach "equilibrium" only by
"complete negation."

I13. Rohrberger, Mary. "Betrayer or Betrayed: Another View of 'Flowering Judas.'" *Notes on Modern American Literature*, 2 (Winter 1977), Item 10.

Laura's "No" in the dream passage signifies that she will remain "true to herself." Eugenio stands for Christ, and thus the Church, which she realizes is as corrupt as all other institutions.

I14. Walsh, Thomas F. "Braggioni's Jockey Club in Porter's 'Flowering Judas.'" *Studies in Short Fiction*, 20 (Spring–Summer 1983), 136–38.

The allusions to the Jockey Club "suggest that the Braggioni's of the Revolution do not represent change, only frightening continuity."

I15. ———. "Braggioni's Songs in 'Flowering Judas.'" *College Literature*, 12 (Spring 1985), 147–52.

The songs Braggioni sings in "Flowering Judas" reveal two intertwined strands of Laura's personality. "'A la Orilla de un Palmar' exposes sexual fears behind her nunlike devotion to her ideals, while 'La Norteña' commemorates her heroic if vain struggle to cling to those ideals."

I16. ———. "The Making of 'Flowering Judas.'" *Journal of Modern Literature*, 12 (March 1985), 107–30.

A careful exploration of the people and events of Porter's experiences in Mexico in 1920–21. The figure of Laura is based on Porter, not Mary Doherty. By May 1921 Porter had been convinced that "Mexico as a potential paradise was and could be nothing but a dream. . . . If Mexico could not assuage her troubled psyche, it compelled her to contemplate the entwined betrayals of revolution and of self, and to transform her disillusion and spiritual isolation into Laura's."

I17. Walter, James. "Revolution and Time: Laura in 'Flowering Judas.'" *Renascence*, 38 (Autumn 1985), 26–38.

A close examination of the story shows that the Judas tree symbolizes "a creative love that communicates itself temporarily through nature." Porter believed that art has a redemptive value, representing "a spiritual action originated in time's openness contextually ordered by nature."

I18. West, Ray B., Jr. "Katherine Anne Porter: Symbol and Theme in 'Flowering Judas.'" *Accent*, 7 (Spring 1947), 182–88.

An analysis of the story's three types of symbols—those of religion, of revolution, and of love. These can be seen as three circles, all of which Laura is outside of. "Her life seems to be a sense-less kind of existence similar to the drugged sleep of the prisoners." The story thus has more than just a superficial resemblance to T.S. Eliot's "Gerontion."

Reprinted in West and Robert Wooster Stallman (eds.), *The Art of Modern Fiction* (1949); John W. Aldridge (ed.), *Critiques and Essays on Modern Fiction: 1920–1951* (1952); Lodwick Hartley and George Core (eds.), *Katherine Anne Porter: A Critical Symposium* (H51); and as "A Critique of 'Flowering Judas'" in Robert Stallman and Robert Waldhorn (eds.), *American Literature: Readings and Critiques* (1961).

"Gertrude Stein: Three Views"

I19. Herbst, Josephine. "Miss Porter and Miss Stein." *Partisan Review*, 15 (May 1948), 568–72.

Critical of the essay "Gertrude Stein: A Self Portrait." Porter's picture of Stein as a "gloomy, low-pressure, possessive slug" can be contrasted with Picasso's portrait in which "the whole being is saturated with patience and eagerness." Porter's seeing Stein's prose as "irresponsible" and chaotic and her implying that it contributed to the political chaos of the thirties and forties is wrongheaded. Similar narrowminded reaction against the *avant garde* has been felt by Hitler and the leaders of the Soviet Union.

I20. McCormick, John. *The Middle Distance: A Comparative History of American Imaginative Literature 1919–1932.* New York: Free Press, 1971, pp. 90–91.

Concern's Porter's criticism of Gertrude Stein's experimental style.

"The Grave"

I21. Bell, Barbara Currier. "Non-Identical Twins: Nature in 'The Garden Party' and 'The Grave.'" *T h e Comparatist: Journal of the Southern Comparative Literature Association*, 12 (May 1988), 58–66.

Not examined by compiler.

I22. Bell, Vereen M. "'The Grave' Revisited." *Studies in Short Fiction*, 3 (Fall 1965), 39–45.

Curley's interpretation of "The Grave" (I24) in terms of Christian symbolism and Christian resurrection is misleading. Futhermore, this may not be one of those stories which can be scientifically dissected.

I23. Brooks, Cleanth. "On 'The Grave.'" *Yale Review*, 55 (Winter 1966), 275–79.

Of Porter's stories, "The Grave" most clearly indicates her artistic genius. One can see "how skilfully, and apparently almost effortlessly, the author has rendered the physical and social context that gives point to Miranda's discovery of truth and has effected the modulation of her shifting attitudes—toward the grave, the buried ring, her hunting clothes, the dead rabbit— reconciling these various and conflicting attitudes and, in the closing sentence, bringing into precise focus the underlying theme."

Reprinted in Lodwick Hartley and George Core (eds.), *Katherine Anne Porter: A Critical Symposium* (H51) and Robert Penn Warren, (ed.), *Katherine Anne Porter: A Collection of Critical Essays* (H113).

I24. Curley, Daniel. "Treasure in 'The Grave.'" *Modern Fiction Studies*, 9 (Winter 1963–64), 377–84.

Assuming that "The Grave" is largely autobiographical, we can see it as a masterful blending of childhood experience and adult epiphany. It shows that "the mind of the writer is the grave of the past and that the art of the writer resurrects the past to a new life and a new meaning." The story is a "Christian fable."

I25. Gardiner, Judith Kegan. "'The Grave,' 'On Not Shooting Sitting Birds,' and the Female Esthetic." *Studies in Short Fiction*, 20 (Fall 1983), 265–70.

Both Porter's "The Grave" and Jean Rhys's "On Not Shooting Sitting Birds" "dramatize the female esthetic brilliantly and succinctly." But, unlike the female esthetic as defined by Elaine Showalter (in *A Literature of Their Own*), this view of the esthetic is a positive one. The stories "validate the special nature of female creativity." Both stories concern initiation into the mysteries of sexuality and death, and both have the female protagonist repressing the experience. But in each the buried memory serves as the inspiration for art— "uncontrollable female memory and desire generate the untellable core truth of female story telling."

I26. Joselyn, Sister M., O.S.B. "'The Grave' as Lyrical Short Story." *Studies in Short Fiction*, 1 (Spring 1964), 216–21.

Short stories can be divided into two classes: "mimetic" and "lyrical." "The Grave" belongs to the latter group, for it not only has "the essentials of narrative," but it also incorporates "elements generally associated with poetry to reflect and enrich consciousness."

I27. Kramer, Dale. "Notes on Lyricism in 'The Grave.'" *Studies in Short Fiction*, 2 (Summer 1965), 331–36.

Sister Joselyn's analysis of "The Grave" (I26) is valid but limited. True, the symbolism can be seen as religious. But the story can also be read on "the level of initiation" and "the psychological level." This last level is quite important, for it shows that Miranda, "having been granted knowledge, pulls back from it."

I28. Prater, William. "'The Grave': Form and Symbol." *Studies in Short Fiction*, 6 (Spring 1969), 336–38.

The two-part structure of "The Grave" serves to point out the tendency of human beings to repress horrifying experiences.

I29. Rooke, Constance, and Bruce Wallis. "Myth and Epiphany in Porter's 'The Grave.'" *Studies in Short Fiction*, 15 (Summer 1978), 269–75.

Former criticism of "The Grave" has ignored "the story's paradigm of our most primitive racial myth, that of the fall of man, which is itself the pattern of a primal experience in the life of each individual." The cemetery suggests the Garden of Eden; Miranda's name suggests innocence. In taking the ring, she yields to temptation. With the discovery of the unborn rabbits within the body of their mother, Miranda has fallen into a knowledge of good and evil. "Additionally, she has taken on the knowledge of life, birth, and death as they relate specifically to herself as sinner, as a woman, and as mortal being." In Paul's wanting her to conceal the incident, we see the suggestion of Adam's attempt to conceal his disobedience. When the memory of the event is reawakened in Miranda many years later, she has a vision of Paul turning over the silver dove. The epiphany reveals him as the Apostle Paul and the dove as the

symbol of redemption. The dove came from the grave, just
as Adam and Eve's fall was necessary for Christian
redemption.

Reprinted in Harold Bloom (ed.), *Katherine Anne
Porter* (H11).

I30. Welker, Robert L., and Herschel Gower. "'The Grave':
Investigation and Comment." In *The Sense of Fiction.*
Englewood Cliffs, N.J.: Prentice-Hall, 1966, pp. 150–54.

In "The Grave" Porter "unveils the aesthetics by which
man may live if he is to confront decay and waste in his
world and transform mere existence into the art of
living." Paul has the secret of living meaningfully; his
aesthetic (as symbolized by the dove screwhead) is both
beautiful and practical. In the childhood scene, Miranda
learns half of his secret—that waste is bad. In the adult
epiphany, she learns the other half—"the redeeming art
of creative preservation."

"Hacienda"

I31. Hendrick, George. "Katherine Anne Porter's 'Hacienda.'"
Four Quarters, 12 (Nov. 1962), 24–29.

Porter has skillfully woven together the various
literary, social, and political elements to create "a
brilliantly executed story of disengagement, of spiritual,
physical, moral, and psychological isolation, a short
novel of the lost generation." The critics who complain
that the narrator is detached from the action do not
realize that this quality successfully reinforces "the
totality of her isolation."

I32. Perry, Robert L. "Porter's 'Hacienda' and the Theme of
Change." *Midwest Quarterly,* 6 (Summer 1965), 403–15.

The basic theme of "Hacienda" concerns "the illusion of
change." Throughout the story the political and social
situations, as well as each of the major characters,

reinforce the irony that, if examined beneath the surface, matters are still nearly the same as before.

I33. Walsh, Thomas F. "In Porter's 'Hacienda.'" *New York Review of Books*, 16 June 1983, pp. 52–53.

A Letter to the Editor concerning the basic symbolism in "Hacienda."

"He"

I34. Deasy, Br. Paul Francis, F.S.C. "Reality and Escape." *Four Quarters*, 12 (Jan. 1963), 28–31.

"He" concerns Mrs. Whipple's failure to face reality. At the end, she comes close to a realization but "escapes" once more.

I35. Jorgenson, Bruce W. "'The Other Side of Silence': Katherine Anne Porter's 'He' as Tragedy." *Modern Fiction Studies*, 28 (Autumn 1982), 395–404.

In reading "He" many critics fall error to one of two dangers: either they sentimentalize the character of Mrs. Whipple or they condemn her as self-serving and heartless. However, with a close reading, "an ironic narrative voice, always qualified by context so as to preclude easy, simplistic condemnation, requires us to make ... complex judgments, allowing the validity of Mrs. Whipple's natural motherly feelings but also insisting on the reality of her unadmitted guilt and hostility." The story is a tragedy, the recognition scene coming in the final scene, as He breaks into weeping "and there is no way Mrs. Whipple can ignore it or attribute it to anything except her present or past actions."
Reprinted in Harold Bloom (ed.), *Katherine Anne Porter* (H11).

I36. Liberman, M.M. "The Publication of Porter's 'He' and the Question of the Use of Literature." *Midwest Educational Review*, 4 (Spring 1972), 1–7.

Not examined by compiler.

I37. Moddelmog, Debra A. "Narrative Irony and Hidden Motivations in Katherine Anne Porter's 'He.'" *Modern Fiction Studies*, 28 (Autumn 1982), 405–13.

As in many of her other stories, in "He" Porter is concerned "with self-deception, vanity, and hypocrisy." Mrs. Whipple is "not a weak but well-meaning mother of a retarded child, but rather one whose pride and hypocrisy make her a moral monster." Her hypocrisy is revealed both through her own words and through the irony of the third-person narrator. Her resentment of her son builds to the point where, over and over, she unconsciously wishes for his death, and even places him in danger.

Reprinted in Harold Bloom, *Katherine Anne Porter* (H11).

"Holiday"

I38. Core, George. "Holiday': A Version of Pastoral." In *Katherine Anne Porter: A Critical Symposium*, ed. Lodwick Hartley and George Core. Athens: Univ. of Georgia Press, 1969, pp. 149–58.

A revised, enlarged version of a section of "The *Best* Residuum of Truth" (H21). "Holiday" can be approached in terms of Empson's definition of a "pastoral"—a story reflecting man's longing to return to the Garden of Eden. "In many respects this story is a celebration of the soil which is tilled by those who know and understand it deeply and intuitively." But it is a "double story," also including a "tragic dimension." The death of Mrs. Müller and the coming of Spring provide a framework for revelation and acceptance.

Reprinted in Robert Penn Warren (ed.), *Katherine Anne Porter: A Collection of Critical Essays* (H113).

139. Hardy, John Edward. "Katherine Anne Porter's 'Holiday.'" *Southern Literary Messenger*, 1 (1975), 1–5.

   Not examined by compiler.

140. Peden, William. "Porter and the Promising." *Saturday Review*, 45 (21 April 1962), 30–31.

   A review of *Prize Stories of 1962: The O. Henry Awards* (ed. Richard Poirier), which includes "Holiday." This story shows "no diminution of [Porter's] sure command of characters," but it is "slightly topheavy."

141. Rood, William B., Jr. "Guest Commentary by a Student." In *The Art of Fiction*, ed. Barbara Pannwitt. Boston: Ginn, 1964, pp. 398–400.

   "The success of 'Holiday' in achieving vitality is a result of Miss Porter's using a literary form suitable to and consistent with content. An internally developed theme is externalized and given color, and irony is used to provide suspense."

Introduction to *A Curtain of Green*

142. Boyle, Kay. "Full-Length Portrait." *New Republic*, 105 (Nov. 1941), 707.

   A review of Eudora Welty's short story collection, *A Curtain of Green*, that has an introduction by Porter. Regarding Welty, Porter "has said a number of profoundly true and sensitive things." Disagrees with Porter's feeling that Welty should not attempt a novel.

The Itching Parrot

143. Duff, Charles. *Nation*, 156 (6 March 1943), p. 358.

    A Letter to the Editor concerning Porter's translation of
    The Itching Parrot. The novel is magnificent, and by
    translating it, Porter has "rendered a great service," even
    if she "has not succeeded in producing the perfect last
    word translation."

"The Jilting of Granny Weatherall"

144. Barnes, Daniel R., and Madeline T. "The Secret Sin of
    Granny Weatherall." *Renascence*, 21 (Spring 1969),
    162–65.

    A close reading of the story shows that Granny
    Weatherall has for years been haunted by her secret sin:
    her daughter Hapsy was the child of her sweetheart
    George, not of her husband John.

145. Becker, Laurence A. "'The Jilting of Granny Weatherall':
    The Discovery of Pattern." *English Journal*, 105 (Dec.
    1966), 1164–69.

    Not examined by compiler.

146. Cobb, Joanne P. "Pascal's Wager and Two Modern Losers."
    Philosophy and Literature, 3 (Fall 1979), 187–98.

    Porter's "The Jilting of Granny Weatherall" and
    Flannery O'Connor's "A Good Man Is Hard to Find" give
    modern examples of characters who are confronted with
    the choice posed by Pascal's wager regarding the
    acceptance of the Christian God. After being jilted on her
    wedding day, Granny Weatherall centered her life on
    her belief in a God and rewards in the afterlife.
    Although the story's ending shows the belief to have
    been a mistaken one, Granny, nevertheless, has "won"
    (rather than merely "not lost," as Pascal would have
    described it). Her belief has enabled her to fight off the

despair that would have been a denial of the positive during her lifetime. She "has been a successful mother, a compassionate neighbor, and her children remain as a testament to her achievement."

Reprinted in Harold Bloom (ed.), *Katherine Anne Porter* (H11).

147. Cowser, Robert G. "Porter's 'The Jilting of Granny Weatherall.'" *Explicator* 21 (Dec. 1962), 34.

Porter skillfully and ambiguously uses the title of her story to refer to both of Granny's "jiltings."

148. Detweiler, Robert. "The Moment of Death in Modern Fiction." *Contemporary Literature*, 13 (Summer 1972), 269–94.

The death of Granny Weatherall is one of the literary deaths analyzed to show that: "The death moment in literature lends itself well to an analysis from the standpoint of phenomenology and structuralism. The element of being and nothingness, of the ego and identity, of the rupture of time and space inherent in the death moment are resonant in the language of phenomenological and structuralist methodologies."

149. Estes, David C. "Granny Weatherall's Dying Moment: Katherine Anne Porter's Allusions to Emily Dickinson." *Studies in Short Fiction*, 22 (Fall 1985), 437–42.

References to three Emily Dickinson poems—"Because I Could Not Stop for Death," "I Heard a Fly Buzz When I Died," and "I've Seen a Dying Eye"—serve "to make the intensity of Granny's disillusionment believable."

150. Goodman, Charlotte. "Despair in Dying Women: Katherine Anne Porter's 'The Jilting of Granny Weatherall' and Tillie Olsen's 'Tell Me a Riddle.'" *Connecticut Quarterly*, 1 (March 1979), 47–63.

An examination of stories by Porter and Tillie Olsen (in which the protagonists are dying women) and stories by Thomas Mann and Tolstoi (in which the protagonists are dying men) reveals contrasts "which appear to reflect the differing social roles that the female and male characters have played during their lifetimes. Porter's Granny Weatherall and Olsen's Eva (from "Tell Me a Riddle") are concerned with domestic chores and children as they approach death. But there is also a "bitterness which is threaded through the memories of each and is counterpointed against her past achievements." The male protagonists—Mann's Aschenbach and Tolstoi's Ivan Ilych—"regret their own past actions and the choices they themselves have made, while the female protagonists, viewing themselves as victims, bemoan the ways that males have acted towards them and adversely affected the course of their lives."

I51. Mayer, David R. "Porter's 'The Jilting of Granny Weatherall.'" *Explicator*, 38 (Summer 1980), 33–34.

By blowing out the lamp (in an ironic allusion to the Biblical parable of the wise and foolish virgins), Granny herself becomes the jilter; she chooses not to "wait" for God.

I52. Meyers, Robert. "Porter's 'The Jilting of Granny Weatherall.'" *Explicator*, 44 (Winter 1986), 37.

The unidentified male who kept Ellen Weatherall from collapsing after George jilted her was probably her father.

I53. Timson, Stephen. "Katherine Anne Porter and the Essential Spirit: The Pursuit and Discovery of Truth in 'The Jilting of Granny Weatherall.'" *Kyushu American Literature*, no. 27 (Sept. 1986), 71–80.

"The Jilting of Granny Weatherall" shows the human need to gain insight into one's own nature. The story "is about the discovery of a truth, however insignificant, about ourselves." By the end of the story, "Granny has at last come to the realization that she has not overcome her resentment against George; a resentment so strong that it threatens her with eternal damnation."

I54. Wiesenfarth, Joseph. "Internal Opposition in Porter's 'Granny Weatherall.'" *Critique*, 11 (no. 2, 1969), 47–55.

Granny reacted to George's jilting by creating a new life of order—founded in work, family, and religion. But, at her death, this order is shown to have been insufficient. She remembers George and feels again the fear and humiliation caused by the jilting.

I55. Wolfe, Peter. "The Problem of Granny Weatherall." *College Language Association Journal*, 11 (Dec. 1967), 142–48.

"The key to the story's teleological implications lies in the ironic relation between Granny's mental events and her diminishing volition." At the center of her dying thoughts is the illegitimate baby (fathered by George and delivered by the black servant Hapsy) whom she gave up for adoption.

"The Leaning Tower"

I56. Givner, Joan. "'Her Great Art, Her Sober Craft': Katherine Anne Porter's Creative Process." *Southwest Review*, 62 (Summer 1977), 217–30.

An examination of the people and events from Porter's life that served as sources for "The Leaning Tower" yields insight into her creative process. Letters to Josephine Herbst from Berlin describe Porter's fellow boarding house residents who were obvious inspirations for the residents of Charles's boarding house. Porter's meeting Hermann Goering influenced her creation of the character Hans von Gehring. Porter's memories of her childhood friend Erna Schlemmer were transformed into Charles's friend Kuno Hillentafel. The symbolism of the Leaning

Tower of Pisa reflects the tenuousness of German society; its association with Canto 33 of *The Inferno* adds "sinister overtones." The tower is "the center around which all the themes, moral implications, and images converge, harmonize, and arrange themselves into a coherent whole."

157. ———. "Two Leaning Towers: Viewpoints of Katherine Anne Porter and Virginia Woolf in 1940." *Virginia Woolf Quarterly*, 3 (1977, 1–2), 85–90.

Porter and Virginia Woolf had similar ideas about the writer's responsibility, as can be seen in two works composed at about the same time, near the beginning of World War II: Woolf's essay "The Leaning Tower" and Porter's story of the same title. Both writers were appalled by the horrors of their time, and both believed that the writer had a significant social responsibility.

"Magic"

158. Leath, Helen. "Washing the Dirty Linen in Private: An Analysis of Katherine Anne Porter's 'Magic.'" *Proceeding of Conference of College Teachers of English of Texas*, 50 (Sept. 1985), 51–58.

Although several critics have labeled "Magic" a "dramatic dialogue," they have failed to see the complete implication of this. We should look for the story's central significance in the relationship between the maid narrating the story-within-a-story and her audience, Madame Blanchard. Viewed thus, "Magic" can be seen as focusing on a conflict between these two women—as the maid, with threats of magic, seeks to gain dominance over her mistress.

"The Martyr"

159. Unrue, Darlene Harbour. "Diego Rivera and Katherine
    Anne Porter's 'The Martyr.'" *American Literature*, 56
    (Oct. 1984), 411–16.

    "The Martyr" sheds light on Porter's "artistic method."
    A study of the real-life models for its central characters
    and of the social context of its composition reveals that it
    depicts "the dangers the artist faces when his art is tied
    to a hollow ideal," "the Mexican revolution and one of its
    weakest links," "the cultural renaissance led by Diego,"
    his "fall from the pedestal where he was placed by
    adorers," and "false gods as obstacles in the progress
    toward truth."

"María Concepción"

160. Hafley, James. "'María Concepción': Life Among the
    Ruins." *Four Quarters*, 12 (Nov. 1962), 11–17.

    This story is more a "drama of words" than a "drama of
    events." Pattern and language convey the theme that
    "primitive man's own resinous heart furnishes him with
    modes of conduct essentially like those sanctioned by
    civilized cultures."

"Noon Wine"

161. Beards, Richard D. "Stereotyping in Modern American
    Fiction: Some Solitary Swedish Madmen." *Moderna
    Språk*, 63 (1969, no. 4), 329–37.

    Porter, like Stephen Crane, Ernest Hemingway, and
    Ken Kesey, has failed to overcome the stereotype in
    creating a Swedish character. Helton, in "Noon Wine,"
    fits the image of a solitary, non-communicative,
    physically competent, mad Swede.

162. Groff, Edward. "'Noon Wine': A Texas Tragedy." *Descant*, 22 (Fall 1977), 39–47.

Not examined by compiler.

163. Hoffman, Frederick J. "Katherine Anne Porter's 'Noon Wine.'" *CEA Critic*, 18 (Nov. 1956), 1, 6–7.

From a paper read at a CEA meeting in April 1956. "Noon Wine" is effective classroom material; discussion of it "involves the understanding of narrative pace, the challenge of sudden, violent and uncalculated action, and the agony of slow appraisal of one's acts."

164. Howell, Elmo. "Katherine Anne Porter and the Southern Myth: A Note on 'Noon Wine.'" *Louisiana Studies*, 11 (Fall 1972), 252–59.

Only in "Noon Wine" does Porter portray the plain people of the South. She does so vividly and with sympathy. But the story is not a complete success because she cannot be satisfied with this. "Mr. Thompson must be updated, arbitrarily lifted out of time and place and confronted with a psychological problem that his generation in his part of the world would have had little patience with."

165. Keppler, C.F. *The Literature of the Second Self.* Tucson: Univ. of Arizona Press, 1972, pp. 84–87, 194, 196.

"Noon Wine" is discussed in the chapter "The Second Self as Vision of Horror." Without realizing it consciously, Mr. Thompson sees a grotesque version of himself (jovial, cliché-spouting, nonproductive) in Mr. Hatch and is filled with rage.

166. Leiter, Louis. "The Expense of Spirit in a Waste of Shame: Motif, Montage, and Structure in *Noon Wine*. In *Seven Contemporary Short Novels*, ed. Charles Clerc and Louis Leiter. Glenview, Ill.: Scott, Foresman, 1969, pp. 185–219.

"Noon Wine" is a story of strangers—Helton, Hatch, and Thompson, "who always remains a stranger in the strange land of human wisdom." Its main theme concerns "the daily expense of moral and intellectual stamina, its attrition through the flabbiest kind of action and reaction to existence. Through symbolic and linguistic motifs and through the story's nine-part structure, Porter effectively conveys this theme. The focal point, "like the center of a spider web," is the scene between Hatch and Thompson.

167. Male, Roy R. "The Short Story of the Mysterious Stranger in American Fiction." *Criticism*, 3 (Fall 1961), 281–94.

"Noon Wine" is a good example of an American work dealing with the appearance of a stranger and his effects on others. It can be compared with Robert Penn Warren's "Blackberry Winter" in the authors' showing of "the sensibilities of their characters and the texture of a certain experience."

168. Pierce, Marvin. "Point of View: Katherine Anne Porter's 'Noon Wine.'" *Ohio University Review*, 3 (1961), 95–113.

It is her mastery of point of view that makes Porter's fiction such an achievement. "Noon Wine" is a good example of such mastery. Here "the point of view, beginning and ending with Mr. Thompson but shifting outside of him, is the key to the story."

169. Smith, J. Oates. "Porter's *Noon Wine*: A Stifled Tragedy." *Renascence*, 17 (Spring 1965), 157–62.

Mr. Thompson seeks to define for himself the nature of the killing of Mr. Hatch. "And his quest leads not to an articulation of his act (and therefore his humanity) but rather to a negation of further thought; it is precisely the man's refusal to be irresponsible that leads to his final act, suicide."

170. Stout, Janis P. "Mr. Hatch's Volubility and Miss Porter's Reserve." *Essays in Literature* (Macomb, Ill.), 12 (Fall 1985), 285–93.

Porter's distinctive reserved style and her use of reserve and volubility as keys to character can be seen in "Noon Wine." The reader immediately dislikes Mr. Hatch; "he talks too much." Mr. Helton, a sympathetic character, is taciturn. Mr. Thompson progresses from a volubility almost as great as Mr. Hatch's to the dignity and restraint of his suicide note.

171. Thomas, M. Wynn. "Strangers in a Strange Land: A Reading of 'Noon Wine.'" *American Literature*, 47 (May 1975), 230–46.

A study of the language of "Noon Wine" shows that these seemingly ordinary characters are actually "strangers in a strange land." The story has direction; its "order" is "finally sensed in the fine confusion of people's talk. It cannot be extracted: it must be left where it is. There is a depth of dignity and reticence to the story, and all the garrulity of explanation should finally rest on this."

172. Walsh, Thomas F. "Deep Similarities in 'Noon Wine.'" *Mosaic*, 9 (Fall 1975), 83–91.

In "Noon Wine" Mr. Helton and Mr. Hatch, in addition to being individual characters, serve as doubles to Mr. Thompson. In each case the double's appearance "does not begin a process, but symbolizes a psychic struggle already in process." Mr. Helton is "the secret, alienated, violent self." Mr. Hatch shows "the forced amiability of his public self." In Thompson's encounter with Mr. Hatch the "opposing elements of his character have grown so large that they can no longer be contained within him." The tragedy that ensues shows Mr. Thompson's failure to achieve self-knowledge.

173. ———. "The 'Noon Wine' Devils." *Georgia Review*, 22 (Spring 1968), 90–96.

"Noon Wine" has a "submerged Faustian pattern" that, in several ways, makes it comparable to Stephen Vincent Benet's "The Devil and Daniel Webster." However, Porter's purpose goes beyond that of Benet. She, "like Marlowe and Goethe, is attracted to the Faust myth for its tragic potential."

"Notes on the Texas I Remember"

174. Falcon, Amelia. Letter to the Editor. *Atlantic*, 235 (May 1975), 26.

Points out factual errors.

"Old Mortality"

175. Brooks, Cleanth. "The Southern Temper." In *A Shaping Joy: Studies in the Writer's Craft*. London: Methuen, 1971, pp. 205–08.

First given as a lecture in 1965. Viewing Cousin Eva and Miranda and their different relationships to tradition serves to tell us something about the "Southern temper."

176. Johnson, James William. "The Adolescent Hero: A Trend in Modern Fiction." *Twentieth Century Literature*, 5 (April 1959), 3–11.

Only in modern literature is the adolescent mind thoroughly examined. This mind is "half-child, half-adult; and the novelist is learning to use its emotional and intellectual vantage point as the focus for his own perceptions of life." In "Old Mortality" Porter uses Miranda for such a purpose.

177. Miyata, Toshichika. "On 'Old Mortality.'" *Chu-Shikoku Studies in American Literature*, No. 20 (March 1984), 31–37.

"In 'Old Mortality,' except for the final page, the author's human, passionate, natural side strengthened by the story's seven-year gestation, manages to balance her artistic consciousness. This results in a piece that is both entertaining and literary, and, in consequence, a highly successful work."

I78. Sullivan, Walter. "The Decline of Myth in Southern Fiction." *Southern Review*, 12 (Jan. 1976), 16–31.

Concerning the nature of "the Southern myth," an examination of "Old Mortality" is helpful. The disintegrating family, held together only by the myth of Amy, reflects the disintegrating culture held together (if only temporarily) by the myth of the Old South. Cousin Eva—like Quentin Compson—sees through the myth but cannot fully reject it. Miranda, having been rejected by it, is "a part of the old order and apart from it." She "sees the glory and the doom."

I79. Walsh, Thomas. "Miranda's Ghost in 'Old Mortality.'" *College Literature*, 6 (Winter 1979), 57–63.

In "Old Mortality" Aunt Amy is a ghost haunting Miranda's past and present and affecting her future. The parallels between the two are several: They resemble one another physically; each is high-spirited; each feels weighed down by family expectations; each rebels against her father; each escapes into marriage but regards it as an illness. And in the conversations with Eva, Miranda feels herself compelled to defend Amy. It is as though "Amy's 'restless ghost in a frame' were doomed to live her unhappy life all over again by taking possession of her niece."

"Pale Horse, Pale Rider"

180. Booth, Wayne C. *The Rhetoric of Fiction.* Chicago: Univ. of Chicago Press, 1961, pp. 274–77.

    Porter uses point of view very well in "Pale Horse, Pale Rider." By our being placed directly in Miranda's mind, we can feel her overwhelming isolation.

181. Cheatham, George. "Fall and Redemption in 'Pale Horse, Pale Rider.' *Renascence*, 39 (Spring 1987), 396–405.

    An "undertone" of imagery beneath the surface of "Pale Horse, Pale Rider" shows the story to be one of Christian fall and redemption. Adam is both the pre-lapsarian innocent Adam and also the sacrificial lamb, a Christ figure who dies from saving Miranda. The world of the war is, of course, a fallen one. At first, Miranda despairs over Adam's death, but after receiving his final letter, she begins "careful preparations to live." "She is a feeble Lazarus, yes, but a Lazarus who nevertheless now chooses to live."

182. Flanders, Jane. "The Other Side of Self-Reliance: The Dream Visions of 'Pale Horse, Pale Rider.'" *Regionalism and the Female Imagination*, 4 (Fall 1978), 8–13.

    Not examined by compiler.

183. Gernes, Sonia. "Life after Life: Katherine Anne Porter's Version." *Journal of Popular Culture*, 14 (Spring 1981), 669–75.

    The scene of Miranda's apparent (or near) death in "Pale Horse, Pale Rider" has been given validity "by research done in the past five years on persons who have been clinically 'dead' and have been resuscitated." The account, if based on Porter's actual experience, is, perhaps, "less of an allegory than a rare subjective experience, recorded long before current research on the subject of what it is like to 'die.'"

184. Krishnamurthi, M.G. "Katherine Anne Porter's 'Pale Horse, Pale Rider': A Minority View." In *Indian Response to American Literature*, ed. C.D. Narasimhaiah. New Delhi: The United States Educational Foundation in India, 1967, pp. 215–36.

Reprinted in *Katherine Anne Porter: A Study* (H67) and Harold Bloom (ed.), *Katherine Anne Porter* (H11).

185. Loe, Thomas. "Plot and Anti-Plot in Katherine Anne Porter's *Pale Horse, Pale Rider*." *Mid-Hudson Language Studies*, 9 (1986), 85–93.

Concerning "Pale Horse, Pale Rider," "three major sources of evidence in terms of structure appear to argue for the reappearance of Miranda at the end of the story as a rugged individualist who has learned from her experience about the fallacies of plotting. First is the series of allusions which link Miranda's psychological discoveries to the motif of the journey; second, and most important, is the layering of the love story or romance against a story whose implications are not only realistic, but specifically anti-romantic; third is the final rejection of possibilities, the freedom from plot that leads to negation, the death-in-life that Miranda ultimately retains."

186. Matthiessen, F.O. "The Pattern of Literature." In *Changing Patterns in American Civilization*, ed. Dixon Wechter, *et al.* Philadelphia: Univ. of Pennsylvania Press, 1949, pp. 52–53.

When compared with *The Grapes of Wrath* (published the same year), *Pale Horse, Pale Rider* gives evidence of "a more exacting skill."

187. Walsh, Thomas F. "The Dream Self in 'Pale Horse, Pale Rider.'" *Wascana Review*, 14 (Fall 1979), 61–79.

The five dream sequences of "Pale Horse, Pale Rider" enable the reader to understand [Miranda] in a way that she never understands herself." These dreams show that war and illness are only the forces that bring her despair to the surface; they are not the causes of it. "The opening dream is a paradigm of Miranda's unbearable dilemma throughout the story; fearing life and death, she reluctantly chooses life which she likens to death. Her condition is similar to that of Laing's ontologically insecure person." In the second dream, "a mixture of memory and delirium," we see her fears concerning war, sex, and life itself. The third dream "expresses Miranda's guilt in exposing Adam to contagion, but it also confirms the ambivalence of her love for him." The fourth dream not only "reveals Miranda's unconscious surrender to the war hysteria"; it also reveals fears that she had felt before the war. The fifth dream is of two parts: "In the first part she attempts to blot out experience by becoming insensate, while in the second part she attempts to purify experience to make it conform to the dictates of her feelings." The dreams show that at the story's end we need not accept Miranda's view of herself. They allow us "to know more about her than she knows about herself, but that does not diminish the force of our sympathy for her as unwitting victim of overwhelming circumstances and of her ontological insecure personality."

Reprinted in Harold Bloom (ed.), *Katherine Anne Porter* (H11).

I88. Yanella, Philip R. "The Problems of Dislocation in 'Pale Horse, Pale Rider.'" *Studies in Short Fiction*, 6 (Fall 1969), 637–42.

Porter's world is one of bleak modernity and dislocation, a world that can be seen quite easily in "Pale Horse, Pale Rider." Although the story's "ending is faintly optimistic," it is "a dismal assessment of modern selfhood. Its gloom is pervasive."

189. Youngblood, Sarah. "Structure and Imagery in Katherine Anne Porter's 'Pale Horse, Pale Rider.'" *Modern Fiction Studies*, 5 (Winter 1959–60), 344–52.

   The structure and imagery of this story successfully present Miranda's progress from a dream to reality to delirium and illness and, finally, to her preparations for rejoining the world.
   Reprinted in Lodwick Hartley and George Core (eds.), *Katherine Anne Porter: A Critical Symposium* (H51).

Ship of Fools

190. Abrahams, William. "Progression Through Repetition." *Massachusetts Review*, 4 (Spring 1963), 805–09.

   Although it is wrong to emphasize the allegorical in *Ship of Fools*, Porter does present characters in terms of their basic qualities. Characterization is achieved not through development and change, but through repetition, in which the salient traits of each figure are shown at various points throughout the novel. "Repetition here is a way of getting at the truth."

191. Alexander, Jean. "Katherine Anne Porter's Ship in the Jungle." *Twentieth Century Literature*, 11 (Jan. 1966), 179–88.

   Porter's shorter fiction is "bound to the affective world and to heart-mysteries, for it gives us poetic nuances of promise." On the other hand, *Ship of Fools* "brilliantly question[s] the motions of personality and society, gives us no promise, but only the mind's pleasure in seeing the worst."

192. Daniels, Sally. "The Foundering of *Ship of Fools*, I." *Minnesota Review*, 3 (Fall 1962), 124–27.

   The novel's morally deficient characters undergo no change or awakening of the sort we expect from characters in a novel, even though Porter surpasses other living writers in "her harsh, wise, wonderfully humorous, painfully compelling knowledge of the human condition."

193. DeVries, Peter. "Nobody's Fool." *New Yorker*, 38 (16 June 1962), 28–29.

A parody of *Ship of Fools*. A procrastinating woman writer travelling by ship taunts a fellow passenger, who is her publisher.

194. Fox, Renée C. "The Ship of This World." *Columbia University Forum*, 5 (Summer 1962), 50–51.

One overlooked theme of *Ship of Fools* is "a testament of faith in art." Art, to Porter, is something that allows human beings to deal with the tragedies of existence.

195. "The Ghost of Promise Past." *Saturday Review*, 45 (29 Dec. 1962), 32.

"This has been a year of disappointments, of which the greatest was Katherine Anne Porter's 'Ship of Fools.'"

196. Givner, Joan. "The Genesis of *Ship of Fools*." *Southern Literary Journal*, 10 (Fall 1977), 14–30.

A Porter letter to Caroline Gordon—long thought lost but recently found among the Gordon papers at Princeton—sheds remarkable light upon the creation of *Ship of Fools*. The twenty-page, single-spaced typescript details Porter's experiences and fellow passengers on her 1931 sea journey to Europe. Many of these passengers and experiences have their counterparts in the novel. Some characters (e.g., Herr Glocken) have been changed only slightly from the original. With others, one real passenger served to inspire two fictitious ones; at other times two real-life passengers merged to inspire one fictitious one. Interestingly, the characters who seem to have no basis in the letter are three who closely resemble Porter herself—Jenny Brown, Mrs. Treadwell, and Frau

Rittersdorf. Many of the journey experiences of Porter and
Eugene Pressly have been transformed into those of Jenny
Brown and David Scott.

197. Glicksberg, Charles. *The Sexual Revolution in Modern
    American Literature.* The Hague: Martinus Nijhoff,
    1971 (New York: Humanities Press), 148, 150–54.

    In *Ship of Fools* "love is . . . instinct with cruelty and
    conflict." Porter portrays the human animal as
    oscillating between the two poles of affection and
    antagonism, sensual union and fractious separateness. The
    male is governed by the desire to dominate; he wishes to
    lord it over the female. The conflict of wills goes on all
    the time, each partner struggling hard against the fate of
    being absorbed by the other. Each seeks a way out of his
    subjective prison of loneliness, each craves the beatitude
    of love, but few in this novel are capable of the loyalty,
    the devotion and the sacrifice of self that love demands."

198. Hartley, Lodwick. "Dark Voyagers: A Study of Katherine
    Anne Porter's *Ship of Fools.*" *University Review,* 30
    (Winter 1963), 83–94.

    Ship of Fools is a grim, horror-evoking book. The
    characters are miserable and detestable, "recorded quite
    often in loathing and indignation rather than in pity."
    Although Porter's stated theme concerned the "collusion"
    of "good and virtuous people" with evil, the book doesn't
    have enough good and virtuous people to bear this out.
    The series of violent and cruel acts do not structurally
    lead to a climax. The main reason for reading the novel
    lies not in its theme, characterization, or structure; it lies
    in Porter's successful portrayal of "the dark chaos of life
    itself."

    Reprinted in Lodwick Hartley and George Core (eds.),
    Katherine Anne Porter: A Critical Symposium (H51).

199. Heilman, Robert B. *"Ship of Fools*: Notes on Style." *Four
    Quarters,* 12 (Nov. 1962), 46–55.

Porter's "style has strong affiliations with the Austen and [George] Eliot styles," and "its main lines are traditional rather than innovative." Also, "it is markedly devoid of singularities, mannerisms, private idioms, self-indulgent or striven-for uniquenesses that give a special coloration."

Reprinted in Lodwick Hartley and George Core (eds.), *Katherine Anne Porter: A Critical Symposium* (H51) and Harold Bloom (ed.) *Katherine Anne Porter* (H11).

I100. Hendrick, George. "Hart Crane Aboard the *Ship of Fools*: Some Speculations." *Twentieth Century Literature*, 9 (April 1963), 3–9.

In *Ship of Fools* certain qualities and experiences of Hart Crane are present in the characters of Denny, Echegaray, and Baumgartner.

I101. Hertz, Robert N. "Sebastian Brant and Porter's *Ship of Fools*." *Midwest Quarterly*, 6 (Summer 1965), 389–401.

It is wrong to see *Ship of Fools* as merely a modern adaptation of Sebastian Brant. Porter borrows Brant's symbol but uses it for more complex purposes. Also, her purpose is too ambitious for the book to be seen as a kind of "floating *Grand Hotel*." She has dramatically arranged characters and events to present "the fundamental issue of common human motives and impulses." One of the most common of these is man's selfishness, which leads to "the failure of love . . . the greatest universal failure."

I102. Joselyn, Sister M., O.S.B. "On the Making of *Ship of Fools*." *South Dakota Review*, 1 (May 1964), 46–52.

With additions and "bridges" of varying lengths, Porter carefully transformed eleven separately published pieces into *Ship of Fools*.

I103. Karl, Frederick R. "Pursuit of the Real." *Nation*, 194 (21 April 1962), p. 348.

In this essay on the American writer's attempts to present the disorder of reality, *Ship of Fools* is referred to as a novel in which "everyone is on the run."

I104. Kazin, Alfred. *Bright Book of Life: American Novelists and Storytellers from Hemingway to Mailer*. Boston: Little, Brown, 1973, pp. 38, 49, 165–73. (Reprinted in paperback—Notre Dame, Ind.: Univ. of Notre Dame, 1980.)

"*Ship of Fools* was designed as an epic, but is really a harsh personal statement." It suffered from being so many years in the writing: "The older Miss Porter got in the writing of it, the more she fell into the thought that life is a voyage to nowhere, and time makes monkeys, dwarfs, dupes of us all."

I105. Kirkpatrick, Smith. "*Ship of Fools*." *Sewanee Review*, 71 (Winter 1963), 94–98.

The characters in the novel are, to be sure, fools, and in the time-honored manner of fools, they wear masks. Some of the characters wear the same mask throughout, but the masks of most characters "shift and change like the postures of a dance." The novel thus reflects the journey of each of us—as we "cover our naked selves for the swift passage . . . into eternity."

Reprinted in Robert Penn Warren (ed.), *Katherine Anne Porter: A Collection of Critical Essays* (H113).

I106. Liberman, M.M. "Responsibility of the Novelist: The Critical Reception of *Ship of Fools*." *Criticism*, 8 (Fall 1966), 377–88.

Critics who have reacted with either "bitter resentment or acute disappointment" to *Ship of Fools* have failed to recognize it for what it is—an "apologue," as its relationship to Sebastian Brant would suggest. "*Ship of Fools* argues that romantic literary conventions do not work in the modern world, and emerges as even more remote from the idea of the novel than a study of its

formal properties alone would suggest. One can see it finally as anti-novel."
Reprinted in *Katherine Anne Porter's Fiction* (H68) and in Lodwick Hartley and George Core (eds.), *Katherine Anne Porter: A Critical Symposium* (H51).

I107. ———. "The Short Story as Chapter in *Ship of Fools.*" *Criticism*, 10 (Winter 1968), 65–71.

Ship of Fools can be seen as a series of short stories in which each returning character repeatedly personifies the same character traits. But it is more than this; the stories are not only interlocked but give forth implications beyond the events of *Ship of Fools* itself (as shown clearly by the episode in which Jenny and David quarrel over inviting Freytag to their table). The cumulative effect conveys the theme that "avoidance of collective responsibility invites collective disaster."
Reprinted in *Katherine Anne Porter's Fiction* (H68).

I108. ———. "Some Observations on the Genesis of *Ship of Fools*: A Letter from Katherine Anne Porter." *PMLA*, 84 (Jan. 1969), 136–37.

A previously inaccessible letter from Porter to Malcolm Cowley leads to our viewing *Ship of Fools* "as an apologue by felicitous predisposition, rather than as a novel by misguided intention."

I109. McIntyre, John P. "*Ship of Fools* and Its Publicity." *Thought*, 38 (Summer 1963), 211–20.

The negative reviewers of *Ship of Fools* "fail to see that Miss Porter's theme has precedents in American fiction and that the chief structural principle she uses is parody." Porter's portrayal of a dehumanizing rationalism might remind us of Hawthorne; her portrayal of isolation and of moral emptiness might remind us of Melville's *Confidence Man*. However, with the two earlier writers evil was an individual calamity. "Miss Porter's novel derives much of its moral strength not from any private encounter with evil but from its distressing social picture." But the evil inherent in society can be explained—ultimately—by the characters' inability to love.

I110. Miller, Paul W. "Katherine Anne Porter's *Ship of Fools: A Masterpiece Manqué." University Review*, 32 (Winter 1965), 151–57.

A flaw of *Ship of Fools* is that some of the characters can easily be confused with one another. Other flaws of characterization are that Captain Thiele is inconsistently developed and that some of the characters are developed further than their role in the book warrants.

I111. Murphy, Edward F. Letter to the Editor. *America*, 107 (26 May 1962), 309–11.

A defense of *Ship of Fools* against Harold C. Gardiner's review (J182). Porter's view is much more positive than Gardiner has realized. With such saintly characters as the woodcarver and Dr. Schumann, she provides a balance to human evil.

I112. Plante, Patricia R. "Katherine Anne Porter: Misanthrope Acquitted." *Xavier University Studies*, 2 (Dec. 1963), 87–91.

Ship of Fools does not show Porter to be misanthropic and cynical about human nature. Instead, her "near-despair" is the result of "an intellectual vision of divine possibility and promise." She is calling for a "re-beginning."

I113. Rubin, Louis D., Jr. "We Get Along Together Just Fine. . . ." *Four Quarters*, 12 (March 1963), 30–31.

"The point about *Ship of Fools* is that only a writer of great compassion for her fellow humans, and equally great revulsion at cruelty to humans, could have written it."

I114. Ruoff, James, and Del Smith. "Katherine Anne Porter on *Ship of Fools*." *College English*, 24 (Feb. 1963), 396–97.

Porter discusses the genesis of *Ship of Fools* and makes comments on its theme.

I115. Solotaroff, Theodore. "'Ship of Fools' and the Critics." *Commentary*, 34 (Oct. 1962), 277–86.

Ship of Fools in no way deserves the wildly laudatory reviews it has received. "Its claim to allegory is a sham; its concerns are not as serious as Porter would have us think. Also, the characters are merely caricatures of moral infirmity." Politically, it is "a matter of implying that the fate of Germany and its Jews reduces to the encounter of two particularly obnoxious breeds of inhumanity." The novel gives "little more than misanthropy and technique."
Reprinted in Robert Penn Warren (ed.), *Katherine Anne Porter: A Collection of Critical Essays* (H113) and as "*Ship of Fools*: Anatomy of a Best Seller" in *The Red Hot Vacuum* (1970).

I116. Spence, Jon. "Looking-Glass Reflections: Satirical Elements in *Ship of Fools*." *Sewanee Review*, 82 (Spring 1974), 316–30.

Perhaps those who criticize *Shop of Fools* negatively would be more approving were they to recognize it as satire, "a criticism of mankind by a woman who cares deeply about humanity." Among the lost, self-deceived characters, only Dr. Schumann "moves from foggy self-delusion to an acceptance of truth." The others are trapped in their bigotry, their lack of emotional capacity, their selfishness, or their grandiose self-conceptions. They are unable to love on either a personal or an impersonal level. Every attempt at a love relationship is either thwarted or turned into a parody of what it should be. But Porter's hope is that the reader will see himself in "her mirror of satire" and "strive to correct those failures which deprive him of his own humanity."

I116a. Sullivan, Walter. "Katherine Anne Porter: The Glories and Errors of Her Ways." *Southern Literary Journal*, 3 (Fall 1970), 117–21.

Ostensibly a review of Porter's *Collected Essays* and of H51, but discusses *Ship of Fools* at some length.
Reprinted in *Death by Melancholy: Essays in Modern Southern Fiction* (1972).

I117. Walcutt, Charles C. *Man's Changing Mask*. Minneapolis: Univ. of Minnesota Press, 1966, pp. 92, 145–55.

Porter's novel suffers from the characters' being "a collection of grotesques whom she impales on the point of her pen and holds up to ridicule. She does not grant them any free life, any power to make a vital decision and so affect their destinies."

I118. Walton, Gerald. "Katherine Anne Porter's Use of Quakerism in *Ship of Fools*." *University of Mississippi Studies in English*, 7 (1966), 15–23.

Not examined by compiler.

I119. Weber, Brom. "The Foundering of *Ship of Fools*, II." *Minnesota Review*, 3 (Fall 1962), 127–30.

From her stories Porter has deserved her reputation as a superb writer. But *Ship of Fools* is so bad that it should not have been published.

"Theft"

I120. Givner, Joan. "Katherine Anne Porter, Eudora Welty and *Ethan Brand*. *International Fiction Review*, 1 (Jan. 1974), 32–37.

A comparison of Hawthorne's "Ethan Brand," Eudora Welty's "The Petrified Man," and Porter's "Theft" "provides an effective illustration of the nature and use of the grotesque in contemporary literature." All three concern "characters who are so spiritually maimed that have lost the basic human qualities."

I121. ———. "A Re-Reading of Katherine Anne Porter's 'Theft.'" *Studies in Short Fiction*, 6 (Summer 1969), 463–65.

The theme of "Theft" is one that runs throughout Porter's fiction and is most fully developed in *Ship of Fools*. This theme is "self-delusion in the face of evil." By allowing herself to be victimized, the protagonist encourages the "evil-doers" to hurt others.

I122. Prager, Leonard. "Getting and Spending: Porter's 'Theft.'" *Perspective*, 11 (Winter 1960), 230–34.

The protagonist of "Theft" is "a woman and the purse which she has lost can readily be seen as a sexual symbol; her problem of self-identity is concretely presented as the problem of an 'emancipated' career woman who is starving emotionally in the Wasteland of urban anonymity and alienation." But on a more significant level, "*purse* means value, the lost purse uncertainty of values, the stolen purse betrayal of self. In the act of recalling the past, the protagonist takes an initial step in self-explanation."

I123. Smith, Charles W. "A Flaw in Katherine Anne Porter's 'Theft': The Teacher Taught." *CEA Critic*, 38 (Jan. 1976), 19–21.

"Theft" "allows the teacher to demonstrate that even very talented writers occasionally make mistakes." Porter uses the past tense in the story's first sentence, whereas past perfect would have been correct. (See I124 and I126).

I124. ———. "Rebuttal." *CEA Critic*, 39 (May 1977), 9–11.

Professor Stern's justification (I126) of Porter's use of the simple past in the first sentence of "Theft" is based on faulty reasoning. She seems to irrationally believe that Porter could not make mistakes. Also, she sees the point of view in the story as more complex than it is. She is also wrong to believe that the unorthodox use of tense in the first paragraph is "necessary to the story's complexity."

I125. Stein, William Bysshe. "'Theft': Porter's Politics of Modern Love." *Perspective*, 11 (Winter 1960), 223–28.

"Theft" reflects Porter's "view on the decline of traditional religious authority." The protagonist "suffers from a dissociation of sensibility. Unable to inact the natural roles of woman in society, she substitutes passion for love, bohemian careerism for marriage and motherhood."

I126. Stern, Carol Simpson. "'A Flaw in Katherine Anne Porter's "Theft": The Teacher Taught': A Reply." *CEA Critic*, 39 (May 1977), 4–8.

Porter has not made a grammatical mistake in the first sentence of "Theft." "The choice of the simple past tense in the first sentence followed by the switch to the past perfect in the third is quite deliberate." The use of the simple past emphasizes the protagonist's initial emotional confusion about having had her purse when she entered the room; the past perfect then shows that she is distancing herself from the situation. (See I123 and I124).

I127. Wiesenfarth, Joseph. "The Structure of Katherine Anne Porter's 'Theft.'" *Cithara*, 10 (May 1971), 65–71.

"Theft" concerns the realization of both loss and guilt. The details of each incident in the story lead to this realization by the protagonist and the ensuing loss of innocence. "Theft," like other stories by Porter, "dramatizes the disorder which lurks below an order that does not develop from a personal commitment to love."

"A Wreath for the Gamekeeper"

I128. Aldington, Ricard. "A Wreath for Lawrence?" *Encounter*, 14 (April 1960), 51–54.

Porter is one of those critics who see D.H. Lawrence from a mechanical, lifeless viewpoint. She is, evidently, incapable of understanding Lawrence's "unique life-giving quality which no other person of his epoch possessed."

"Xochimilco"

I129. Walsh, Thomas F. "Identifying a Sketch by Katherine Anne Porter." *Journal of Modern Literature*, 7 (Sept. 1979), 555–61.

"Xochimilco" (C6) is the published version of "The Children of Xochitl"—a manuscript among the Porter papers. It has an affinity with contemporary Mexican art and records Porter's personal response to an attractive aspect of Mexican life.

SECTION J
BOOK REVIEWS

In this section, entries are listed according to the book reviewed (in chronological order) and alphabetically within the listings for each title. Reprints are listed with the original entry.

Flowering Judas

J1. Bogan, Louise. *New Republic*, 64 (22 Oct. 1930), 277–78.

Although these stories deal with unusual subject material, Porter "rejects the exclamatory tricks" and depends upon "straightforward writing," "patience in detail," and "a thorough imaginative grasp in cause and character." No other writer has a talent quite like hers. Reprinted in *Selected Criticism* (1955).

J2. *Boston Evening Transcript*, 28 Jan. 1931, p. III-2.

A brief, vaguely unfavorable review.

J3. Dawson, Margaret Cheney. "A Perfect Flowering." *New York Herald Tribune, Books*, 14 Sept. 1930), pp. 3–4.

"It is a dramatic moment in the life of a patient reader when, after all efforts to be judicial, all carefully balanced yeas and nays, a book presents itself that compels a loud, hearty, unqualified *yes.*" *Flowering Judas* is such a book.

Reprinted in *Mexican Life*, 6 (Nov. 1930), 35–36.

J4. McDonald, John. "Chamber Music." *The Boulevardier*, 6 (Dec. 1930), 22.

The stories "are chamber music in the sense that all the experience that has come into the writer's mind, has been reborn, not loudly enough for an auditorium, but genuinely, slickly, with a touch that belongs to a chamber."

J5. *New York Times, Book Review*, 28 Sept. 1930, p. 6.

Porter is "of that youngest generation of American artists from which one dares to hope much." This group is known for careful, disciplined craftsmanship.

J6. Richardson, Eudora Ramsay. *Bookman*, 72 (Oct. 1930), 172–73.

These six stories "indicate that the career of Katherine Anne Porter is worth watching."

J7. Salpeter, Harry. *New York World*, 13 Sept. 1930, p. 9.

"The stories are delicate and sure, complete and true."

J8. Tate, Allen. "A New Star." *Nation*, 131 (1 Oct. 1930), 352–53.

Porter has a brilliant style, feels comfortable with her material, shows versatility and maintains objectivity. Hers "is a fully matured art."

J9. Weeks, Edward. "The Atlantic Bookshelf." *Atlantic Monthly*, 147 (May 1931), front section, p. 32.

The stories are superb in "their range of subject and their strength of treatment."

J10. Winters, Yvor. "Major Fiction." *Hound & Horn*, 4 (Jan.–
      March 1931), 303–05.

Although "Magic," "Rope," and "He" deal with
themes that are sharply limited and "María Concepción"
is "marred a little by over-decoration," "The Jilting of
Granny Weatherall" and "Flowering Judas" (along with
"Theft") are "major fiction. I can think of no living
American who has written short stories at once so fine in
detail, so powerful as units, and so mature and intelligent
in outlook, except W.C. Williams."

Katherine Anne Porter's French Song-Book

J11. "French Song-Book." *New York Herald Tribune* (Paris), 25
      Dec. 1933, p. 5.

"Miss Porter has accomplished a difficult task in a way
that may be described, without exaggeration, as both
remarkable and admirable."

J12. *New York Herald Tribune, Books*, 28 Jan. 1934, p. 18.

Porter "has managed to convey more of the original
spirit than is usually conveyed in song translations."

J13. *Poetry*, 43 (Feb. 1934), 290.

"Miss Porter's felicity is as apparent here as in her
exquisite fiction. ... Although the book is too expensive
for popular circulation, we can imagine no more
delightful edition of such classics."

J14. Root, Waverly Lewis. "Poet and Printer Vie in Adoring
      Old French Airs." *Chicago Daily Tribune* (Paris), 27
      Nov. 1933, p. 2.

"We can only admire the delicacy of taste and the skill
in translation which have gone into the making of this
book."

Hacienda

J15. Baker, Howard. "Some Notes on New Fiction." *Southern Review*, 1 (July 1935), 188–89.

Likes the work for Porter's ability to capture "the elusive properties of people and things," but laments the lack of "a bold theme."

J16. Chamberlain, John. "Books of the Times." *New York Times*, 10 Dec. 1934, p. 19.

Cites the work as an example of the thesis that life in Mexico changes slowly.

J17. Cowley, Malcolm. "Conscience Fund." *New Republic*, 83 (29 May 1935), 79.

Only one paragraph. Refers to the hostilities involved in the making of Eisenstein's film. "Miss Porter is the only writer who has dealt with the quarrel impartially; she treats all sides and parties with even-handed malice."

J18. Hart, Elizabeth. "Slight and Short Stories." *New York Herald Tribune, Books*, 16 Dec. 1934, p. 15.

The story is disappointing; perhaps it is "the polished-up notes for a future novel."

J19. *Nation*, 140 (27 March 1935), 369.

One long paragraph. "'Hacienda' ought to be the first, or the last, chapter of a memorable novel. But it is worth reading as it stands."

J20. Poore, Charles G. "A New Story by Katherine Anne Porter." *New York Times, Book Review*, 23 Dec. 1934, p. 4.

"A quiet, diabolic work," but not as fine as her earlier stories.

J21. Wolfe, Bertram D. "Books of the Age." *Workers' Age,* 4 (19 Jan. 1935), 2.

Praises the story for showing the deficiencies of the Mexican upper and middle classes, but points out that Porter did not include "the new Mexican, the worker."

Flowering Judas and Other Stories

J22. Angoff, Charles. "An Honest Story Teller." *American Spectator,* 3 (Nov. 1935), 11.

Porter writes with "obvious maturity and unimpeachable honesty" that raises her fiction above the "plausible fraud" found in the stories of O'Hara, Hemingway, and the "later Faulkner." "The immemorial bewilderments of the heart are her chief topic, as they should be those of every genuine writer of fiction."

J23. *Booklist,* 32 (Dec. 1935), 110.

Very brief. Praises Porter's style.

J24. *Christian Century,* 52 (Nov. 1935), 1426–27.

Admires the "economy and distinction" of Porter's style; the stories are "remarkably good stuff."

J25. Chamberlain, John. "Books of the Times. *New York Times,* 11 Oct. 1935, p. L-23.

The stories are examples of Porter's superb prose style.

J26. Clark, Eleanor. "Cameos." *New Republic,* 85 (25 Dec. 1935), 207.

Dislikes "Hacienda" and two of the other stories, but "these few failures can be forgiven in a book that is primarily one of small patterns written with subdued and exceptional brilliance."

J27. "Complexity and Depth." *Saturday Review of Literature*, 13 (14 Dec. 1935), 16.

    Likes the book, admires Porter's style and her "considerable range." The four added stories are "rather more experimental" than the earlier ones.

J28. Connolly, Cyril. "New Novels." *New Statesman and Nation*, 11 (25 April 1936), 634–35.

    The stories are "about as good as any short stories that have been written lately." The stories set in Mexico "do much to rid it of the Bogeyman quality with which it was invested by Lawrence."

J29. Dickson, Thomas. "Absorbing Characters." *New York Daily News*, 13 Oct. 1935, p. 84.

    The stories are successful.

J30. "Greene, Graham. "Legend." *Spectator*, 156 (24 April 1936), 766.

    "These seem to me the best short stories that have come out of America since the early Hemingways, and there is more promise of future life in them, the sense of a consciousness open to any wind, a style adaptable to any subject."

J31. Herbst, Josephine. "More than Style." *New Masses*, 18 (21 Jan. 1936), 24–25.

    Porter deserves to be known as something more than just a superb stylist. Her better stories have a vitality, a powerful feeling that mere style could not have evoked.

J32. Higgins, Cecile. "Short Stories." *New York Sun*, 26 Oct. 1935, p. 10.

    "Despite the rigid discipline to which the narratives have been subject they abound in depth and naturalness."

J33. La Rocquetinker, Edward. "New Editions, Fine and Otherwise." *New York Times, Book Review*, 29 Sept. 1940, p. 25.

These stories "have charm and honesty sufficient to serve as an anodyne in these times." (A review of the 1940 Modern Library edition.)

J34. "Mexican Contrasts." *Times Literary Supplement*, 18 April 1936, p. 333.

Porter's stories depend too much on the workings of the characters' minds and suffer from lack of pattern.

J35. Nash, Anne. "A Vivid Awareness." *Pacific Weekly*, 11 Nov. 1935), 228.

"Atmosphere Miss Porter can create as a painter can, and it is atmosphere that makes these stories rare and valuable."

J36. Nicholas, Esther K. "Katherine Anne Porter Collects." *Brooklyn Daily Eagle*, 3 Nov. 1935, Section C, last page.

Praises Porter's style and the "wide variety of subject and mood.

J37. O., C.D. "Etches with Clarity." *Los Angeles Times*, 27 Oct. 1935, p. II-6.

All of the stories "are superbly and exquisitely done."

J38. Troy, William. "A Matter of Quality." *Nation*, 141 (30 Oct. 1935), 517–18.

Although some of the stories do not have adequately focused themes, Porter is still "among the most distinguished masters of her craft in this country."

J39. Walton, Eda Lou. "An Exquisite Story-Teller." *New York Herald Tribune, Books*, 3 Nov. 1935, p. 7.

Rather than use "the sociological approach," Porter "holds to the true artist's position: that the character must, in words, in thought, in action, explain himself or herself."

J40. Walton, Edith H. *Forum and Century*, 94 (Dec. 1935), ix.

Porter is "clearly one of the best ... of modern short story writers."

J41. ———. "Katherine Anne Porter's Stories and Other Recent Works of Fiction." *New York Times, Book Review*, 20 Oct. 1935, p. 6.

Porter's stories show humor and vitality, and her style is distinguished.

Noon Wine

J42. Belitt, Ben. "South Texas Primitive." *Nation*, 144 (15 May 1937), 571.

The story shows a technical skill, that is somewhat concealed by "an effort of gangling artlessness."

J43. Brewster, Dorothy. "Worth Waiting For." *New Masses*, 23 (25 May 1937), 25–26.

"A beautifully wrought story" but Porter's "insistence on a blind and pointless will to evil" is not credibly presented.

J44. Morse, Samuel French. "Style—Plus." *Reading and Collecting*, 1 (April 1937), 14.

The story successfully conveys a sense of innocence overtaken by irrational doom.

J45. Walton, Edith H. "An Ironic Tragedy." *New York Times, Book Review*, 11 April 1937, p. 7.

The work is "simple and clear-edged, full of a dry, colloquial humor." But the theme is not clear; the story is "too ironic for ordinary mortals."

Pale Horse, Pale Rider: Three Short Novels

J46. "Away from Near-War Consciousness." *Times Literary Supplement*, 27 May 1939, p. 311.

The book is recommended as "first choice" of the "novels of the week." Porter's work is distinguished by a "strain of poetry," but this strain too often "appears more bravely than to discreet advantage."

J47. *Booklist*, 35 (15 April 1939), 271.

Only one paragraph. "Beautiful writing, of special interest for its technical skill."

J48. Collins, Margaret. "Of New Books and Authors." *Correct English*, 39 (April 1939), 80.

"A collection of three distinctive short novels."

J49. Crume, Paul. *Southwest Review*, 25 (Jan. 1940), 213–18.

Porter's newspaper background is evident in her fiction. "Her approach is a curious blend of impressionism with the hardness and exactness of a writer who reports."

J50. Fadiman, Clifton. "Katherine Anne Porter." *New Yorker*, 15 (1 April 1939), 77–78.

Porter's strengths lie in her ability to "create by suggestion" and in the fact that she "calculates her effects, which is not to say that she gives the effect of calculation." The title story is the most powerful; "Old Mortality" is the least effective.

J51. Gannet, Lewis. "Books and Things." *New York Herald Tribune*, 30 March 1939, p. 23.

Brief but laudatory review. "This is insight; this is real writing."

J52. Hartung, Philip T. *Commonweal*, 30 (19 May 1939), 109–10.

"Precise, poetic and decidedly feminine, Miss Porter paints her pictures in lovely soft tones and then sharply runs a line of bitter satire through them."

J53. Isherwood, Christopher. "Miss Porter and Mr. Todd." *New Republic*, 98 (19 April 1939), 312–13.

Porter's stories show a great deal of talent, but she is too restrained, too "cautious."

J54. Moult, Thomas. "Mr. Coppard and Others." *Manchester Guardian*, 30 June 1939, p. 7.

"Noon Wine" and "Old Mortality" are so subtle in effect that "the connoisseur alone will appreciate them at their proper value." But the title story is "a straightforward example of tale-telling, poignant, witty, charming."

J55. *North American Review*, 247 (Summer 1939), 399.

One brief paragraph. "Miss Porter's new book will solidify her already envious position in contemporary fiction."

J56. Page, Evelyn. "The Novel as Poetry." *Washington Post*, 20 Aug. 1939, Section 3, p. 10.

"One attribute that distinguishes Miss Porter sharply from most writers in her field is her sense of time."

J57. "Promise Kept." *Time*, 33 (10 April 1939), 75.

This work lives up to the artistic promise shown in *Flowering Judas*; it "has the subtlety that has marked all

Miss Porter's writing, none of the preciousness that has previously marred it."

J58. Rahv, Philip. "A Variety of Fiction." *Partisan Review*, 6 (Spring 1939), 113.

One paragraph. Praises Porter's style.

J59. Reid, Forrest. "Fiction." *Spectator*, 162 (9 June 1939), 1010.

"Miss Porter has discovered the form [the long short story] which exactly suits her particular gifts."

J60. Rice, Philip Blair. "The Art of Katherine Anne Porter." *Nation*, 148 (15 April 1939), 442.

"Old Mortality" and "Noon Wine" successfully immerse the reader in their events, but the title story is, in places, "slick magazine writing." Porter's work so far shows "range and versatility as well as polish"; it seems to lack depth.

J61. Rosenfeld, Paul. "An Artist in Fiction." *Saturday Review of Literature*, 19 (1 April 1939), 7.

Compares Porter to Hawthorne, Flaubert, and Henry James, "story tellers whose fiction possesses distinct esthetic quality, whose feelings have attained harmonic expression in their work."

J62. S., M.W. "More Flowering." *Christian Science Monitor*, 13 May 1939, p. 10.

Porter writes for readers who enjoy "not only what an author says, but what he whispers."

J63. Sherman, Caroline B. "Comments on Current Literature." *Southern Literary Messenger*, 1 (May 1939), 366–67.

Each story is "absorbing" and "well-nigh faultless."

J64. Soskin, William. "Rare Beauty of Good Writing." *New York Herald Tribune*, 9 April 1939, Section 9, p. 5.

"Incisively through her beautifully molded sentences and through the rhythmic sweep of feeling in her stories, she reduces a whole lifetime of observation to the carefully wrought pattern of a single story like 'Old Mortality.'"

J65. Stegner, Wallace. "Conductivity in Fiction." *Virginia Quarterly Review*, 15 (Summer 1939), 444–45.

"I found myself reading all three novelettes with admiration, but only "Noon Wine" with excitement."

J66. Straus, Ralph. "At Home and Abroad." [London] *Sunday Times*, 4 June 1939, p. 8.

Porter "shows what an impression can be made with a clear theme only sparsely embroidered."

J67. Swinnerton, Frank. "New Novels." *Observer*, 4 June 1939, p. 6.

"While my final impression is of a little Southern languor I have no doubt of the originality and value of the talent the three stories express."

J68. Thompson, Ralph. "Books of the Times." *New York Times*, 30 March 1939, p. L-21.

In these stories, especially the title story, Porter "has contrived to produce an emotional effect that few, if any, of her contemporaries would have been able to match."

J69. Walton, Edith H. "The Delicate Art of Katherine Anne Porter." *New York Times, Book Review*, 2 April 1939, p. 5.

"Noon Wine" is clever, "but somehow it does not quite ring true." "Old Mortality" is "flawless," while the title story "has a sensitive, a haunting quality."

J70. Wescott, Glenway. "Praise." *Southern Review*, 5 (Summer 1939), 161–73.

Porter's artistry is apparent in that her stories communicate moral judgment (as in the character of Mr. Hatch in "Noon Wine") through suggestion rather than statement. Also, it is wrong to label her a "stylist" in the traditional sense of one who embellishes or who loves words for their own sakes. In her works, "it is simply the story that is laid bare." Her people "are not phenomenal characters; and they do not, to be sure, see heaven very often. But when they do ... or when there is a vision of good and evil ... it is a direct and veritable sight."

J71. West, Anthony. "New Novels." *New Statesman and Nation*, 17, n.s., (27 May 1939), 832, 834.

"These stories, which go no deeper than the emotions of a particular people in special circumstances, have the power to please and charm in a completely satisfying way."

The Itching Parrot

J72. Chamberlain, John. "Books of the Times." *New York Times*, 20 March 1942, p. L-23.

Porter's "introduction is alone worth the price of the book; it is the best background material on the last days of Spanish Mexico that I have ever encountered."

J73. Jones, Howard Mumford. "Lizardi...." *Saturday Review of Literature*, 25 (4 April 1942), 14.

Praises Porter's introductory essay and concedes that the translation is "adequate," but finds the novel itself boring.

J74. *New Yorker*, 18 (21 March 1942), 70–71.

One paragraph. Finds the book "rather dull."

J75. Rugoff, Milton. *New York Herald Tribune, Books*, 22 March 1942, p. 9.

> The novel "is, in Miss Porter's adaptation at least, the rash and racy chronicles of a knave."

J76. Ryan, Edwin. *Commonweal*, 36 (24 July 1942), 331–32.

> The translation is well done; the novel is entertaining.

J77. Trilling, Lionel. "Mexican Classic." *Nation*, 154 (28 March 1942), 373–74.

> Porter's introduction makes Lizardi seem fascinating, but the novel itself (or perhaps the translation) is a bore.

J78. "Unintentional Best Seller." *Time*, 39 (23 March 1942), 79–80.

> Finds the novel fascinating, does not say much about Porter.

J79. Walton, Edith H. "Bygone World." *New York Times, Book Review*, 10 May 1942, p. 22.

> "There can be no doubt as to the excellence of Miss Porter's introduction, which supplies the necessary background in a most clear and telling fashion."

J80. Wolfe, Bertram D. "Picaresque." *New Republic*, 106 (22 June 1942), 868–70.

> The book is "well translated, well edited."

The Leaning Tower and Other Stories

J81. *American Mercury*, 59 (Dec. 1944), 766.

> In the title story, Porter is not up to par; the other stories are better.

J82. Baker, Herschel. "Katherine Anne Porter's Art." *Dallas Morning News*, 1 Oct. 1944, Section 3, p. 12.

Porter has "proved herself once again to be of the sisterhood that includes Jane Austen and Rebecca West.

J83. Beach, Joseph Warren. "Self-Consciousness and Its Antidote." *Virginia Quarterly Review*, 21 (Spring 1945), 292–93.

Sees Porter as "the perfect antidote" to Steinbeck's "self-consciousness" in *Cannery Row*. In her stories "the spiritual state of the character is delicately but firmly dramatized in a personal situation that has the impact of sober truth."

J84. *Booklist*, 41 (15 Oct. 1944), 59.

One paragraph. "Skillful and beautiful writing that, unfortunately, may appeal only to discriminating readers."

J85. "Books Received." *Christian Century*, 61 (11 Oct. 1944), 1170.

Only a few lines. All of the stories "exhibit a calculated and skillful technique."

J86. Buckman, Gertrude. "Miss Porter's New Stories." *Partisan Review*, 12 (Winter 1945), 134.

Although these stories are not as good as Porter's earlier ones, "her essential qualities of purity and delicacy are again revealed."

J87. Daiches, David. *Tomorrow*, Nov. 1944, p. 79.

The stories have many virtues, but they lack "the imaginative compulsion which enables the writer to break the bounds of a story and expand its significance almost indefinitely." Perhaps we can anticipate "a full-scale major opus" from Porter soon.

J88. Downing, Francis. "More Books of the Week." *Commonweal*, 40 (29 Sept. 1944), 572.

Porter is an artist "whose sensitiveness and subtlety of spirit are a tribute to the intellect and to the spirit."

J89. Hansen, Harry. "The First Reader." *New York World-Telegram*, 14 Sept. 1944, p. 22.

"Miss Porter is particularly interested in character and in the relations of human beings to one another."

J90. Jones, Howard Mumford. "A Smooth Literary Texture." *Saturday Review*, 30 Sept. 1944, p. 15.

Admits that Porter's style has "exquisite rightness" but wonders "if the straightforward narrative manner formerly characteristic of the short story" might not be more effective than the obvious artistry of contemporary stories.

J91. Kelley, Gilbert H. *Library Journal*, 69 (1 Sept. 1944), 699.

One paragraph. The book is "recommended."

J92. Kristol, Irving. "This Majestic and Terrible Failure." *New Leader*, 27 (16 Dec. 1944), 11.

Most contemporary literature is of two trends: that preoccupied with specific social issues (Steinbeck, Farrell) and that preoccupied with "myth-making" (Kafka's imitators). Porter fits into neither group. She may "redeem literature as a private, reflective activity which, through the grace of technical exposition becomes socially shared."

J93. M., F.W. "Some Books in Brief Review." *Chicago Sun Book Review*, 24 Sept. 1944, p. 8.

These stories, like most of Porter's other work, are "a collection of episodes suggestive of far more than meets the eye."

J94. Matthiessen, F.O. *Accent*, 5 (Winter 1945), 121–23.

> The Miranda stories show Porter's "searching originality"; they show "the living intricacy of any relationship." "A Day's Work" and "The Downward Path to Wisdom" are not Porter at her best. But in "The Leaning Tower" she superbly interweaves symbolism, character, atmosphere, and theme.
>
> Reprinted as "That True and Human World" in Kerker Quinn and Charles Shattuck (eds.), *Accent Anthology* (1946) and in John Rackliffe (ed.), *The Responsibilities of the Critic: Essays and Reviews of F.O. Matthiessen* (1952).

J95. Molloy, Robert. "The Book of the Day." *New York Sun*, 15 Sept. 1944, p. 20.

> This volume "further establishes her as an artist of the most fastidious sort."

J96. Morgan, Charles. "A Lady of Quality." (London) *Sunday Times*, 2 Dec. 1945, p. 3.

> These stories are commendable, but Porter suffers from an "unwillingness to commit herself to the full hazard of story-telling."

J96. Morley, Christopher. *Book-of-the-Month Club News*, Oct. 1944, p. 13.

> The stories show Porter's "subtle skill."

J97. "New Books." *Catholic World*, 160 (Nov. 1944), 189.

> These stories are valued for Porter's controlled but relaxed style and for the genius of the characterizations.

J98. Prescott, Oliver. "Books of the Times." *New York Times*, 18 Sept. 1944, p. 17.

Although these stories show Porter's "special gifts and special approach to the craft of fiction," they are not as "impressive" as those in her first two collections.

J99. ———. "Outstanding Novels." *Yale Review*, 34, n.s. (Autumn 1944), 190.

The stories are all good; "The Downward Path to Wisdom" is the best.

J100. Read, Martha. "The Mind's Delineation." *Quarterly Review of Literature*, 2 (1945), 150–52.

The stories have "dramatic emotional intensity."

J101. Sapieha, Virgilia. "By Katherine Anne Porter." *New York Herald Tribune, Book Review*, 17 Sept. 1944, p. 2.

All of these stories give evidence of Porter's excellent craftsmanship, but the title story goes beyond mere craftsmanship.

J102. Spencer, Theodore. "Recent Fiction." *Sewanee Review*, 53 (Spring 1945), 300–01.

These stories show Porter's special gift of being "*inside* the situation she is describing."

J103. "Tears and Berlin." *Time*, 44 (25 Sept. 1944), 103–04.

The Miranda stories are "gentle, affectionate epitaphs for a dead world, which read more like a continuous record of nostalgic memories than like separate short stories." The title story is a "sombre, horrifying picture."

J104. *Times Literary Supplement*, 10 Nov. 1945, p. 533.

Since the death of Katherine Manfield, only American writers have produced short stories which are "told simply and unaffectedly and with the lightest, implicit emotion." From this volume, "The Source" is a good example.

J105. Trilling, Diana. "Fiction in Review." *Nation*, 159 (23 Sept. 1944), 359–60.

This is Porter's best book so far; the title story, especially, is deserving of high admiration. Unlike her contemporary women writers, Porter does not deviate into "preciousness."

J106. Warren, Robert Penn. "Reality and Strength in These Tales." *Chicago Daily Tribune, Books,* 15 Oct. 1944, p. 17.

Porter's stories "for all their polish, fastidiousness, and calculated understatement, spring from issues of the real and frequently unpleasant business of living."

J107. Weeks, Edward. "The Atlantic Bookshelf." *Atlantic Monthly,* 174 (Nov. 1944), 131, 133.

The stories are stylistically competent but lack warmth and vitality.

J108. Wescottt, Glenway. "Stories by a Writer's Writer." *New York Times, Book Review,* 17 Sept. 1944, p. 1.

These stories indicate that, if she turns to larger fiction, Porter may give American literature a better novel than it has ever known.

J109. Whicher, George F. "Books and Things." *New York Herald Tribune,* 14 Sept. 1944, p. 19.

Porter's prose is more than "flawless.... It is utterly flexible, undulant and colorless save for little iridescences, like some transparent marine organism that one can just discern in a glass, almost impalpable but palpitating, and somewhere in its secret concealing an unforeseen power to sting."

J110. Wilson, Edmund. "Books." *New Yorker,* 20 (30 Sept. 1944), 72–74.

Porter is "absolutely a first-rate artist, and what she wants other people to know she imparts to them by creating an object, the self-developing organism of a work of prose."

Reprinted as "Katherine Anne Porter" in *Classics and Commercials: A Literary Chronicle of the Forties* (1950); *A Literary Chronicle: 1920–1950* (1952), and Robert Penn Warren (ed.), *Katherine Anne Porter: A Collection of Critical Essays* (H113).

J111. Young, Marguerite. "Fictions Mystical and Epical." *Kenyon Review*, 7 (Winter 1945), 152–54.

Sees Porter's stories as dealing with the necessity of order and values, even in situations in which these are only "dimly remembered." The Miranda stories are nostalgic renderings; the title story concerns a harsher reality.

The Days Before

J112. Allen, Charles. *Arizona Quarterly* 9 (Spring 1953), 71–73.

"Here is a maturity born out of good breeding and a fine intelligence and disciplined reading—a sea of maturity which floods around small islands of frail skittishness."

J113. "Author and Critic—Essays in Literary Dissection." *London Times*, 3 Oct. 1953, p. 9.

"In these non-fiction contributions everything she sets down is positive. She criticizes members of her own craft to some purpose; she is the literary surgeon dissecting with skill the worth and craftsmanship, the shortcomings and foibles of the authors she has chosen for the table in her operating theater. . . . She is at her best in writing on Mexico."

J114. Baker, Carlos. "Good Reading: Review of Books Recommended by the Princeton Faculty." *Princeton Alumni Weekly*, 4 (14 Nov. 1952), 3.

"Crystal-clear, continuously entertaining collection of essays-in-narrative, the harvest of thirty years."

J115. ———. "A Happy Harvest." *New York Times, Book Review*, 1 Nov. 1952, p. 4.

Reading these essays "is as easy, as pleasant, and as rewarding as reading a fine novel." The reward "mainly consists in the strong intimation, perpetually renewed, of power, vitality and . . . a measure of greatness." The essays "show a criticism flowering naturally in the midst of the narrative, with the narrative supporting it, nourishing it by a continual accession of particulars." "These essays combine without forcing, into a magnificent book about artistic growth and its enemies, the perennial pests, the recurrent blights."

J116. *Booklist*, 49 (1 Nov. 1952), 86.

"However varied they are in subject, the essays all bear the imprint of their author's conviction of the high mission of the artist."

J117. "Books Briefly." *Progressive*, 17 (March 1953), 38.

"In an admirable collection of her non-fiction pieces written over a 30-year span, Miss Porter shines in her judgment and taste, her rejections and affirmations."

J118. Chapin, Ruth. "They Wrote with Differing Purpose." *Christian Science Monitor*, 4 Dec. 1952, p. 18.

Porter's "usual high standards of workmanship are everywhere apparent." The "unifying factor in all these critiques is Miss Porter's single-minded devolution to her art." Her art "orders as best it can, out of its own materials, one corner of what seems an enigmatic universe."

J119. Daiches, David. "A Master." *Manchester Guardian*, 30 Oct. 1953, p. 4.

"The great precision of Miss Porter's prose, the lucidity and clarity of her intelligence, the honesty and perceptiveness of her observation are clearly revealed in this wholly delightful book. There are few writers who combine such sensitivity with such lack of pretentiousness or affectation, whose thought is so luminous and undoctrinaire."

J120. F., M. "Writers and Books." *Winnipeg Free Press*, 10 Jan. 1953, p. 8.

Porter is "reticent, and wise, and compassionate, and eloquent with an individual note that, once heard, never can fade from memory. She signs even the most casual piece with the heraldry of her genius."

J121. Fiedler, Leslie A. "Love is Not Enough." *Yale Review*, 42 (Spring 1953), 456, 458–59.

Porter's "best critical writing . . . as well as her more fashionable absurdities . . . are connected with her involvement in a tradition that has outlived its usefulness."

J122. Entry deleted.

J123. Fremantle, Anne. "Yesterdays of Katherine Anne Porter." *Commonweal*, 57 (7 Nov. 1952), 122–23.

In the more personal and domestic essays, Porter "is comfortably close to us, and cosy: we need pay no mind, we can take it or leave it. But when she speaks about literature, then we *must* listen."

J124. Hardy, John Edward. "Interesting Essays by a Novelist." *Baltimore Evening Sun*, 20 Jan. 1953, p. 16.

Hardy is "uneasy" with the "evenness, constancy, of tone" in the volume, "the calm, wise, tolerant, . . . charming, already almost consciously old-fashioned liberal—that spoke from the pages written only this or last year." Because Porter "seems to have read, written about, done exactly and only what she pleased, in the way she pleased," her style is "more sensibility, more glow, than critical cogency." A "person with so much sensibility can at times get on very nicely without understanding."

J125. Hartley, Lodwick. "A White-Robed Priestess with a Pagan Shrine." *Raleigh* (N.C.) *News and Observer*, 9 Nov. 1952, p. IV-5.

"Katherine Anne Porter is and always has been a writer's writer." "The present volume provides an illuminating index not only to the excellence of Miss Porter's art but also to its limitations. . . . As always, Miss Porter writes with such precision, compactness, and fine fluency that no perceptive reader can fail to be charmed by what she has to say. . . . Art is apparently the nearest thing to a be-all and end-all in Miss Porter's existence . . ., but "her championship of art as comprehending both morality and religion may seem at times less like a confession of faith than an act of desperation. . . . And whatever may be the vigor, the vitality, and even the nicely calculated violence of some of her stories and whatever may be the strength of her utterance in other fields, she is likely to continue being regarded as something like a beautiful, white-robed priestess of an immaculate pagan shrine—a role she has deliberately and expertly written for herself."

Reprinted as "The Lady and the Temple" in Lodwick Hartley and George Core (eds.), *Katherine Anne Porter: A Critical Symposium* (H51).

J126. Hobson, Laura Z. "Trade Winds." *Saturday Review*, 35 (13 Sept. 1952), 6, 8.

"It will be a book for thoughtful readers, and thoughtful reading, and good talk afterwards."

J127. Jackson, Katherine Gauss. *Harper's*, 205 (Dec. 1952), 108.

"In her essays and criticism, as in her fiction, in sentences flawless in their deceptive simplicity, Katherine Anne Porter has always been able to open up new worlds to mind, heart, and spirit. Reading here her sharp, wise, and compassionate judgments on life, on writers, their craft, and their works gives a new dimension to them all."

J128. K[ilstoffe], J[une]. "Katherine Anne Porter's Essays Are Joy to Read." *San Antonio Express*, 2 Nov. 1952, p. 16-C.

"What pleases her is writing of the story that is all too rare, precise without being precious, simple without being austere, intensely moving when she wants it to be, and biting when she chooses." The essays here form "a sort of self-portrait, for they reveal Miss Porter's likes and dislikes, her beliefs."

J129. *Kirkus*, 20 (15 Oct. 1952), 697.

"Katherine Anne Porter is a discriminating writer for a discriminating audience, and these pieces, fastidious in discernment, subtle in judgment, have a definite destination."

J130. LeRoy, Gaylord C. "Katherine Anne Porter as Critic, Autobiographer." *Philadelphia Inquirer*, 4 Jan. 1953, "Society," p. 16.

Porter's "talent in criticism is as perfect as her talent in the short story." As a critic, Porter "is satisfied to concern herself with one or two books, one aspect of the man, one special point of view of her own."

J131. McDonald, Gerald D. *Library Journal*, 77 (15 Oct. 1952), 1807–08.

Porter has given these assigned essays with "her own artist's integrity, sure intelligence, and literary grace."

Her responses to the works of writers "are contributions whose value seems permanent."

J132. McDowell, Frederick P. "An Autobiography of an Artist's Mind." *Western Review*, 17 (Summer 1953), 334–37.

"These essays are, all told, most valuable for their relevance to the themes of Miss Porter's fiction."

J133. McGrory, Mary. "Essayist Katherine Anne Porter Reflects on Art, Life and Love." *Washington Star*, 7 Dec. 1952, p. E-7.

The credo that "people true to themselves, their values and gifts will prevail" runs through this collection of "meticulously fashioned reflections on art, life and love."

J134. Mizener, Arthur. "A Literary Self-Portrait." *Partisan Review*, 20 (March-April 1953), 244–46.

"These occasional pieces show her mind at work." "The book's value for us is what we can learn about a fine mind on informal occasions." The "interplay of imaginative understanding and firm, common sense appraisal" constitute "the style of her mind."

J135. Monroe, Harold. "New Porter Collection Notable." *Fort Worth Star-Telegram*, 16 Nov. 1952, Section 2, p. 11.

"She achieves that most desired of all feats in literature—to write so precisely what she means that all her sentences seem to have flown with ease from her pen. . . . Her discussions of the current scene . . . are gems . . . [her] essays on Mexico . . . are written with charm and understanding."

J136. Morse, S.F. "Of Durable Beauty." *Hartford Courant, Magazine*, 2 Nov. 1952, p. 18.

Porter's work has "the tensile strength and durable beauty of that of E.M. Forster." This collection "is a great satisfaction": the critical essays are "impressive not only

for the justness of their judgments but also for their
integrity and independence."

J137. Munford, Howard M. "Personal Record and Artistic Credo
in Essays of Katherine Anne Porter." *Louisville
Courier-Journal*, 9 Nov. 1952, Section 3, p. 14.

Having these pieces "available between the covers of a
book gives them the added dimension of a personal record
and artistic credo." The essays "bear the distinctive
stamp of Miss Porter's incomparable style and reveal an
unusually deep insight, feminine and firm. She knows
what and whom she likes and can say exactly why."

J138. P., R.G.G. *Punch*, 225 (11 Nov. 1953), 587–88.

"This enjoyable collection of reprinted literary and
general articles is distinguished by a curt commonsense
that presents the gains of a lifetime's reading and feeling
as though to an audience of cultured but calm matrons."

J139. *New Statesman & Nation*, 46 (31 Oct. 1953), 540.

In these essays Porter "is most often too mannered and
too inexact in her meaning. . . . She settles down hardly
ever on the cool and precise comment which is an equally
essential element in compelling criticism."

J140. *New Yorker*, 28 (1 Nov. 1952), 134.

The critical articles and reviews are finely drawn,
characterized by a "tough-minded sensitivity," and
perceptive. The personal writings "make a fine sheaf of
sketches for a self-portrait."

J141. Parrish, Stephen Maxfield. "Critics Academic and Lay."
Virginia Quarterly Review, 29 (Winter 1953), 158–59.

"Miss Porter's essays sparkle with vitality. She has
strong convictions, but she is never doctrinaire, never
pompous or fussy, nor darkly allusive, and the icy clarity

of her style makes every word she writes a delight to read." What "principally emerges" is "the portrait of the artist."

J142. Poore, Charles. "Books of the Times." *New York Times*, 23 Oct. 1952, p. 29.

"The pieces are alive with the vigor of strong opinions expressed in a style of singing clarity.... Although her main theme is literature, her main interest is life."

J143. *Publishers Weekly*, 162 (27 Sept. 1952), 1462.

"A notable volume of essays by the distinguished author."

J144. Putcamp, Luise, Jr. "Another Texas Book: Ponderings of Porter." *Dallas Daily Times Herald*, 30 Nov. 1952, Section 7, p. 6.

"Miss Porter is readable in the extreme." "In her critical pieces Miss Porter affirms a passion for integrity of intent and a mania (that a poet might envy) for the precise word in both her own and other people's writing."

J145. Rolo, Charles J. "Reader's Choice." *Atlantic Monthly*, 190 (Dec. 1952), 97–98.

"Close to being a self-portrait," the collection has as its "central preoccupation" "'the passion for individual expression without hypocrisy.'" "In these articles, there is an intelligence that races along; there is sanity, charm, and a love of the world."

J146. Schorer, Mark. "Biographia Literaria." *New Republic*, 127 (10 Nov. 1952), 18–19.

"The first hundred and nineteen pages, devoted to criticism, are the most valuable in the book.... But much in [the] second and third sections hardly bears re-reading": in fact, a few of these pieces are "vulgar" or "dull." Porter's literary criticism "is almost always human rather than critical, highly personal, degenerating occasionally into vague impressionism." "If Miss Porter had a 'continuous, central interest' in her life, that interest is the life of the imagination in relation to tradition, more concretely, the life of Miss Porter's imagination in relation to the social and literary tradition in which she has been involved."

J147. Schwartz, Edward. "Miss Porter's Essays." *Nation*, 175 (15 Nov. 1952), 452–53.

Porter, like Hardy, "is committed to the faith of 'the Inquirers,'" is devoted to truth-telling, is skeptical of abstract theories, and holds an exalted view of the devout artist. "These implicit values unify the book, but the subject matter is highly diversified."

J148. Sherman, John K. "Intuition Speeds Her Sharp Mind." *Minneapolis Tribune*, 26 Oct. 1952, Feature-News Section, p. 6.

"This book has varied riches for those who enjoy the workings of a sharp discriminating brain linked with wide sympathies—and a few healthy antipathies." "Miss Porter has humor and art, heart and mind. Reading her is a good exercise in clearing mental cobwebs and chasing the cliches away."

J149. Sibley, Celestine. "'The Days Before'—Katherine Anne Porter Talks About Writing, Writers, Love, and A-Bombs." *Atlanta Journal*, 26 Oct. 1952, p. 7-F.

Porter's "character, her taste and personality . . . may be found in this new collection of her nonfiction works." The volume "is good reading and a satisfying way to round out an acquaintance with a great artist and a great craftsman."

J150. Spiller, Robert E. "Wiles & Words." *Saturday Review*, 36 (10 Jan. 1953), 12.

This book succeeds because Porter is "unusually unified and interesting as a personality" and has a unified and interesting "point of view." As one of the finer artists of our time, every word she says on these topics is worth listening to. Porter's education "was not only a matter of training in craftsmanship; it was a consecration to art because art is more than life."

J151. Stallings, Sylvia. "Deft Touch." *New York Herald Tribune, Book Review*, 2 Nov. 1952, p. 8.

"Whether she writes critically, as an artist speaking of her own kind, or personally, as a visitor in Mexico or as an intelligent individual surveying the crises of the times, her quick eye and sure command of language never fail." "Concerned for people, with the situations in which they find themselves and with which they must deal, whether as artists or as well-diggers, she is never jaded with life."

J152. Sullivan, Richard. "More Distinguished Prose from a Fascinating Mind." *Chicago Tribune, Books*, 26 Oct. 1952, p. 4.

The qualities of her fiction are evident here: "sensitivity and control, intensity and scrupulous selectivity, so that the writing seems restricted to essentials." This is "a considerable book."

J153. Taylor, Norris. "Art, Not Artifice, Is Key to Porter Writing." *Houston Post*, 26 Oct. 1952, Section 7, p. 7.

"Her viewpoint is the classical position of the artist in society: as commentator, as a dissenter, as a seeker after the truth not bound by any group or special interest. She escaped this tyranny by developing slowly in her own way, through her own efforts, and in her own time, the personal viewpoint and uncompromising integrity that marks this book." "Porter writes a kind of prose that is inimitable: one phrase pulling another like a linked chain, the whole not to be unstrung from any of the parts."

J154. Tinkle, Lon. "Reading and Writing." *Dallas Morning News*, 14 Dec. 1952, Part VI, p. 11.

Porter's works "are organic growths of a fruitful and highly original mind, and scrupulously offered as real nourishment.... Quality of mind blends in Miss Porter with a quite original quality of emotional response."

J155. Weston, Mildred. "Katherine Anne Porter Claws Stein, Whitman." *New York Post*, 14 Dec. 1952, p. 12M.

Porter "sums up the collection as parts of a journal of her thinking and feeling, and as such it will delight her many admirers." "We are made particularly aware of her warm antipathies in her essays on writers, and it is here that some of her readers, even devoted ones ..., will disagree with her."

J156. "A Writer's Reflections." *Times Literary Supplement*, 2698 (16 Oct. 1953), 663.

This collection of essays "shows the combination of intellectual acuity and delicate perception that makes many of Miss Porter's stories memorable." Her "vague generous liberalism is here an inadequate substitute for a general system of ideas embodying the relationship of life to literature."

J157. Yeiser, Frederick. "Mixed Bag." *Cincinnati Enquirer*, 26 Oct. 1952, p. 62.

"In spite of the drudgery and effort they [the essays] cost her, they attain the same high quality of her stories. She seems incapable of writing badly."

Ship of Fools

J158. Arimond, Carroll. "Books." *Extension*, 57 (Aug. 1962), 25.

The novel is worthy for its character studies and for its style.

J159. Auchincloss, Louis. "Bound for Bremerhaven—and Eternity." *New York Herald Tribune, Books*, 1 April, 1962, pp. 3, 11.

This long-awaited novel is not a disappointment. It is "rich enough to be read on many levels and will keep the lovers of symbols happy," and it is "bathed in intelligence and humor."
Reprinted in Robert Penn Warren (ed.), *Katherine Anne Porter: A Collection of Critical Essays* (H113).

J160. Beck, Warren. "Masterly Novel Crowns Author's Notable Career." *Chicago Sunday Tribune, Magazine of Books*, 1 April 1962, pp. 1–2.

The book "goes beyond explicit tragedy, to frame appalling reality with a commensurate pathos."

J161. Bedford, Sybille. "Voyage to Everywhere." *Spectator*, 209 (16 Nov. 1962), 763–64.

In spite of its bulk, its static characters, and its emphasis on the grotesque, *Ship of Fools* is a "great universal novel."
Reprinted in Robert Penn Warren (ed.), *Katherine Anne Porter: A Collection of Critical Essays* (H113).

J162. Bode, Carl. "Katherine Anne Porter, *Ship of Fools*." *Wisconsin Studies in Contemporary Literature*, 3 (Fall 1962), 90–92.

"*Ship of Fools* is an honest, disheartening book. It is not over-written or over-blown. Quite the reverse; it has been revised downward. Its basic image is old but as the author develops it, it becomes modern and more complex. I do not believe that *Ship of Fools* reaches the heights of Miss Porter's earlier work but I am sure it will find a place, if a small one, in our literary histories."
Reprinted as "Miss Porter's *Ship of Fools*" in *The Half-World of American Culture* (1965).

J163. Bond, Alice Dixon. "New Porter Novel Worth the Wait."
       Boston Herald, 1 April 1962, Section 2, p. 8.

   Porter's "insights are myriad, her depictions superb."

J164. Booth, Wayne C. "Yes, But Are They Really Novels?"
       Yale Review, 51 n.s. (Summer 1962), 632–34.

   The novel is disappointing. It has "no steady center of
   interest except the progressively more intense
   exemplification of its central truth: men are pitifully,
   foolishly self-alienated."

J165. Bradbury, Malcolm. "New Novels." *Punch*, 243 (21 Nov.
       1962), 763–64.

   At times Porter's "manner becomes mechanical, and she
   shows a tendency to repeat her effects; but the whole is
   undoubtedly a very remarkable book."

J166. Bradley, Van Allen. "Sailing on Into Eternity." *Chicago
       News*, 31 March 1962, p. 10.

   The novel is "an impressive achievement" and "offers
   us vivid evidence of almost every kind of human
   malevolence, of the inhumanity of man to man."

J167. C., E. "Books in English." *Books Abroad*, 36 (Summer
       1962), 322–23.

   Ship of Fools is "in the great tradition of the novel," of
   the calibre published "perhaps not more than once in a
   generation."

J168. Chamberlain, John. "The Devil for a Captain." *Wall
       Street Journal*, 2 April 1962, p. 14.

   The novel, though "a compendium of short stories or
   novelettes," is successful in its style and its "subtle
   psychological analysis."

J169. Clepper, Patrick. "The Plot Isn't Much, But the Prose Is Brilliant." *St. Paul Dispatch*, 9 June 1962.

The plot is bare; the characters are "unappealing"; the style is "brilliant."

J170. Cournos, John. "Sea Voyage Kindles Passion, Greed, Prejudice and Laughter." *Philadelphia Evening Bulletin*, 1 April 1962, Section 2, p. 3.

"Not a dull page; not a word you want to skip."

J171. Culligan, Glendy. "Shipload of Eternal Pilgrims." *Washington Post*, 1 April 1962, p. E-6.

The novel may suffer from too bleak a view of human nature. Still, it is technically a "marvel," and the remarkable style effectively reflects the writer's feelings.

J172. Day, Franklin. "Mankind Includes Those Confined to Steerage." (San Francisco) *People's World*, 25 Aug. 1962, p. 7.

The novel is a success only if we see it as "an intensive study of the relatively narrow range of middle class types she is most at home with."

J173. Dorr, Bill. "Ship is Safe in Port for Novelist Porter." *Publishers' Auxiliary*, 97 (7 April 1962), 2.

The publication of *Ship of Fools* is "the greatest moment for one of our greatest writers."

J174. Drake, Robert. "A Modern Inferno." *National Review*, 12 (24 April 1962), 290–91.

The novel is worth the twenty-year wait. Porter's view of hell is all encompassing; the yearning for something beyond is evident. However, Porter's "descent into the Inferno may ... have been too much even for her, and the book's structure and power [has] suffered accordingly."

Ship of Fools is "not so much a novel as a textbook in the pathology of sin."

J175. Duchene, Anne. "Twenty Years Agrowing." *Manchester Guardian*, 2 Nov. 1962, p. 12.

"This is a very good novel, voluminous yet concentrated, but it lacks the pulse of nervous communication so often present in Miss Porter's smaller works."

J176. English, Charles. "A Long-Awaited Masterpiece." *Jubilee*, 10 (May 1962), 46–48.

"Miss Porter's economy of words, her high humor, special power of discernment and powerful ability to create atmosphere, is combined with a magnificent style that is even more evident here than in her shorter works."

J177. Fadiman, Clifton. *Book-of-the-Month Club News*, March 1962, pp. 2–4.

At last we have "Miss Porter's magnum opus." The novel gives us her vision of today's world. She "has her eye on the object, and, though her object is the dehumanization of our day, who never assumes the robe of the preacher or philosopher."

J178. Fefferman, Stan. "Books Reviewed." *Canadian Forum*, 42 (Aug. 1962), 115.

Through this "moral experiment," Porter is able to comment on the nature of original sin.

J179. "Fiction." *Booklist and Subscription Books Bulletin*, 58 (15 April 1962), 565.

One paragraph. Favorable.

J180. Finklestein, Sidney. *Mainstream*, 15 (Sept. 1962), 42–48.

"The novel is all finely wrought surface with no depth. Its craftsmanship is honest; its pretensions at serious thought can only be called unwitting fraud." Porter's view of fascism is too limited to be revealing.

J181. Finn, James. "On the Voyage to Eternity." *Commonweal*, 76 (18 May 1962), 212–13.

Although *Ship of Fools* fails to live up to the high expectations aroused over the years of its composition, it is an accomplishment. Porter "has been true to her harsh, clear vision and has communicated it with high imaginative intensity."

J182. Gardiner, Harold C. "New Fiction." *America*, 107 (14 April 1962), 54.

This is not a novel but "an extremely long series of character sketches." Also, the novel gives "no positive vision to counterbalance the depressing picture."
See the 26 May issue, pp. 309–12, for Letters to the Editor concerning this review.

J183. Goldsborough, Diana. "The Ship and the Attic." *Tamarack Review*, 24 (Summer 1962), 104–07.

The book is a marvelous but despair-producing work.

J184. Gorn, Leslie. "Septuagenarian Writes Her First Novel." *San Francisco Examiner, Highlight*, 1 April 1962, p. 2.

The novel is technically successful but Porter's pessimistic vision is not valid.

J185. Greene, A.C. "Prediction: Greatness." *Dallas Times-Herald*, 1 April 1962.

J186. Greene, Maxine. "Beyond Compassion." *The Humanist*, 22 (Nov.–Dec. 1962), 197.

As we move through the book, "we are continually forced to confront the failure of love." Humanists should not be offended by the bleak view of humanity shown here.

J187. Hartley, Lodwick. "A Voyage in Relentless Reality." *Raleigh* [N.C.] *Times*, 8 April 1962.

Since Porter is completely successful only in short fiction, *Ship of Fools* is flawed. But it has a "nightmare" quality that makes it powerful.

J188. Hicks, Granville. "Voyage of Life." *Saturday Review*, 45 (31 March 1962), 15–16.

"The novel, for all its lucidity and all its insights, leaves the reader a little cold. There is in it, so far as I can see, no sense of human possibility."

J189. Hogan, William. "A Devil's Mix from a Blender." *San Francisco Chronicle, This World*, 1 April 1962, p. 28.

Porter seems to have "poured a variety of short stories into some literary Waring blender and . . . this devil's mix is the result."

J190. Holmes, Theodore. "The Literary Mode." *Carleton Miscellany*, 4 (Winter 1963), 124–28.

The book consists of "the whole dreary fare of the middle-class woman's magazine during the thirty years [in which it] was written."

J191. Humboldt, Charles. "The Porter Novel." *National Guardian*, 14 (4 June 1962), 9.

There are a few characters in the novel with a few positive qualities, but the evil pervading the book renders these qualities powerless. Still, there is hope for the future—reflected in the increasing number (seven births) of the steerage passengers.

J192. Hutchens, John K. "Ship of Fools." *New York Herald Tribune*, 2 April 1962, p. 19.

The novel is not as successful as Porter's short stories. The characters are static; the plot does not have enough movement; even her style at times has "a sort of flabbiness."
Reprinted as "Shipload of Fools" in *Philadelphia Inquirer*, 8 Dec. 1962, p. D-6.

J193. Hyman, Stanley Edgar. "Archetypal Woman, Archetypal Germans." *New Leader*, 45 (2 April 1962), 23–24.

The main presences in the novel are Woman (a composite of Jenny Brown, Mrs. Treadwell, and La Condessa) and The German (a composite of the various German characters). The other characters are "brilliantly drawn grotesques." The plot centers on "the wild eruption of a repressed mixture of violence and sex." Unfortunately, the reader is likely to be "disgusted rather than moved."

J194. Jarrett, Thomas D. "Ship of Fools—Evil Voyage." *Atlanta Journal*, 9 Dec. 1962, p. D-8.

The novel shows Porter's "ability to probe the human heart, to present an interplay of characters in struggle with themselves. But in dealing only with "evil, frustration, and self-delusion," it has too limited a point of view.

J195. Jones, Frank N. "A Master Storyteller." *Baltimore Sun*, 1 April 1962, p. A-5.

After reading the novel, we know "that we have been in the presence of a master story-teller, a genius in painting human nature."

J196. Kasten, Maurice. *Shenandoah*, 13 (Summer 1962), 54–61.

Ship of Fools is too "real" to be seen as grandly universal. But seen on a more narrow level, it has its "victories."

J197. Kauffmann, Stanley. "Katherine Anne Porter's Crowning Work." *New Republic*, 146 (2 April 1962), 23–25.

For the most part the novel is "a disappointment." Porter's style is "less pure" than previously; there is "little development in depth" of the characters; the German and the Jewish characters are caricatures.

J198. Kirsch, Robert R. "The Long-Awaited 'Ship of Fools' Flounders." *Los Angeles Times-Mirror*, 25 March 1962, "Calendar," p. 22.

The novel fails to "command interest, generate excitement."

J199. Kohler, Dayton. "Miss Porter Writes of Allegorical Voyage." *Louisville Courier-Journal*, 1 April 1962, Section 4, p. 7.

This is an honest, well-structured, powerful, great novel.
Reprinted in *Richmond* [Va.] *New Leader*, 11 April 1962.

J200. Lalley, J.M. "Gaudeamus Omnes!" *Modern Age*, 6 (Fall 1962), 440–42.

In taking "sin as the universal phenomenon" for her topic, Porter has produced a work of "cumulative tedium."

J201. Lasswell, Mary. "'Ship of Fools' a Realist Shocker." *Houston Chronicle*, 15 April 1962, "TV Pullout," p. 10.

The novel is reminiscent of "Spanish realism and humor"; it is a masterpiece of the gruesome and the cruel. Mrs. Treadwell is its "only ray of humanity."

J202. Lease, Benjamin. "Dramas of Life on Ship and Dunes." *Chicago Sun-Times*, 15 April 1962, Section 3, p. 1.

"A rare and wonderful achievement," the novel is exciting and significant.

J203. Lehan, Richard. "Under the Human Crust." (Austin) *American-Statesman*, 8 April 1962, p. E-8.

By ending the novel with the characters unchanged in their indifference or bitterness, Porter has remained true to her vision. "She chose to write an allegory about modern man and war." At this, she is "brilliantly convincing."

J204. "The Longest Journey." *Newsweek*, 59 (2 April 1962), 88–89.

The novel's central theme is "the terrifying inability of most of these people to extend any comprehension of mind, magnanimity of feeling, or compassion of heart to those around them."

J205. M., M.E. "Current Fiction." *Christian Century*, 79 (18 April 1962), 492.

Only a few lines. Favorable.

J206. Maddocks, Melvin. "Miss Porter's Novel." *Christian Science Monitor*, 5 April 1962, p. 13.

This is Porter's "magnum opus," making "most contemporary novels seem trivial and amateurish by comparison."

J207. Martin, Ron. "Her Ship Finally Came In." *Detroit Free Press*, 1 April 1962, p. B-5.

The book will no doubt be a bestseller; it is, nevertheless, disappointing.

J208. McDonnell, Thomas P. "New Books." *Catholic World*, 195 (June 1962), 180–81, 184.

Porter has taken the image of the journey further than has usually been done in contemporary literature. "She has made of it both a panorama and a microcosm of the modern world." Also, she shows that she is one of the few American writers (such as Henry James) who can completely "enter the European consciousness—if not conscience."

J209. McGrory, Mary. "Style and Irony: A Porter Blend." *Washington Star*, 1 April 1962, p. B-5.

Although technically commendable, the novel is too crowded with emotionally intense scenes and with unlikable characters.

J210. Morse, J. Mitchell. "Fiction Chronicle." *Hudson Review*, 15 (Summer 1962), 292–94.

Coming from such a superb writer, *Ship of Fools* is a major disappointment. It is not innovative; the language is commonplace; its people have no depth of characterization; it theme is nothing new.

J211. Mortimer, Raymond. "A Scathing Microcosm of Eternity." (London), *Sunday Times, Magazine*, 28 Oct. 1962, p. 31.

The book is "outstanding"; Porter's thinking is "clear and keen"; the language never gives a "phrase that is pretentious, clumsy, or commonplace."

J212. Moss, Howard. "No Safe Harbor." *New Yorker*, 38 (28 April 1962), 165–66, 169–70, 172–73.

The novel is moral without being dogmatic; Porter's style is effectively simple. "The missing ingredient is impulse"; the twenty years of composing it have ruled out the effect of spontaneity, found so often in her short stories.

Reprinted in *Writing Against Time: Critical Essays and Reviews* (1962), Robert Penn Warren (ed.), *Katherine Anne Porter: A Collection of Critical Essays* (H113), and Harold Bloom (ed.), *Katherine Anne Porter* (H11).

J213. Murphy, Edward F. "Book Reviews." *Ramparts,* 1 (Nov. 1962), 88–91.

Those who have criticized *Ship of Fools* as overwhelmingly pessimistic are guilty of not having read it carefully. All of the characters are capable of reaching safe harbor if they only realize the need for supernatural guidance.

J214. Murray, James G. "Ship of Fools." *Critic,* 20 (June–July 1962), 63–64.

The novel turns up themes worth considering and contains "little masterpieces in episodic form." But it is rather a "splendid failure" than a success. "Its realism contends with its allegory, and it take a wrong direction in emphasizing evil rather than folly."

J215. Murray, Michele. "Reality of Evil Faced in Long-Awaited Novel." *Catholic Reporter,* 6 April 1962.

To Porter evil is not an illusion, nor is it "accidental"; it is a metaphysical reality. "Although *Ship of Fools* is by no means the conventional 'religious' book, every page has its ground in a religious ordering of the world and its possibilities."

J216. "Notes on Current Books." *Virginia Quarterly Review,* 38 (Summer 1962), lxxii.

Although Porter's literary gifts are displayed forcefully, her "unrelieved pessimism" makes reading the novel a sobering experience.

J217. "Novels Distinctive and Significant." *Wisconsin Library Bulletin*, 58 (May–June 1962), 178.

"The writing is superb, the craftsmanship is masterful and the tone is one of despair."

J218. O'Brien, John H. "Katherine Anne Porter's Latest: An Allegory in Search of a Symbol." *Detroit News*, 8 April 1962, p. F-3.

The novel is puzzling regarding meaning and symbolism, but it is well worth reading.

J219. O'Connor, William Van. "Katherine Anne Porter Ignores Power of Love." *Minneapolis Sunday Tribune*, 8 April 1962, p. F-10.

Ship of Fools presents a kind of truth, but Porter ignores "the transforming power of love."

J220. "On the Good Ship Vera." *Times Literary Supplement*, 2 Nov. 1962, p. 837.

The novel has "moments of great power and compassion." However, "the achievements are those of a great short-story writer." The attempts at universality are mechanical and superficial; the characters are stereotypes; there is no "dramatic centre."

J221. Parker, Dorothy. "Book Review." *Esquire*, 58 (July 1962), 129.

The characters are depressing; its message is harsh. But "My God, here is a book."

J222. Pickerel, Paul. "After the Death of Plot." *Harper's*, 204 (April 1962), 84, 86.

The novel gives rigid authoritarianism in the captain and chaotic primitiveness in the steerage passengers. Between these two extremes are the first-class passengers trying to work out a mid-course. But there is no satisfactory course; there is "no relationship that endures in happiness, no revelation that is more than momentary." Stylistically, the novel has "a glow of perfection that is seldom seen achieved in contemporary fiction."

J223. Poore, Charles. "Books of the Times." *New York Times*, 3 (April 1962), 37.

Ship of Fools is "a miraculously brilliant book ... a cathedral for the damned."

J224. Powers, Dennis. "Porter Novel is A Compelling View of Human Experience." *Oakland Tribune*, 1 April 1962, p. E-2.

The novel gives "the follies and flaws in human nature responsible for the growth to power of a phenomenon like Nazism."

J225. Reitz, Rosetta. "Sick Ship." *Village Voice*, 2 Aug. 1962, "Books," p. 10.

Porter's "passion is reportage made with detachment. ... She handles her characters like geometric forms in a finely woven tapestry, each of a different color, but all bearing a similar hue. ... There is no vibrance or dramatic play."

J226. Rubin, Louis D., Jr. "A Work of Genius." *Baltimore Evening Sun*, 30 April 1962, p. A-24.

The novel shows a sense of "psychological motivation" and Porter's "deep compassion for human beings and her detestation of bigotry, cruelty, and sham." The characters are either cruel or weak, but some are saved by the ability to love.

J227. Ryan, Marjorie. "Katherine Anne Porter: *Ship of Fools*." *Critique*, 5 (Fall 1962), 94–99.

It is, to be sure, a quite pessimistic work, but it also has sympathy and humor. Its major theme is that "we are involved with and responsible for one another."

J228. Schorer, Mark. "We're All on the Passenger List." *New York Times, Book Review*, 1 April 1962, pp. 1, 5.

Ship of Fools is universal; "it will be a reader myopic to the point of blindness who does not find his name on her passenger list." It is truly a masterpiece—"the 'Middlemarch' of a later day."
Reprinted in Robert Penn Warren (ed.), *Katherine Anne Porter: A Collection of Critical Essays* (H113).

J229. Sherman, Thomas B. "Reading and Writing." *St. Louis Post-Dispatch*, 22 April 1962, p. C-4.

Although the basic scheme of *Ship of Fools* is formulaic, the book is a success because Porter makes the reader care about the characters.

J230. "Sight and Sound." *McCall's*, 89 (April 1962), 14.

Although the book has "a bitter view," the story is told with "skill and suspense."

J231. Smith, Miles A. "All Life is Portrayed in New Porter Novel." *Cleveland Plain Dealer*, 8 April 1962, p. E-42.

The novel is never dull; the characters' "passages through good and evil—particularly the latter—are depicted graphically and without literary affectation."

J232. Southern, Terry. "When Fiction Gets Good. . . ." *Nation*, 195 (17 Nov. 1962), 330.

Ship of Fools "could be a good, entertaining movie; but it is not a good book, almost for that reason."

J233. "Speech after long Silence." *Time*, 79 (6 April 1962), 97.

Although "optimists" might demur, Porter has successfully conveyed the theme that "all passages of the world's voyage are dismal, and the entente of ignorance and evil is forever in command."

J234. Stoker, Ben. "Chablis, Bordeaux, and Courvoisier." *The New Guard*, 2 (Sept. 1962), 15.

The novel is "like the finest Chablis, dry as desert air and only appreciated when served very chilled."

J235. Taubman, Robert. "A First-Class Passenger." *New Statesman*, 64 (2 Nov. 1962), 619–20.

The novel is "solid up to a point—solid and soft at the same time, like a fruit-cake." On the whole, it is not satisfying.

J236. Theall, D. Bernard. "'Ship of Fools' Portrays Man's Life on Earth." *San Francisco Monitor*, 11 May 1962.

The book is depressing but "immensely readable."

J237. Thompson, John. "The Figure in the Rose-Red Gown." *Partisan Review*, 29 (Fall 1962), 608–12.

Unlike Porter's short stories and novelettes, *Ship of Fools* suffers from a too obvious theme. And the theme itself is given as "a curse, a cold, joking remorseless, unpitying curse."

J238. Troy, George. "A Passenger's Report on a Ship of Fools." *Providence Journal*, 1 April 1962, p. W-22.

The novel is too gloomy; the characters are too flat.

J239. "What's Wrong with American Novels?" *Books and Bookmen*, Nov. 1962, p. 21.

Porter's twenty years of revising this novel have had a negative effect; it "has become academically perfect but lacks heart."

J240. Wilson, Angus. "The Middle-Class Passenger." *London Observer*, 28 Oct. 1962, p. 27.

Ship of Fools is disappointing, muddled, and "middle-brow."

J241. Wilson, Tom. "A Load of Mortal Mischief in This Liner's Cargo." *Denver Post, Roundup*, 1 April 1962, p. 9.

The book "is an outstanding work of literature and human understanding."

J242. Yanitell, Victor R., S.J. "Fiction." *Best Sellers*, 22 (15 April 1962), 25–26.

The novel has superb character portrayals and effective symbolism. However, it is too long and has too many characters to really be successful.

J243. Yeiser, Frederick. "Porter Writes First Novel." *Cincinnati Enquirer*, 1 April 1962, p. B-6.

The book contains effective caricature, memorable characters, and an outstanding style.

J244. Ylvisaker, Miriam. *Library Journal*, 87 (15 March 1962), 1152.

"A rich, complex novel of rare distinction in both aim and execution."

Collected Stories

J245. Aldridge, John W. "Hors d'oeuvres for an Entree." *New York Herald Tribune, Book Week*, 19 Sept. 1965, pp. 4, 22.

Although critics are generally laudatory in dealing with Porter's works, they seem hard put to find specific merits. If looked at objectively "a good deal of her writing does indeed seem pale. . . . She has been careful to take no imaginative risks which she could not easily and gracefully put into words." Her stories of Texas have "an air of relaxation and warmth, as well as a seeming natural richness of texture." Unfortunately, in most of her work Porter seems to have "turned away" from the southern childhood experiences and tried "to serve an ideal of complete artistic objectivity."

Reprinted as "Art and Passion in Katherine Anne Porter" in *Time to Murder and Create: The Contemporary Novel in Crisis* (1966), *The Devil in the Fire* (1972), and Lodwick Hartley and George Core (eds.), *Katherine Anne Porter: A Critical Symposium* (H51).

J246. Bordwell, Harold. "The Stories of Katherine Anne Porter." *Today*, Dec. 1965, pp. 30–31.

These lucid stories effectively focus on a single moment in a way that "encompasses past and future in the present."

J247. Bradbury, Malcolm. "Perspectives." *Manchester Guardian*, 10 Jan. 1964, p. 7.

"So densely is life, in the past and in the present, created for us, so firm and precise and delicate is Miss Porter's awareness of its flux and flow, that she clearly stands, in her best stories, as a very important writer."

J248. Burgess, Anthony. "A Long Drink of Porter." *Spectator*, 212 (31 Jan. 1964), 151.

Although *Ship of Fools* was disappointing, this volume guarantees Porter's literary permanence. "The secret of her stories is flow. . . . The flow is checked by the solidity of a symbol."

J249. *Choice*, 2 (Nov. 1965), 582–83.

"Should be purchased by all libraries, no matter what their size or type."

J250. "Clear Colours." *Times Literary Supplement*, 9 Jan. 1964, p. 21.

Porter cannot be labeled either a Southern writer or a political writer, nor should she be compared to Hemingway or Katherine Mansfield. "She is one of those original artists who half-deliberately develop their talents in isolation rather than by the exchange of ideas with friends."

J251. Connolly, Cyril. "Deep in the Heart." (London) *Sunday Times*, 5 Jan. 1964, p. 29.

"The stories go deep, deeper than the deceptively well-mannered prose suggests."

J252. Donadio, Stephen. "The Collected Miss Porter." *Partisan Review*, 33 (Spring 1966), 278–84.

Most of Porter's stories suffer from being too craftsmanlike. "Technique is exaggerated at the expense of content; details are rendered as if they existed under glass." Her most successful stories—"Flowering Judas," "Pale Horse, Pale Rider," and "The Leaning Tower"— manage to avoid such a snare. In them, human relationships and individual conflict are superbly conveyed.

J253. Donoghue, Denis. "Reconsidering Katherine Anne Porter." *New York Review of Books*, 5 (11 Nov. 1965), 18–19.

"In Miss Porter's best stories the past is so rich that it suffuses the present and often smothers it, and even when there is nothing more there is enough. But this means that her characters are utterly dependent on the past for their development." Thus stories such as "Flowering

Judas," "Old Mortality," "Holiday," and "Noon Wine" are successes, while *Ship of Fools* and the "Irish-American pieces" are not.

J254. Featherstone, Joseph. "Katherine Anne Porter's Harvest." *New Republic*, 153 (4 Sept. 1965), 23–26.

Porter has achieved "the wisdom of those whose identity is a conscious reconstruction of their instincts, who have come to terms with the past they rebelled against, and who see themselves in the world with lucid impersonality."
Reprinted as "Katherine Anne Porter's Stories" in Gilbert A. Harrison (ed.), *The Critic as Artist* (1972).

J255. "Fiction." *Booklist*, 62 (1 Nov. 1965), 263.

A very brief review. The book is "a convenient compilation."

J256. Goldberg, Barbara. "Bleakness." *Canadian Forum*, 45 (Jan. 1966), 240.

"Katherine Anne Porter is unquestionably an excellent writer but five hundred pages of bickering bleakness and unhappy endings can be pretty hard to take."

J257. Gullason, Thomas A. "Tragic Parables." *Boston Herald*, 3 Oct. 1965, Section 1, p. 57.

Seeing the stories in the context of the original collections (rather than as individual works) will yield "new insights and richer patterns of meaning."

J258. Hagopian, John V. "Reviews." *Studies in Short Fiction*, 4 (Fall 1966), 86–87.

In Porter's stories "the theme, more often than not, is Camusian in its existentialism: the central character discovers that neither society nor the universe is so ordered as to yield the possibility of meaning of love."

J259. Hicks, Granville "A Tradition of Story Telling."
      Saturday Review, 48 (25 Sept. 1965), 35–36.

      Although it is difficult to isolate the outstanding
      virtues of Porter's fiction, "one has the feeling, with
      almost every story, that it is absolutely right."

J260. Higgins, John. "Dangerous Briefing." (London) *Telegraph*,
      5 Jan. 1964.

      The stories suffer from deliberate "literariness."

J261. Hill, William B., S.J. "Fiction." *America*, 113 (27 Nov.
      1965), 686.

      A very brief, favorable review.

J262. Kiely, Robert. "Placing Miss Porter." *Christian Science
      Monitor*, 24 Nov. 1965, p. 15.

      Porter is "deliberately the least romantic of
      contemporary writers." She shows the "sham and
      illusion" inherent in her "exotic settings" and "the tender
      sentiments" of her characters. Still, her graceful prose
      and "the cool order of her thoughts maintain the saving
      balance."

J263. Kilcoyne, Francis P. "New Books." *Catholic World*, 202
      (Jan. 1966), 250.

      The superb characterization, presentation of setting,
      dialogue, and style make the stories well worth reading.

J264. *Library Journal*, 91 (15 Jan. 1966), 448.

      A very brief, favorable review.

J265. McDonald, Gerald D. *Library Journal*, 90 (1 Oct. 1965),
      4111.

      A brief, favorable review.

J266. "Misanthrope." *Time*, 86 (5 Nov. 1965), 122.

Porter's stories reflect her progress toward misanthropy. They show "too little warmth and softness. But hardness endures, and six or eight of her stories will endure like diamonds."

J267. Moore, Harry T. *Chicago Tribune, Books Today*, 3 Oct. 1965, p. 3.

Compares Porter with Willa Cather, as a writer who has been influenced by both rural areas and city scenes. "A more distinctly feminine writer than Willa Cather, Miss Porter is often more complex."

J268. Moss, Howard. "A Poet of the Story." *New York Times, Book Review*, 12 Sept. 1965, pp. 1, 26.

In Porter's stories, "the ambiguity of good and evil is the major theme." Her characters "struggle to escape the necessity of confronting themselves." Most of the stories are good, but "Noon Wine" overshadows the others and puts Porter in the company of Joyce, Mann, Chekhov, James, and Conrad.

J269. O'Brien, E.D. "A Literary Lounger." *Illustrated London News*, 244 (25 Jan. 1964), 142.

Sees only "a weary narcissism" in Porter's stories.

J270. Piercy, Esther. "Eloquent, Satisfying." *Baltimore Sun*, 31 Oct. 1965, p. D-7.

"It is a matter of joyous celebration . . . to find that a cherished writer speaks to one as eloquently and as satisfyingly today as she did yesterday."

J271. *Playboy*, 12 (Dec. 1965), 63.

"Between the covers of this collection are caught the agony points of much of this century, in private life and public affairs."

J272. Pritchett, V.S. "Stones and Stories." *New Statesman*, 67 (10 Jan. 1964), 47–48.

Porter's "singularity as a writer is in her truthful explorations of a complete consciousness of life. Her prose is severe and exact; her ironies are subtle and hard." She solves the basic problem of a short story writer: "how to satisfy exhaustively in writing briefly."
Reprinted in Robert Penn Warren (ed.), *Katherine Anne Porter: A Collection of Critical Essays* (H113).

J273. Pryce-Jones, Alan. "Katherine Anne Porter's Stories— Proof of Her Talent." *New York Herald Tribune*, 26 Oct. 1965, p. 27.

"'He,' 'The Jilting of Granny Weatherall,' 'Pale Horse, Pale Rider,' and 'Holiday' would, any one of them, suffice to put their creator among the unforgettable."

J274. Wardle, Irving. "Touring with a Lady from Texas." (London) *Observer*, 5 Jan. 1964, p. 21.

The stories show Porter's "distaste for life outside the South" and her "fondness for voluptuous self-communication and symbolic dreams, both asserting an affronted sensibility withdrawn from the ugliness of the world."

J275. Washburn, Beatrice. "It's Katherine Anne Porter, But Is It Art?" *Miami* (Florida) *Herald*, 3 Oct. 1965, p. F-7.

Because Porter's stories are so lacking in life, it is hard to understand her status as a first-rate artist.

J276. Wheeler, John. "Fiction in Brief." *Books and Bookmen*, March 1964, p. 30.

One brief paragraph. Dislikes the Miranda stories, like "The Leaning Tower."

The Collected Essays and Occasional Writings

J277. *American Libraries*, 1 (July–Aug. 1970), 715.

"Written with a stringency of style and honesty of opinion richly representative of the intellectual probings of this brilliant literary figure."

J278. *American Literature*, 42 (Nov. 1970), 427.

A brief descriptive review.

J279. *Booklist*, 66 (1 July 1970), 1314.

"Porter reveals herself as a woman wise about literature and life and as perceptive about herself as about others."

J280. Bufkin, E.C. *Georgia Review*, 25 (Summer 1971), 248–51.

The volume is important because it publishes the statements "of a great artist who, by virtue of that unique trait and power of genius, reveals to us fresh and hitherto unthought-of ways of seeing." Porter's work is "classical." "It evinces, through and through, the standard classical characteristics of clarity, economy, control, objectivity, form, veneration for tradition (historical and social as well as artistic).

J281. *Catholic Library World*, 42 (May 1971), 557.

"Sometimes one feels ... that Miss Porter is almost better at criticism and letter-writing than at fiction— certainly much of the material here is far more valuable than all of *Ship of Fools*."

J282. "The Critics Are Saying." *New York Post*, 4 April 1970, p. 39.

Excerpts from Geoffrey Wolff (J301), Glendy Culligan (J283), Hilton Kramer (J286), and Thomas Lask (J287) reviews of *Collected Essays*.

J283. Culligan, Glendy. "Belles-Lettres." *Saturday Review*, 53
(28 March 1970), 29–30.

La Condesa and Mrs. Treadwell of *Ship of Fools*
"represent *in extremis* the polarities of Miss Porter's own
nature as revealed in her 'occasional' writing. When
extremes like these can be balanced, they produce—as in
her best work—the intensity and insight of great
literature. When the slip out of balance, they can produce
banal enthusiasms on the one hand, defensive bitterness
on the other." Her best essays "exhibit a splendid fusion
of passion and discipline, blending the lyrical and
didactic impulses in a prose fabric of remarkable
brilliance." There is an "undercurrent of violence that
pulsates in much of Miss Porter's criticism, vitalizing her
vaunted style." This collection "is far too heavily
burdened with writing that is, indeed,
'occasional' . . . fragments of uneven quality and of
impermanent interest except to biographers yet unborn."

J284. Highsmith, James Milton. "The Other Side of the Desk."
San Francisco Examiner & Chronicle, 19 April 1970,
"This World," pp. 36, 42.

"Her honesty and, even more disarming, her downright
exultation of her own subjectivity defy the reader to say
anything he doesn't believe or to be anything except
what he is."

J285. *Kirkus Reviews*, 37 (15 Dec. 1969), 1360.

"Although she speaks always with directness and
sometimes with desolating accuracy, only a quarter of the
contents of this hefty collection covering four decades of
marginal activity has the mastery of style associated
with her name."

J286. Kramer, Hilton. "At Her Very Best and at Her Unhappy
Worst." *New York Times, Book Review*, 22 March 1970,
p. 4.

The volume is "a literary miscellany that displays her talents at their very best and at their very worst." Porter is "only at her best" as a critic "when she is in perfect sympathy with her subject." "Her critical intelligence is completely hostage to what she likes—and likes extravagantly; in the presence of what she dislikes, it fades into gossip and polemic."

J287. Lask, Thomas. "Miss Porter Speaks Her Mind." *New York Times*, 16 March 1970, p. 41.

Porter "will never write a more revealing memoir" than *Collected Essays*: "contradictions are part of the unity" of her personality. In her prose, "word and thought are so united that her writing has the quality of an art song: each element increases the beauty of the other."

J288. Lawson, Lewis A. "Books: A Fine Story Teller as Essayist." *Washington Sunday Star*, 29 March 1970, p. C-2.

The "work here reviewed contains essays that will surely stand the test of time." "Composed mainly of the living tissue of personal experiences," these pieces describe Porter's "own experiences in such a way that my own experiences are either confirmed or enriched." The pieces are informed by Porter's femininity, "an accepting, tolerant, compassionate regard for the universe and its inhabitants, foolish or otherwise."

J289. Liberman, M.M. "Circe." *Sewanee Review*, 78 (Oct.–Dec. 1970), 689–93.

Although "not very ambitiously edited and without sufficient apparatus to satisfy the professional," the volume "makes a great deal of sense as a collection. It gives us Miss Porter over the years as a writer, critic, woman, aunt, friend, and above all, unflaggingly hard-headed, clear-minded, and sublimely eloquent enemy of the puking dragon, Error." The subject of the collection is "always Miss Porter . . . works of definition of herself."

J290. McDonald, Gerald D. *Library Journal*, 94 (15 Dec. 1969), 4527–28.

"As a critic she is partisan..., but in her considerations of literature and life she is a writer we can not only admire but trust."

J291. McPherson, William. "Porter at 80—In Print." *Washington Post*, 15 May 1970, pp. C1–C2.

"Some of these pieces could have been left out but the best of them are very, very good—and the worst are a reminder that we all have a bad day now and then."

J292. *New York Times, Book Review*, 7 June 1970, pp. 39–40.

"Some of the best work of one of our finest writers." Also appears in the 6 Dec. 1970 issue, pp. 99–100.

J293. "Notes of a Survivor." *Time*, 95 (4 May 1970), 99–100.

"It is the caustic, illusionless side of Miss Porter that pervades much of this collection. . . . Only a few well-made literary essays . . . reflect morning freshness and intelligence at high noon."

J294. Overmeyer, Janet. "Roving Lady Novelist at Large." *Christian Science Monitor*, 7 May 1970, p. B-9.

"This collection should enhance Miss Porter's already exalted reputation by adding the essay to the short story on her list of accomplishments."

J295. Pritchard, William H. "Tones of Criticism." *Hudson Review*, 23 (Summer 1970), 365–66.

Critical of some of the pieces and admiring of others: "One doesn't have to be interested in all these occasional writings to appreciate the superb intelligence of them at their best."

J296. *Publishers Weekly*, 196 (1 Dec. 1969), 38.

This collection shows Porter "more sententious than illuminating. Often, too, one senses a highly charged fastidiousness in her response. . . . But her rich variety of appreciations and insights . . . are continuously interesting."

J297. *Publishers Weekly*, 203 (2 April 1973), 67.

"At all times and in many forms Ms. Porter is always a privilege to read." (Concerns the paperbound edition.)

J298. Rogers, W.G. "The Literary Scene." *New York Post*, 2 March 1970, p. 36.

Her "starting point is usually a writer or writing, but she branches out courageously, thanks to native inquisitiveness, a propensity for taking nothing for granted, a habit of developing a chain of argument and holding on to the last link, thanks to a man's sort of mind in point of vigor and a woman's in point of subtlety and finesse."

J299. Samuels, Charles Thomas. "Placing Miss Porter." *New Republic*, 162 (7 March 1970), 25–26.

Ostensibly a review of *Collected Essays*, most of which Samuels feels does not warrant reprinting, especially since the volume contains no explanation as to why pieces were included. Samuels assesses all Porter's work. Porter "does not so much have a 'vision,' or a point of view, as a suspicion of people less uncommitted"; she is not "a writer of rich imagination, and this fact, more than any other, seems to account for her difficulty in producing much fiction. . . . Distinctive neither in style nor vision, Miss Porter, after all, is at the mercy of her material. Only when she touches something truly rich [as in 'The Jilting of Granny Weatherall,' 'Magic,' 'Noon Wine,' and 'Old Mortality'] is her skepticism undiminishing and her rhetorical clarity a pure advantage."

J300. Sullivan, Walter. "Katherine Anne Porter: The Glories and Errors of Her Ways." *Southern Literary Journal*, 3 (Fall 1970), 114–17.

This volume "lays the worst parts of Miss Porter's mind and soul bare before the world." Porter "is quickly out of her intellectual depth, and she flounders in currents that swirl above her head without seeming to realize that she has lost her footing.... Again and again, reading *The Collected Essays*, one is struck by the narrowness of Miss Porter's view and her willingness to accept as final wisdom whatever cliché comes to hand."

J301. Wiesenfarth, Joseph. *Commonweal*, 92 (7 Aug. 1970), 396–98.

"Those who read Katherine Anne Porter's stories will find this collection of writings a necessary complement; those interested in modern literature will match wits with the critical intelligence of a contemporary."

J302. Wolff, Geoffrey. "Miss Porter." *Newsweek*, 75 (6 April 1970), 91.

"It's a little as though Katherine Anne Porter cleaned out her desk and sent it all off to be published, and it was." The review is critical of some of the pieces but praises those on Cotton Mather, Gertrude Stein, and D.H. Lawrence.

J303. Y[oder], E[d]. *Harper's*, 240 (March 1970), 112.

The collection "discloses a career of impressive scope" characterized by "tough-minded humanism" and "autobiographical" basis for her criticism. "There is no dead wringer of salvation in these essays; there is merely the lifetime's contemplation of one's duty to language, to people and places—by out first lady of letters."

The Never-Ending Wrong

J304. *Booklist*, 74 (15 Sept. 1977), 116–17.

"Porter's name alone is what gives this flaccid, self-serving essay consequence."

J305. Deedy, John. "Sacco and Vanzetti." *Commonweal*, 104 (2 Sept. 1977), 571–72.

The book is "sketchy and rambling, the confusions of a very old person whose interest in the case turns out to have been, and remains still, more institutional than individual—the probable innocence of Sacco and Vanzetti being secondary to whether they got a fair trial—and whose latter-day preoccupation is whether she was 'used' a half-century ago by radicals (read Communists) seeking to exploit the fate of Sacco and Vanzetti for their own ideological purposes."

J306. Fludas, John. *Saturday Review*, 4 (3 Sept. 1977), 32.

"Not always coherent, random and shifting as memory itself, it gains power and reveals some indelible pictures."

J307. F[remont]-S[mith], E[liot]. "Summer Hopes and Fears." *Village Voice*, 22 (27 June 1977), 56.

"This short, vivid memoir recalls the author's efforts in their [Sacco and Vanzetti's] cause, and reassesses the political consequences."

J308. Heymann, C. David. "Sacco and Vanzetti: Fifty Years of Doubt." *Washington Post*, 21 Aug. 1977, pp. G-1, G-4.

"A kind of haphazard memorial record of the inquisition that adds not an iota of information to what we already knew about it."

J309. *Kirkus Reviews*, 45 (1 July 1977), 715.

This work is "marked" by "confused, paper-thin moralism combined with a resolute political ignorance."

J310. Leonard, John. "Reasonably Doubtful." *New York Times*, 22 Aug. 1977, p. 21.

"An unsubstantial and inconsequential essay, from which we learn very little about the case, nothing new about the Communists who came late to the cause and too much about how Miss Porter feels on every occasion of human betrayal."

J311. Marcus, Greil. "Books." *Rolling Stone*, No. 250 (20 Oct. 1977), 101.

"Porter has one thing to say in this skimpy memoir."

J312. Mathewson, Ruth. "Writers and Writing—Remembering Sacco and Vanzetti." *New Leader*, 60 (12 Sept. 1977), 15–16.

When "it departs from personal experience, this little book is so careless of the most elementary, easily ascertainable truths, it blunts her contribution to a broader understanding of the tragedy."

J313. *New Yorker*, 53 (29 Aug. 1977), 87–88.

"She writes like an angel—a shining style, gleaming candor."

J314. Preston, Gregor A. *Library Journal*, 102 (Aug. 1977), 1640.

"The work reveals more about its author than about Sacco and Vanzetti."

J315. *Progressive*, 42 (Feb. 1978), 45.

"The brief memoir of her experiences is primarily a bitter tirade against the communists' cynical manipulation of the young liberals' idealistic beliefs."

J316. *Publishers Weekly*, 211 (13 June 1977), 103.

"It is, in the noblest sense, the memory-laden statement of one of the grand women of American letters about the tragedy which she feels, at 87, to be the moment of our moral and spiritual decline."

J317. Starr, Roger. "Sacco and Vanzetti." *Commentary*, 64 (Dec. 1977), 95–96.

Porter here recognizes that "the Sacco and Vanzetti episode marked a turn in her own development as a writer where the hazy landscape of youth fades from view."

J318. Symons, Julian. "Injustice Department." *Times Literary Supplement*, 3960 (17 Feb. 1978), 198.

The work "is written with her customary brilliant clarity, but the argument from which it proceeds is distinctly confused."

J319. Welty, Eudora. "Post Mortem." *New York Times, Book Review*, 21 Aug. 1977, pp. 9, 29.

"The essence of the book's strength lies in its insight into human motivations, and the unique gifts she has brought to her fiction have been of value to her here as well—even in the specific matter of her subject. . . . This book she has written out of her own life is of profound contemporary significance."

J320. Whitehead, Philip. "Wolf's Prey." *Listener*, 99 (30 March 1978), 418.

"Miss Porter's fragment also deserves to survive, as part of the memory of all the great hopes and muddled ideals of those who took time off to fight when man was wolf to man."

SECTION K
PH.D. DISSERTATIONS

Entries in this section are in alphabetical order.

K1. Adams, Robert Hickman. "The Significance of Point of View in Katherine Anne Porter's *Ship of Fools*." Ph.D., University of Southern California, 1965.

Adams closely examines point of view in the novel and concludes that Porter's manipulation of it is here "put to some relatively new uses." Adams examines Brandt's *Narrenschiff* and some of Porter's short stories as a prelude to the study of the novel. Porter uses point of view in the novel to resist sentimentality, to unify the book, to characterize, interpret and/or evaluate, and to convey the idea that egotism is a barrier to commitment.

K2. Albert, Marie Louise Hannibal. "Children of the Confederacy: A Study of New South Themes in Porter, Welty, McCullers, and O'Connor." Ph.D., University of Hawaii, 1982.

Studies the image of the "New South" in the four writers' work—limited to their treatment of child characters and the themes of love and order, good and evil, and progress. In discussing the seven "Old Order" stories, "The Downward Path to Wisdom," "The Witness," "Old Mortality," "He," and "The Fig Tree,"

Albert concludes that Porter (like the other three) portrays a generally affirmative view of the South.

K3. Bevevino, Mary Margaret. "The Metamorphosis of Economic Disillusionment in Katherine Anne Porter's Society." Ph.D., Pennsylvania State University, 1985.

Traces Porter's growing economic disillusionment in her fiction, essays, and letters. The process culminated in 1977 in "disillusionment with all governments and movements." The focus of Porter's economic concerns was the condition of the poor; she turned for a solution first to revolutionary force, then to communism, and last to political campaigns in democracy before abandoning faith in government. Porter is a Jeffersonian democrat.

K3a. Breedlove, Laura D. "Diary of a Craftsman: The Fiction and Nonfiction of Katherine Anne Porter." Ph.D., University of Georgia, 1989.

Isolates in Porter's published nonfiction her major preoccupations throughout her career, examines the development of these concerns in her thinking, and traces their influence on her stories and on *Ship of Fools*. Her nonfiction prose is an index to the mind of the artist who transmuted these ideas into powerful fiction.

K4. Bunkers, Suzanne Lillian. "Katherine Anne Porter: A Re-Assessment." Ph.D., University of Wisconsin, Madison, 1980.

Analyzes the relationships of women in some of Porter's short fiction, primarily the Miranda stories, to assess their importance to her fictional world vision. The bonding process between generations, classes, and races among the women in Porter's fiction reinforces her world vision of hope and belief in the necessity of community among individuals. There are parallels between the work of Porter and that of Virginia Woolf.

K5. Cimarolli, Mary Lou. "Social Criticism as a Structural Factor in Katherine Anne Porter's Fiction." Ph.D., East Texas State University, 1977.

The social criticism in Porter's fiction functions either as of paramount importance in the structure of a work or as separate from the central structure and design. The fine "threads" of Porter's social criticism are the family as an institution, revolution and war, Christianity as an institution, racism, and marriage as an institution.

K6. Crowder, Elizabeth G. "Image, Metaphor, and Symbol in Katherine Anne Porter's Short Fiction." Ph.D., New York University, 1974.

Porter's use of images, symbols, and metaphors reinforces themes in her short fiction. Her two persistent techniques are the creation of symbolic images to suggest motives and feelings of characters and the use of unobtrusive common objects as symbols and metaphors for human relations and experiences. Twenty-one of the stories are discussed.

K7. DeMouy, Jane Krause. "The Seeds of the Pomegranate: A Study of Katherine Anne Porter's Women." Ph.D., University of Maryland, 1978.

Explores the conflicting images of womanhood depicted in Porter's fiction. The conflict of the traditional female role and assertion of self is the motivating force of most of Porter's most significant stories. In her six earliest stories, Porter portrays archetypal female figures. The stories written from 1929 to 1932 depict the conflict in psychological depth, while those of 1935 and 1936 represent a merging period. This conflict is not addressed in *Ship of Fools*. Porter's women may have love or work, but not both. They struggle with the tension between the desire to be feminine and the desire to be free.

K8. Farrington, Thomas Arthur. "The Control of Imagery in Katherine Anne Porter's Fiction." Ph.D., University of Illinois, Urbana-Champaign, 1972.

Examines all of Porter's fiction for her use of imagery. Her fiction may be divided into realistic or symbolic modes, according to her use of imagery. Her control of imagery, or lack thereof, often determines the success of the individual work.

K9. Gaunt, Marcia Elizabeth. "Imagination and Reality in the Fiction of Katherine Anne Porter and John Cheever: Implications for Curriculum." Ph.D., Purdue University, 1972.

Explores "anxiety dreams" and "wish-fulfillment dreams" in the fiction of Porter and John Cheever. In contrast to her view of the past, Porter sees the future as empty ("anxiety dream"). Idealism ("wish-fulfillment") tempers her pessimistic vision. Because Porter is able to reconcile idealism with unpleasant reality, her works are suitable for use in teaching.

K10. Graves, Allen Wallace. "Difficult Contemporary Short Stories: William Faulkner, Katherine Anne Porter, Dylan Thomas, Eudora Welty and Virginia Woolf." Ph.D., University of Washington, 1954.

Graves classifies twenty types of difficulties encountered in short stories in proposing a pragmatic way to approach the interpretation of difficult stories. Eighteen stories by Faulkner, Welty, Dylan Thomas, Woolf, and Porter are dissected. Porter's "Flowering Judas," "Pale Horse, Pale Rider," and "He" are studied primarily as contrasts to the difficult stories of the others. Porter's stories are closer to "traditional narrative prose," exhibiting "intricacy of technical variation" within tradition. Porter is a "highly accomplished craftsman but within a limited vision."

K11. Greene, Annetta Corgeat. "Katherine Anne Porter: Person and Persona." Ph.D., State University of New York at Binghamton, 1978.

Asserts that Porter's art and life shape each other and become one. Explores that premise in Porter's real and created biography and in what Greene calls the Miranda stories: "The Source," "The Journey," "The Witness," "The Circus," "The Last Leaf," "The Fig Tree," "The Grave," "Old Mortality," "Holiday," "Pale Horse, Pale Rider," "Rope," "Theft," and "Hacienda."

K12. Hatchett, Judie James. "Identity, Autonomy, and Community: Explorations of Failure in the Fiction of Katherine Anne Porter." Ph.D., University of Louisville, 1985.

Takes as Porter's theme "the majestic and terrible failure of the life of man in the Western World" and traces it through her fiction. Porter feels the crisis of modern life in the individual; she portrays four different types of characters who illustrate the various degrees of success and failure in maintaining an autonomous identity relating to others.

K13. Hertz, Robert Neil. "Rising Waters: A Study of Katherine Anne Porter." Ph.D., Cornell University, 1964.

The basic conflict in Porter's fiction, articulated as well in *The Days Before*, is selflessness versus self love. Chapters are devoted to *The Days Before*, "Women Without Men," "Downward Paths to Wisdom," and *Ship of Fools*.

K14. Jensen, Lucile Rae. "The Ideas of Failure and Affirmation in the Short Fiction of Katherine Anne Porter." Ph.D., University of Utah, 1984.

Porter's short fiction examines the causes of failure in the lives of men in the Western world: weaknesses in cultures and in individuals. But by means of the Miranda character, Porter also illustrates that an individual can overcome such weaknesses. Because of Porter's ability to portray failure and her sympathy for her characters, she articulates an acceptance of life and its failure, as well as a sense of affirmation.

K15. Kiernan, Robert F. "The Story Collections of Katherine Anne Porter: Sequence as Context." Ph.D., New York University, 1971.

Kiernan studies the story collections *Flowering Judas, Pale Horse, Pale Rider,* and *The Leaning Tower* as conscious works of art. "Miss Porter's sequences are admirably devised, in part, indispensable contexts for the right understanding of her total statement." In general, the sequences are organized around themes and the manipulation of point of view. Understanding the art of the sequences provides a means to understand the technique of *Ship of Fools.*

K16. Krishnamurthi, Matighatta Gundappa. "Katherine Anne Porter: A Study in Themes." Ph.D., University of Wisconsin, Madison, 1966.

Examines many of Porter's short stories and *Ship of Fools* for common themes. "Miss Porter's fiction dramatizes failure in life and the causes of that failure."

K17. Ledbetter, Nan Wilson Thompson. "The Thumbprint: A Study of People in Katherine Anne Porter's Fiction." Ph.D., University of Texas at Austin, 1966.

Studies sixteen of Porter's short stories and *Ship of Fools* to demonstrate Porter's ability to create "complex and unified convincing individual characters." The characters are explored under the rubrics of "The Young Discoverers," "The Self-Deluded," "The Guilt Haunted," and "The Searchers."

K18. Lugg, Bonelyn. "Mexican Influences on the Work of Katherine Anne Porter." Ph.D., Pennsylvania State University, 1976.

Traces the influences of Mexico on Porter by means of a study of her works with Mexican subjects, settings, or associations.

K19. Lyons, Mary Phoebe. "Art and Politics in the Writings of Katherine Anne Porter." Ph.D., University of Rhode Island, 1981.

Explores Porter's politics and aesthetics in her nonfiction and letters as a means to understand and interpret her fiction. Porter's belief in the ability of art to create order informs her themes and techniques. "Porter saw contemporary politics as the perversion of the order she believed in and endeavored to reveal it as such through her art."

K20. McLaughlin, Marilou Briggs. "The Love Dialectic." Ph.D., State University of New York at Binghamton, 1975.

Explores the use and treatment of romantic love in *Ship of Fools*, Joyce Carol Oates's *Them*, Doris Lessing's *The Golden Notebook*, and Christina Stead's *The Man Who Loved Children*. Porter's too polemic treatment in the novel spoils it. All of the novels suggest that women depend too much on romantic love to make their lives rich and full.

K21. Meyers, Judith Marie. "'Comrade-Twin': Brothers and Doubles in the World War I Prose of May Sinclair, Katherine Anne Porter, Vera Brittain, Rebecca West, and Virginia Woolf." Ph.D., University of Washington, 1985.

"Pale Horse, Pale Rider" is an example of a work in which the heroine/author re-enacts combatant experience through a male figure who is a psychological double.

K22. Miles, Lee Robert. "Unused Possibilities: A Study of Katherine Anne Porter." Ph.D., University of California, Los Angeles, 1973.

Miles traces four recurrent themes in Porter's fiction and nonfiction: threat of evil, rarity of love, need for rationality, and importance of childhood in molding personality.

K23. Murphy, Edward F. "Henry James and Katherine Anne Porter: 'Endless Relations.'" Ph.D., University of Ottawa, 1959.

Explores the influence of Henry James on the theory and practice of Porter. Murphy finds affinities in their biographies, philosophies, techniques, and themes. The relations between them are "endless" and provide possibilities for further investigation.

K24. Nance, William Leslie. "The Principle of Rejection: A Study of the Thematic Unity in the Fiction of Katherine Anne Porter." Ph.D., University of Notre Dame, 1963.

Nance defines the "principle of rejection" as the central thematic pattern unifying Porter's fiction. The "principle of rejection impelled Miss Porter into art, but at the same time severely limited that art in both quantity and scope." Outlines the characteristics and motifs of the rejection theme and categorizes the works as either alpha (containing a semi-autobiographical or subjective protagonist) or beta (not containing such a protagonist). Chapters are devoted to *Flowering Judas*, stories of "theme and variations," the Miranda stories, and *Ship of Fools*.

K25. Osta, Winifred Hubbard. "The Journey Pattern in Four Contemporary Novels." Ph.D., University of Arizona, 1970.

Compares Julio Cortazar's *Los Premios, Ship of Fools,* Moacir C. Lopes's *Belona, Latitude Norte,* and Carlos Fuentes's *Cambio de Piel.* All use the journey as their basic structural metaphor to re-create a vision of the chaos of modern society and of modern man's predicament. All add the heroic quest pattern to indicate the possibility of a solution to the conflict in man's mind between chaos and order. Porter's view is expressed through Dr. Schumann's recognition and refusal of the challenge to reach out to another individual.

K26. Pickard, Linda Haskovec. "A Stylo-Linguistic Analysis of Four American Writers." Ph.D., Texas Woman's University, 1974.

Surveys the history of rhetoric and style before making a close analysis based on counts of lexical and syntactic elements in selections from Hemingway's Nick Adams stories, the Miranda stories, Salinger's *The Catcher in The Rye,* and Plath's *The Bell Jar.* Concludes that gender is a lesser factor of literary style than the time in which a writer is born; that is, that Hemingway and Porter have more affinities than do Porter and Plath.

K27. Redden, Dorothy S. "The Legend of Katherine Anne Porter." Ph.D., Stanford University, 1975.

Redden traces the theme of alienation in "Miranda characters" in some of Porter's fiction: "The Old Order," "The Source," "The Witness," "The Last Leaf," "The Jilting of Granny Weatherall," "The Circus," "The Fig Tree," "The Grave," "Virgin Violeta," "Old Mortality," "Pale Horse, Pale Rider," "Flowering Judas," *Ship of Fools,* and "Holiday."

K28. Schwartz, Edward. "The Fiction of Katherine Anne Porter." Ph.D., Syracuse University, 1953.

Porter rejected the "tradition of orthodoxy" and allied herself with "the tradition of dissent"; she is the inheritor of the "tradition of dissent and inquiry, of selfless devotion to the search for truth and beauty and order in the world of art." Discusses Porter' fiction and nonfiction through 1952. Concludes that Porter was devoted to the search for understanding and had a "tragic attitude."

K29. Sugisaki, Kazuko. "Harmonious Motion of Life: A Comparative Study of the Works of Katherine Anne Porter and Kanoto Okamoto." Ph.D., Occidental College, 1973

Porter's search to discover the relationship of art to the artist led her to a belief in her personal experiences. Most of her stories are, in a sense, moral stories. Both Porter and Okamoto were motivated by everyday reality, and both were constantly occupied with the theme of the past. Both writers found in their pasts the existential meaning of their present and future which motivated their most important creative works. Both affirmed the value of life on earth: life is to be lived out wholesomely by individuals who can fulfill its potentiality and give it an order which can be passed on to future generations. Porter's art is proof of her faith in man's future.

K30. Titus, Mary Ellen. "Katherine Anne Porter's Fictions." Ph.D., University of North Carolina at Chapel Hill, 1986.

Explores Porter's biography, fiction, and unpublished writing with the tools of feminist and psychoanalytic critical theory. In her quest for an illusive, imagined perfection in life and work, Porter created fictions which connect her life and her work. These "fictions" repeat the same story: "a lost world associated with love, security and wholeness of identity; a painful, emotionally destructive experience which fragments the secure self; subsequent exile from the 'country of the heart'; a frightening sense of insecure identity, perpetual alienation; and a perpetual quest to locate and so regain the former happiness and sense of self-perfection." Examines the "texts" of Porter's family relations, social and sexual relations, and public identity.

K31. Vliet, Vida Ann. "The Shape of Meaning: A Study in the Development of Katherine Anne Porter's Fiction Form." Ph.D., Pennsylvania State University, 1968.

Porter's work as a whole combines the objective methods of the past with the subjective methods of the newer writers; her thematic development over the course of her work is from optimism to despair. Studies sixteen of Porter's short stories and *Ship of Fools* in detail.

K32. Waldrip, Louise Dolores Baker. "A Bibliography of the Works of Katherine Anne Porter." Ph.D., University of Texas at Austin, 1967.

Attempts to include all translations, stories, poems, essays, books, contributions to periodicals, introductions or afterwords to books, and all other types of contributions to books written by Porter up to 1965.
Published as the first part of Waldrip and Shirley Ann Bauer, *A Bibliography of the Works of Katherine Anne Porter and A Bibliography of Criticism of the Works of Katherine Anne Porter* (F8).

K33. Walters, Dorothy Jeanne. "The Theme of Destructive Innocence in the Modern Novel: Greene, James, Cary, Porter." Ph.D., University of Oklahoma, 1960.

Walters explores both active and passive destructive innocents in Graham Greene's *The Quiet American*, Henry James's *The Golden Bowl*, Joyce Cary's *The Horse's Mouth*, and Porter's "Noon Wine." Olaf Helton is a passive agent of destruction in Porter's study of "the paradox of destructive innocence." Walters also briefly discusses "Flowering Judas," "Pale Horse, Pale Rider," "The Leaning Tower," "Theft," and "He."

K34. Yosha, Lee William. "The World of Katherine Anne
     Porter." Ph.D., University of Michigan, 1960.

   Treats twenty-three of Porter's stories by categorizing
   them under four different themes: the person in conflict
   with his past, the person in conflict with the family, a
   woman in conflict with the male-constructed world, and
   the person in conflict with "foreign attitudes." Does not
   discuss "Virgin Violeta," "The Martyr," "The Journey,"
   and "Holiday."

INDEX OF AUTHORS,
EDITORS, AND TRANSLATORS

Abdullah, Sofie AA2 (a)

Abrahams, William B24, B40, I90

Acosta, Marta AA2(j)

Adams, Robert Hickman K1

Akio, Kudô AA5(n)

Albert, Marie Louise Hannibal K2

Aldington, Richard I128

Aldridge, John W. I18, J245

Alexander, Jean I91

Allen, Charles G78, H1–3, J112

Allen, Henry G1–2

Alvarez, Ruth M. F4

Amory, Cleveland G3

Angoff, Charles J22

Anson, Cherrill G4

Aono, Kouko A25

Archer, Eugene G5

Arimond, Carroll J158

Ashford, Gerald C115

Auchincloss, Louis H6, J159

Aycock, Wendell M. H55

Babcock, Frederic G8

Bain, Robert G 64

Baker, Carlos J114–15

Baker, Herschel J82

Baker, Howard H7–7a, J15

Baldeshwiler, Eileen H8

Bandler, Michael G9

Barnes, Bart G10

Barnes, Daniel I44

Barr, Beryl C102

Barrett, Phyllis W. H9

Bart, Peter G11

Bates, H.E. H10

Bauer, Shirley Ann F8

Bayley, Isabel A23

Baym, Nina B21

Beach, Joseph Warren J83

Beals, Carleton G12

Beards, Richard I61

Beatty, Richard Croom B8, B17

Beck, Warren J160

Becker, Laurence A. I45

Bedford, Sybille J161

Belaguer, Manuel AA2(j)

Belitt, Ben J42

Bell, Barbara Currier I21
Bell, Vereen I22
Benardete, M.J. C30
Benstock, Shari G13
Berg, Paul G14
Bevilacqua, Winifred F. H19
Bevivino, Mary Margaret K3
Birss, John H. F1
Bishop, John Peale B13, G184
Bixby, George F2
Blackwell, Earl G137
Block, Maxine G138
Blomkvist, Torsten AA5(w)
Bloom, Harold H11, H25, H68,
    H114, H116, H122, I4, I29,
    I35, I37, I46, I84, I87, I99,
    J212
Bloom, Lynn Z. B13
Bluefarb, Sam I5
Bo, Adriane AA3(f)
Bockow-Blüthgen, Hansi
    AA1(d), AA3(c)
Bode, Carl J162
Bode, Elroy H12
Bode, Winston G17
Bogan, Louise J1
Bolsterli, Margaret H13
Bonazza, Blaze O. B11–13
Bond, Alice Dixon J163
Booth, Wayne C. I80, J164
Bordwell, Harold J245
Boudin, Leonard B. G20
Boutell, Clip G21
Boyle, Kay C122, I42
Brack, O.M., Jr. H33
Bradbury, John M. H14
Bradbury, Malcolm J165, J245
Bradford, M.E. H15
Bradley, Van Allen J166
Brannan, Dana H16
Breedlove, Laura K. K3a
Breit, Harvey G23
Brewster, Dorothy J43

Bride, Sister Mary, O.P. I6
Brinkmeyer, Robert H., Jr.
    H17
Brooks, Cleanth B21–22, G24,
    I23
Brown, John L. G25
Bruno, Anne Turner G26
Bryer, Jackson R. F4
Buckley, Tim G27
Buckman, Gertrude J86
Bufkin, E.C. G28, J280
Bunkers, Suzanne Lillian K4
Burgess, Anthony J248
Burnett, Hallie C110
Burnett, Whit B13, C56, C110
Byrne, Evelyn B. C132

Cairns, Huntington C41
Camati, Anna Stegh H18
Carr, Virginia Spencer G30
Carson, Barbara Harrell H19
Cassill, R.V. B12–13
Cassini, Igor G31
Chamberlain, John G32, J16,
    J25, J72, J168
Chapin, Ruth J118
Chartburus, Arporn AA3(h)
Cheatham, George H19a–20,
    I81
Chisholm, Elise G129
Cimarolli, Mary Lou K5
Clark, Eleanor G33, J26
Clarke, Gerald G34
Clepper, Patrick J169
Clerc, Charles B22, I66
Clyman, Toby W. H73
Cobb, Joann P. I46
Colby, Veneta C87
Cole, Hunter G34a
Collins, Margaret J48
Connolly, Cyril J28, J251
Core, George G163, G176, H21,
    H50–51, H90–91, H114,

H116, I1, I18, I23, I38, I89, I98–99, I106, J125, J245
Corry, John G35
Cory, Jim H22
Cournos, John J170
Cowley, Malcolm G36, J17
Cowser, Robert G. I47
Crane, Hart G37
Crawford, Kitty Barry G38
Crowder, Elizabeth G. K6
Crume, Paul J49
Cruttwell, Patrick H23
Culligan, Glendy G39–41, J171, J283
Curley, Daniel H24, I24
Cutrer, Thomas W. G42

Daiches, David J87, J119
Daniels, Sally I92
da Silva Ramos, Péricles Eugênio AA2(i)
Davis, Robert Gorham B17
Dawson, Margaret Cheney J3
Day, Franklin J172
Deasy, Br. Paul Francis, F.S.C. I34
Deedy, John J305
DeMouy, Jane F4, H24a–25, K7
Denham, Alice G44
Detweiler, Robert I48
DeVries, Peter I93
Diamond, Arlyn H19
Dickson, Thomas J29
Dlouhý, Karol AA5(a)
Dolan, Mary Anne G46
Dolbier, Maurice G47
Donadio, Stephen J252
Donoghue, Denis J253
Dorr, Bill J173
Dorsey, John G48
Downing, Francis J88
Drake, Robert J174

Duchene, Anne J175
Duff, Charles I43
Duke, Maurice F4

Eagleton, Sanda B11
Edwards, Lee R. H19
Eidlitz, Elizabeth M. B24
Elliott, Emory H26
Emmons, Winfred S. H27
English, Charles J176
Estes, David C. I49
Etulain, R.W. F3

Fadiman, Clifton B8, J50, J177
Farrington, Thomas Arthur K8
Featherstone, Joseph J254
Fefferman, Stan J178
Fetterley, Judith H29
Fiedler, Leslie A. J121
Finkelstein, Sidney J180
Finn, James J181
Flanders, Jane H30–31, I82
Flood, Ethelbert, O.F.M. I7
Flora, Joseph M. G64
Flores, Angel C52
Fludas, John J306
Foley, Martha B22
Ford, Hugh G52
Forkner, Ben B11, B20, B40
Fox, Renée C. I94
Frankel, Haskel G55
Fremantle, Anne J123
Fremont-Smith, Eliot J307
Fries, Maureen G56

Gannett, Lewis G57, J51
Gardiner, Harold C. J182
Gardiner, Judith Kegan I25
Gardini, Carlos AA6(e)
Gaston, Edwin W., Jr. H32
Gaunt, Marcia Elizabeth K9
Gelfant, Blanche H. G58
Gerlach, John I8

Gernes, Sonia I83
Gessel, Michael H33
Gibbons, Kaye H34
Gibson, Rochelle G59
Gilbert, Sandra M. B11
Gilroy, Harry G60
Givner, Joan C1–2, C51, F4, G2,
　　G17, G38, G45–48, G61–71,
　　G73, G82, G105, G108,
　　G124, G128–29, G149–50,
　　G153, G163, G169, G178,
　　G181, H35–38, I56–57, I96,
　　I120–21
Glicksberg, Charles I97
Goldberg, Barbara J256
Goldsborough, Diana J183
Goodman, Charlotte I50
Gordon, Caroline B21, H40
Gorn, Leslie J184
Gottfried, Leon I9
Gower, Herschel I30
Graves, Allen Wallace K10
Gray, Richard H41
Green, Martin G72
Greenbaum, Leonard C119
Greene, A.C. J185
Greene, Annetta Corgeat K11
Greene, George H42
Greene, Graham J30
Greene, Maxine J186
Greiff, Trygve AA5(o)
Gretlund, Jan Nordby H43–44
Groff, Edward I62
Gross, Beverly I10
Grumbach, Doris G73
Gubar, Susan B11
Gullason, Thomas A. J257
Gunn, Drewey Wayne G74
Gustaitis, Rosa G75
Gwin, Minrose H45

Hafley, James I60
Hagopian, John V. H46, J258

Hall, James B. B10
Hamovitch, Mitzi Berger
　　C142–44, G76–77
Hankins, Leslie K. H47
Hansen, Hagmund AA5(b)
Hansen, Harry B24, J89
Hardy, John Edward H48, I38,
　　J124
Harkness, Don H47
Harrison, Gilbert A. J254
Hart, Elizabeth J18
Hartley, Lodwick G163, G176,
　　H49–51, H90–91, H114,
　　H116, I1–2, I18, I23, I89,
　　I98–99, I106, J125, J187,
　　J245
Hartung, Philip T. J52
Hatchett, Judie James K12
Haycraft, Howard C55
Heilman, Robert H52, I99
Hendrick, George H53, I31,
　　I100
Hendrick, Willene H53
Hennessy, Rosemary H54
Herbst, Josephine I19, J31
Hernandez, Frances H55
Hertz, Robert N. I101, K13
Heymann, C. David J308
Hicks, Granville J188, J259
Hiers, John T. G172
Higgins, Cecile J32
Higgins, John J260
Highsmith, James Milton J284
Hill, William B., S.J. J261
Hindle, John J. G184
Hobson, Laura Z. J126
Hoffman, Burton C. C56
Hoffman, Frederick J. G78,
　　H56, I63
Hogan, William G79, J189
Holmes, Theodore J190
Hoopes, Robert B17
Horton, Philip C29, G80

Howard, Maureen C83
Howe, Ilana Wiener B9
Howe, Irving B9
Howell, Elmo H57, I64
Hubbell, Jay B. B18, H58
Hughes, Linda K. I3
Humboldt, Charles J191
Humphrey, William G81
Humphries, Rolfe C30
Hutchens, John K. J192
Hyman, Stanley Edgar J193

Ibieta, Gabriella H59
Ilona, Róna AA5(j–k)
Inge, M. Thomas F4
Isherwood, Christopher J53

Jackson, Katherine Gauss
 J127
Jacobs, Robert D. H52, H119
Jacobsen, Ole AA3(a)
Janeway, Elizabeth G82
Jarrett, Thomas D. J194
Jason, Phillip K. G83
Jefferson, Margo G84
Jensen, Lucile Rae K14
Johnson, James William H60,
 I76
Johnson, Shirley E. H61
Johnston, Laurie G85
Jones, Anne Goodwyn H62
Jones, Frank N. J195
Jones, Howard Mumford J73,
 J90
Jones, Llewelyn H63
Jorgenson, Bruce W. I35
Joselyn, Sister M., O.S.B. H64,
 I26, I102
Josephson, Matthew G86

Kamata, Nobuko G87
Kaplan, Charles B13, H65
Karl, Frederick J. I103

Kasten, Maurice J196
Kauffmann, Stanley J197
Kauppi, Kaija AA5(d)
Kazin, Alfred I104
Kelley, Gilbert H. J91
Keppler, C.F. I65
Kernan, Michael G93
Kiely, Robert H66, J262
Kiernan, Robert F. F5, K15
Kilcoyne, Francis P. J263
Kilstoffe, June J128
Kimper, Kenneth W. B13
Kinney, Arthur F. B13
Kirkpatrick, Smith I105
Kirsch, Robert R. J198
Kobayashi, Kenji AA6(b)
Kohler, Dayton J199
Kostelenos, D.P. AA5(i)
Krähenbuhl, Olivía AA3(e)
Kramer, Dale I27
Kramer, Hilton J286
Krishnamurthi, M.G. H67, I84,
 K16
Kristol, Irving J92
Kunitz, Stanley C26, C55, C87
Kuzumi, Kazushi A24

Lalley, J.M. J200
Langer, Elinor G95–97
La Rocquetinker, Edward J33
Lask, Thomas J287
Lass, Abraham H. B11
Lasswell, Mary G98, J201
Laughlin, James C38, C54
Lawson, Lewis A. J288
Lease, Benjamin J202
Leath, Helen I58
Ledbetter, Nan G99, K17
Lefkowitz, Bernard G100
Lehan, Richard J203
Leiter, Louis B22, I66
Leonard, John J310
LeRoy, Gaylord C. J130

Levitas, Gloria G102
Liberman, M.M. C123, G103,
    H68, I36, I106–08, J289
Litz, A. Walton B13
Loe, Thomas I85
Lopez, Enrique Hank G104–05
Lugg, Bonelyn K18
Lyons, Mary Phoebe K19
Lytle, Andrew G183

Macy, John H63
Madden, David I11
Maddocks, Melvin J206
Male, Roy R. I67
Malfetti, James B24
Malik, Meera H69–70
Marcus, Greil J311
Marian, Eugen B. AA5(t)
Marsden, Malcolm M. H71
Marshall, Margaret H72
Martin, Judith G106
Martin, Ron J207
Mathewson, Ruth J312
Matthiessen, F.O. I86, J94
May, Charles E. H73
Mayer, David R. I51
Mazzolani, Lidia Storoni
    AA2(g), AA6(a)
McAlmon, Robert C122
McClave, Heather H114
McCormick, John I20
McDonald, Gerald D. J131,
    J265, J290
McDonald, John J4
McDonnell, Thomas P. J208
McDowell, Edwin G107
McDowell, Frederick P. J132
McGrory, Mary G108, J133,
    J209
McIntyre, John P. I109
McLaughlin, Marilon Briggs
    K20
McMurtry, Larry H74

McPherson, William J291
McQuade, Donald B21
Mercer, Charles G109
Meyers, Judith Marie K21
Meyers, Robert I52
Miles, Lee Robert K22
Miller, Paul W. I110
Millett, Fred B. G111
Mitgang, Herbert G114
Miyata, Toshichika I77
Mizener, Arthur G115, J134
Moacyr Garcia, Othon AA1(h)
Mochtar Lubis, Diter-
    djemahkan oleh AA2(f)
Moddelmog, Debra A. I37
Molloy, Robert J95
Molz, Kathleen G116
Monroe, Harold J135
Mooney, Harry J., Jr. H75
Moore, Harry T. J267
Moore, Teresa G180
Morgan, Charles J96
Moritz, Charles G139
Morley, Christopher J96
Morse, J. Mitchell J210
Morse, Samuel French J44,
    J136
Mort, John G117
Mortimer, Gail G118
Mortimer, Raymond J211
Moss, Howard J212, J268
Motti, Adriana AA5(l–m)
Moult, Thomas J54
Munford, Howard M. J137
Murphy, Edward F. H76, I111,
    J213, K23
Murray, James G. J214
Murray, Michele J215

Nance, William L. G120, H77–
    78, K24
Narasimhaiah, C.D. I84
Nash, Anne J35

Nathan, Paul S. G121
Naylor, Pauline G121a
Newquist, Roy G124
Nichols, Esther K. J36
Nichols, Lewis G125
Nordell, Rod G127
Novak, Josephine G128–29
Nykoruk, Barbara G46

O'Brien, E.D. J269
O'Brien, Edward J. B12–13,
B17, B20, B24
O'Brien, John H. J218
O'Connor, Flannery G132,
G159
O'Connor, William Van H79,
H98, J219
Okada, Tazuko AA6(b)
Olsen, Tillie G133
Onur, Erdem AA5(x)
Orvis, Mary Burchard H80
Osta, Winifred Hubbard K25
Overmeyer, Janet J294

Packer, Nancy Huddleston
B17
Page, Evelyn J56
Parker, Dorothy J221
Parrish, Stephen Maxfield
J141
Partridge, Colin H81
Peden, William B18, I40
Penzler, Otto M. C132
Pernoud, Régine C85
Perrine, Laurence B11
Perry, Robert L. I32
Phillips, McCandlish G135
Pickard, Linda Haskovec K26
Pickering, James H. B17
Pickerel, Paul J222
Pierce, Marvin I68
Piercy, Esther J270
Pinkerton, Jan H82

Pires do Amorim, Geraldo
AA1(h)
Placzek, Hannelore AA4(a)
Plante, Patricia R. I112
Poirier, Richard B40
Poore, Charles J20, J142, J223
Poore, Dudley C52
Porta, Baldomero AA5(v)
Porter, Paul G140
Poss, S.H. H84
Powers, Dennis J224
Powers, James F. H85
Prager, Leonard I122
Prater, William I28
Prescott, Oliver J98–99
Prescott, Peter S. B12, G141
Pressly, Eugene A11
Preston, Gregor A. J314
Pritchard, William H. J295
Pritchett, V.S. B13, J272
Pryce-Jones, Alan J273
Putcamp, Luise, Jr. J144

Quinn, Kerker J94

Rackliffe, John J94
Rademacher, Susanna AA5(f–
h)
Rahv, Philip J58
Ramsdell, Charles G146
Read, Martha J100
Redden, Dorothy I12, K27
Reid, Forrest J59
Reitz, Rosetta J225
Rice, Philip Blair J60
Richardson, Eudora Ramsay
JJ6
Robinson Cecil H86
Robkin, Leslie Y. B8
Rockwell, Jeanne G147
Rogers, W.G. J298
Rohrberger, Mary I13
Rolo, Charles J. J145

Rood, Karen Lane G63
Rood, William B., Jr. I41
Rooke, Constance I29
Root, Waverly Lewis J14
Rosenfield, Paul J61
Rosson, John G148
Roy, Emil B11–13
Roy, Sandra B11–13
Rubin, Louis D., Jr. B17, G64,
    H52, H119, I113, J226
Rugoff, Milton J75
Ruoff, James G149, I114
Ryan, Edwin J76
Ryan, Marjorie H87–88, J227

Sachs, Barbara Turner C102
Salpeter, Harry J7
Samuels, Charles Thomas
    J299
Samway, Patrick B11, B20, B40
Sapieha, Virgilia J101
Sarcone, Elizabeth G183
Schack, Elizabeth AA3(d)
Schoettler, Carl G150
Schorer, Mark B24, H89, J146,
    J228
Schwartz, Edward F6, H90–91,
    J147, K28
Scott, Shirley Clay H92–93
Secrest, Meryle G151
Shattuck, Charles J94
Shearer, Gordon K. G153
Shenker, Israel G154
Sherman, Caroline B. J63
Sherman, John K. J148
Sherman, Thomas B. J229
Shi, David E. G155
Sibley, Celestine J149
Sibon, Marcelle AA1(c),
    AA2(b), AA3(b), AA5(e)
Sjögren, Erik AA3(g)
Skroczyńska, Maria AA6(d)
Slocum, Kathleen H94

Smith, Charles W. I123–24
Smith, Del I114
Smith, Harrison G156
Smith, J. Oates I69
Smith, Miles A. J231
Smith, Rebecca W. H95
Snell, George H96
Solá de Brinckman, Maria
    Elvira AA1(i)
Solotaroff, Theodore I115
Soskin, William J64
Southern, Terry J232
Spence, Jon I116
Spencer, Theodore J102
Spiller, Robert E. H97, J150
Srinivasan, Seetha G34a
Stallings, Sylvia J151
Stallman, Robert Wooster
    G157, H98, I18
Stanford, Donald E. H99
Starr, Roger J317
Stegner, Mary B8
Stegner, Wallace B8, J65
Stein, William Bysshe I125
Steloff, Frances G158
Stephen, C. Ralph G159
Stern, Carol Simpson I126
Stoker, Ben J234
Stone, Alan A. B24
Stone, Sue Smart B24
Stone Wilfred B17
Stout, Janis P. H100, I70
Straumann, Heinrich H101
Straus, Ralph J66
Stroud, Kandy G160
Subrahmanyam, K.N. AA1(j)
Sugisaki, Kazuko K29
Šuklje, Rapa AA5(u)
Sullivan, Nancy B17
Sullivan, Richard J152
Sullivan, Walter I78, I116a,
    J300
Suzue, Akiko H102

Suzue, Akiko H102
Swinnerton, Frank J67
Sylvester, William A. F7
Symons, Julian J318

Takahashi, Masao AA2(h)
Takano, Fumi A26
Tarnowska, Krystyna AA5(s),
 AA6(c)
Tasman, Norma L. B11
Tate, Allen B13, B21, C41,
 G183–84, J8
Taubman, Robert J235
Taylor, Norris J153
Teixeira, Cristina Maria H103
Thayer, Mary V.R. G161
Theall, D. Bernard J236
Thomas, M. Wynn 171
Thompson, Barbara G163
Thompson, John J237
Thompson, Ralph G164, J68
Thorburn, David B23
Timson, Stephen I53
Tinkle, Lon G165, J154
Titus, Mary H104, K30
Trilling, Diana J105
Trilling, Lionel J77
Trimmer, Joseph F. B11, B13
Troy, George J238
Troy, William J38

Uhlmann, Joachim AA1(e),
 AA3(d)
Ulrich, Carolyn F. G78
Unrue, Darlene Harbour
 H105–06, I59
Unterecker, John C125, G168

Vallandro, Leonel AA5(p–r)
Van Doren, Mark C41, C49–51
Van Gelder, Robert G169
Van Nostrand, A.D. AA3(f)
Van Zyl, John H107

Vliet, Vida Ann K31
von Schweinitz, Maria
 AA2(c–e)
Voss, Arthur H108

Wade, C. B11, B13
Walcutt, Charles C. I117
Waldhorn, Robert I18
Waldron, Ann G170a
Waldrip, Louise F8, K32
Wallis, Bruce I29
Walsh, Thomas F. H109, I14–
 16, I33, I72–73, I79, I87,
 I129
Walter, James I17
Walters, Dorothy Jeanne K33
Walton, Eda Lou J39
Walton, Edith H. J40–41, J45,
 J69, J79
Walton, Gerald I118
Wanning, Andrews H110
Wardle, Irving J274
Warren, Robert Penn B8,
 B21–22, C89, G105, G171,
 G176, H91, H111–17, I23,
 I38, I106, I115, J106, J159,
 J161, J212, J228, J272
Washburn, Beatrice J275
Watkins, Floyd C. B8, B17,
 G172
Webber, Alan C. C173
Weber, Brom I119
Wecter, Dixon I86
Weeks, Edward J9, J107
Weil, Fran G174
Weiner, Rex G175
Welker, Robert L. I30
Welty, Eudora C40, J319
Wescott, Glenway G176, J70,
 J108
West, Anthony J71
West, Ray B., Jr. H117–20, I18
Weston, Mildred J155

Weyland, Ana AA3(f)
Wheeler, John J276
Whicher, George H121, J109
White, Jean G177
Whiteaker, Mildred G178
Whitehead, Philip J320
Wiesenfarth, Joseph H122, I1,
    I54, I127, J301
Williams, Jerry T. F9
Wilson, Angus J240
Wilson, Edmund J110
Wilson, Tom J241
Winslow, Marcella Comes
    G180
Winsten, Archer G181
Winters, Yvor J10
Wolfe, Bertram D. J21, J80
Wolfe, Don M. C86
Wolfe, Peter I55
Wolff, Geoffrey J302
Woodress, James F10
Wykes, Alan H123
Wynn, Ellen C. B17

Yanella, Philip R. I88
Yanitell, Victor R., S.J. J242
Yeiser, Frederick J157, J243
Ylvisaker, Miriam J244
Yoder, Ed J303
Yosha, Lee William K34
Young, Marguerite J111
Young, Thomas D. B17, G183–
    84
Young, Vernon A. H124
Youngblood, Sarah I89

Zyla, Wolodymyr T. H55

INDEX OF PORTER TITLES

Only English-language titles are listed. A title is listed twice only if it applies both to a book and to a piece included within a book. More than one reference is listed after a title only if the contents of the entries are different from one another.

"Acceptance by Miss Porter" C121
"Act of Faith: 4 July 1942" C47
"Actress Lover of Good Books Aspires to Try Hand at Writing" D21
"Adventure in Living" C83
"The Adventures of Hadji: A Tale of a Turkish Coffee House" B4
"Affectation of Praehiminincies" C45
"After a Long Journey" C93
"Airplane Comedy Has Catchy Songs" D66
"Allocution de Mme. Katherine Anne Porter" C76
"American Critics Discredit Fetish to Foreign Artists" D68
"American Statement" C47
"American Statement: 4 July 1942" C47
"Among Our Contributors" C11
"And to the Living Joy" C131
Anniversary in a Country Cemetery A10
"Anniversary in a Country Cemetery" C36
"The Art of Katherine Mansfield" E46
"Artist and Playwright Part over Question of Cut Doorway" D43
"Audubon's Happy Land" C33
"Ay, Que Chamaco" E14

"Beauty Unadorned Attracts When War Hero Is Passed By" D49
"Beerbohm Bailiwick" E60
"'The Best Books I Read This Year'—Twelve Distinguished Opinions" C70
"'Better 'Ole' Pleases Crowd at Broadway" D80
"Big Audience Sees Comedy at Tabor" D99
"'Billeted' Is Clever Comedy of England" D40
"Black, White, Red, Yellow and the Pintos" E21
"Bohemian Futility" E37
"Book Week Symposium on Modern Fiction" C112
"Books I Have Liked" C66, 69, 79
"'The Boss' Is Big Hit with Denham Crowd" D28
"Bouquet for October" C25
"A Bright Particular Faith—A.D. 1700" C27
"Broadway's Last Play Merits High Praise" D83
"Brother Spoiled a Romance" C2

"The Calm, Pure Art of Willa Cather" E54
"'Cameo Kirby' Wins Denham Audience" D32
"Caretakers Guard Stage Genius—Mothers, Husbands and Sisters" D27
"Carle's Big Comedy Scores at Broadway" D45
"The Charmed Life" C44
"Children and Art" C20
A Christmas Story A17
"A Christmas Story" C63
"The Circus" B18
"Clever Little Play Heads Orpheum Bill" D63
The Collected Essays and Occasional Writings of Katherine Anne Porter A20
The Collected Stories of Katherine Anne Porter A19
"Comedians Win Tabor Crowd—Bears Entertain Children" D60
"The Complete Letter Writer" E9
"La Conquistadora" E16
"Corridos" C16
"The Cracked Looking-Glass" B14
"Current Comment—China's Plight C61

"Dancers Top Bill at Orpheum Debut" D103
"The Dark Ages of New England—The Puritan Emerges Alive and Softened" E31
The Days Before A14
"The Days Before" C59

"A Day's Work" B25
A Defense of Circe A15
"A Defense of Circe" C81
"Defoe—*Moll Flanders*," "(c.1661–1731)—" C41
"Denham Presents 'Husband' Comedy" D54
"Denham Presents Real Melodrama" D65
"Denham Saves Time by Revolving Stage" D70
"A Disinherited Cosmopolitan" E41
"Dora, the Dodo, and Utopia" E10
"The Downward Path to Wisdom" B24
"Drama at Denham Has Many Thrills" D44
"Dulce et Decorum Est" E45
"Dylan Thomas" E65-67

"E.M. Forster" E62
"E.M. Forster Speaks Out for the Things He Holds Dear" E62
"Edith Sitwell's Steady Growth to Great Poetic Art" E55
"Eleanor Clark" E64
"Embarkation" B31
"Enchanted" C12
"Enthusiast and Wildcatter" E20
"Enthusiastic Audience Welcomes Haru Omuki" D24
"Etiquette in Action" E13
"Eudora Welty and 'A Curtain of Green'" C40
"Everybody Is a Real One" E19
"Example to the Young" E42
"The Exile" B34
"Extracting Blood from a Population of Turnips" C139
"'The Eyes of Youth' Entertaining Play" D76

"The Fair-Haired Man" E36
"The Faithful Princess" B2
"The Family" E29
"Famous Stars of Past Jokes of Today on Stage, Says Critic" D78
"Famous Tabor Drop Curtain Dusted and Placed in Service" D30
"The Fiesta of Guadalupe" C126
"The Fig Tree" B39
"The First American Saint" E47
"Flannery O'Connor at Home" C108
"The Flower of Flowers" C71
Flowering Judas A4
"Flowering Judas" B13
Flowering Judas and Other Stories A7

"Foreword" C80, 85
"Fresh Vegetable Borscht" C102
"Frivolities of Harmless Sort Billed to Amuse Theater Goers" D8
"From a Mexican Painter's Notebooks" C18
"From the Notebooks of Katherine Anne Porter—Yeats, Joyce, Eliot, Pound" C111
"From the Notebooks: Yeats, Joyce, Eliot, Pound" C111
"The Future is Now" C74

"Gertrude Stein: A Self Portrait" C67
"The Gift of Woman" C90
"Girl with Personality Tops Orpheum's Card D29
"Girls from America Out of Place in Paris, Says Society Woman" D5
"Go Little Book" C113
"A Goat for Azazel (A.D. 1688)" C34
"Good Cast Enlivens 'Cappy Ricks' Farce" D62
"Gracious Greatness" C108
"The Grand and the Tragic" E64
"Grand Opera Artists Please Big Audience" D23
"The Grave" B17
"The Great Catherine" E11
"Great Omar Khayyam Pageant to be Held in Denver July 10" D81
"The Guild Spirit in Mexican Art" C17

Hacienda A6
"Hacienda" B15
"Hand-Book of Magic" E26
"Happy Land" C33
He A21
"He" B8
"Headliner Thrills Orpheum Crowd" D41
"Heiress to Millions Abandons Frivolity to Handle Tractors" D72
"Henry Fielding—*Tom Jones*," "(1707–1754)—" C49
"Henry James—*The Turn of the Screw*," "(1843–1916)—" C51
"Her Legend Will Live" C106
"Here Is My House" C82
"High Rents in Attic Quarters Drive Artists to Mere Hotels" D74
"The High Sea" B29
"His Poetry Makes the Difference" E65
"History for Boy and Girl Scouts" E18
"History on the Wing" E43
"Hofmann's Playing Wins Music Lovers" D16
Holiday A24

"Holiday" B40
"'Home Grown' Music Good, Says Hoffman" D15
"A House of My Own" C39
"Howard's Song Revue Wins Orpheum Crowd" D33
"Huge Audience Hears Grand Opera Singers Render Famous Gems"
    D53
"Human Light" C100
"The Hundredth Role" E30

"Ice Cream, Scenic Railway and Lakeside Joys Make Perfect Day for
    100 Kiddies" D77
"In the Depths of Grief, a Towering Rage" E66
"In the Morning of the Poet" E67
"Introduction" C21, 37, 40, 52
"Introduction—Notes on the Life and Death of a Hero" C53
"It Is Hard to Stand in the Middle" E61
The Itching Parrot A11
"It's Easy to be Mad Nowadays and M.D.'s List You as Genius" D90

"Jacqueline Kennedy" C106
"The Jilting of Granny Weatherall" B11
"The Journey" B20

"Katherine Anne Porter" C127, 132
"Katherine Anne Porter Comments on *Good-Bye Wisconsin*" C109
"Katherine Anne Porter, 1894– " C26
"Katherine Anne Porter [Homage to Ford Madox Ford—1875–1939]"
    C54
"Katherine Anne Porter Remembers: Romany Marie, Joe Gould—
    Two Legends Come to Life" C92
"Katherine Anne Porter Replies" C138
"Katherine Anne Porter Writes Views on Debate" C65
Katherine Anne Porter's French Song-Book A5
"Kein Haus, Keine Heimat" B28

"The Last Leaf" A12
"'The Laughing Heat of the Sun'" E55
"The Leaning Tower" B27
The Leaning Tower and Other Stories A12
"Leaving the Petate" C24
"Let Suzanne Shop for You!" D91, 93, 95
"Let's Shop with Suzanne!" D69, 75, 79, 82, 85, 97, 101, 104
Letter C8, 22

Letter to Donald Ogden Stewart C31
Letter to Frances Steloff C137
Letter to Gerald Ashford C114–15
Letter to Malcolm Cowley C123
Letter to Paul Michael C96
Letter to Philip Horton C29, 125
Letter to R.P. Blackmur C119
Letter to students, Thomas A. Edison High School, Tulsa, Oklahoma
     C95
"A Letter to Sylvia Beach" C105
Letter to the Editor C98
"A Letter to the Editor of *The Nation*" C64
"A Letter to the Editor of *The Saturday Review of Literature*" C128
"A Letter to the Editor of *The Village Voice*" C88
"A Letter to the Editor of *The Washington Post*" C101
"A Letter to the Editor of *The Yale Review*" C98
Letters of Katherine Anne Porter A23
"Letters to a Nephew" C117
"Letters to a Nephew: Observations on—Pets, Poets, Sex, Love, Hate,
     Fame, Treason" C117
Letters to Kerker Quinn C145
Letters to Mitzi Berger Hamovitch C142
Letters to Richard Blackmur, Bernard Bandler, and Lincoln Kirstein"
     C143
Letters to Richard Blackmur, Bernard Bandler, Lincoln Kirstein, and
     Mitzi Berger Hamovitch C144
Letters to Robert McAlmon C122
"Lewis Carroll—*Alice in Wonderland*," "(1832–1858—)" C50
"Lion Interviewing as Opposed to Talk with Foy Children" D61
"A Little Incident in the Rue de l'Odéon" C107
"Little Requiem" C14
"Little Theater Plays Charm First Nighters" D20
"Live Memories of a Growing Season" C88
"Local Amateur Actors Busily Prepare for Season of Drama" D18
"'Lord and Lady Algy' Delights Audience" D7
"'Lottery Man' Given to Close Denham D87
"Love and Hate" C68
"Lovely Evocative Photographs" E48

"'Madmen Flutter By' Latest Thing in Opera" D84
"Magic" B9
"The Magic Ear Ring" B3

"Man Dancer Makes Costumes Even to Sewing on Buttons" D56
"Marc Lescarbot" E27
"María Concepción B5
"Marriage Is Belonging" C75
"The Martyr" B6
"Maud Powell Repeats Triumphs in Concert" D67
"Max Beerbohm" E60
"Maxine Elliott Reviews Play in Which She Scored Success" D6
"Maya Treasure" E4
"Measures for Song and Dance" C72
"The Mexican Trinity" C7
"Mexico" E1
"Mexico's Thirty Long Years of Revolution—A Story Told Simply and Effectively in Text and Photographs" E50
"Misplaced Emphasis" E25
"Miss Porter Adds a Comment" C58
"Miss Porter Gets the Last Word" C116
"Mr. George on the Woman Question" E12
"Moral Waxworks Exposed" E34
"The Most Catholic King" E38
"A Most Lively Genius" E63
"Movie Actress Seen at Denver Theater" D12
"Music of the Jarabe and Versos—Collected in the State of Hidalgo" C23
"Musical Comedy to Supplant Stork in Popular Denver House" D35
"Musical Show Scores with Tabor Audiences" D36
My Chinese Marriage A1
"My First Speech" C129

"The Necessary Enemy" C68
"Neglected Books of the Twentieth Century" C141
The Never-Ending Wrong A22
"The Never-Ending Wrong" C140
"'The New Henrietta' Pleases Theatergoers" D37
"The New Man and the New Order" C5
"New Songs and Gowns Feature Eltinge Show" D71
"1942: Transplanted Writers" C48
"1939: The Situation in American Writing" C32
"No Masters or Teachers" C86
"No Plot, My Dear, No Story" C46
"No Poodles, No Maids, Just Plain Anna Case" D9
Noon Wine A8
"Noon Wine" B19, 22

"'Noon Wine': The Sources" C89
"Not So Lost!" E33
"A Note" C103
"A Note on Pierre-Joseph Redouté" C73
"Note to *A Christmas Story*" C120
"Noted Paris Writer to Address Alliance Francaise Saturday" D34
"Noted Singer Here, Appalled at America's Neglect of Music" D94
"Notes on a Criticism of Thomas Hardy" C35
"Notes on the Life and Death of a Hero" C53
"Notes on the Texas I Remember" C136
"Notes on Writing—From the Journals of Katherine Anne Porter"
     C38
"November in Windham" C84
"Now at Last a House of My Own" C39

"Old Gods and New Messiahs" E35
"Old Melodies Please at Nursery Benefit" D100
Old Mortality A25
"Old Mortality" B21
"The Old Order" B20
The Old Order: Stories of the South from Flowering Judas; Pale Horse,
     Pale Rider; and The Leaning Tower A16
"Ole Woman River" C118
"The Olive Grove" C30
"On a Criticism of Thomas Hardy" C35
"On Christopher Sykes" E69
"On Communism in Hollywood" C65
"On First Meeting T.S. Eliot" C99
"On Modern Fiction" C112
"On Writing" C130
"Opening Speech at Paris Conference, 1952" C76
"An Opinion: Notes on Writing" C38
"Oriental Ballet Vies with Jazz at Ball of Mystic Shrine Nobles" D55
"Orpheus in Purgatory" E56
Outline of Mexican Popular Arts and Crafts A2
"Over Adornment" E8

"Pale Horse, Pale Rider" B23
Pale Horse, Pale Rider: Three Short Novels A9
"Paris: A Little Incident in the Rue de l'Odéon" C107
"Paternalism and the Mexican Problem" E22
"A Philosopher at Court" E23
"Pierre Joseph Redouté" C73

"Playlet Headlines Orpheum Program" D38
"The Poet and Her Imp" E3
"Poetry of Khayyam Depicted by Masque" D89
"Popular Actress Back on Stage Surpasses Former Successes" D31
"Porter, Katherine Anne (May 15, 1894–)" C55, 87
"Portrait: Old South" C60
"Presentation to Eudora Welty of The Gold Medal for the Novel by
    Katherine Anne Porter" C133
"Princesses, Ladies and Adventuresses of the Reign of Louis XIV" E6a
"The Prisoner" B32
"'Public Shame to Our Intelligence as a Nation'—Katherine Anne
    Porter" C62
"Pull Dick, Pull Devil" E53
"'The Purple Poppy' Scores at Orpheum" D46

"A Quaker Who 'Had a Splendid Time of It'" E59
"Queena Mario's Voice Captivates Denver" D25
"Question of Royalties" C42
"Quetzalcoatl" E15

"Readers' Forum—on 'The Wave'" C28
"The Real Ray" C3
Recent Southern Fiction: A Panel Discussion C104
"Recollection of Rome" C134
"Reflections on Willa Cather" C77
"Remarks on the Agenda" C91
"Remarks on the Agenda by Katherine Anne Porter" C91
"Requiescat——" C14
"Rivera's Personal Revolution in Mexico" E44
"Romany Marie, Joe Gould—Two Legends Come to Life" C92
"Rope" B10

"St. Augustine and the Bullfight" C83
"San Carlo Star Singer Captures San Francisco—Opera Company to
    Appear Here This Week" D22
"Saslavsky Concert Presents Contrast" D92
"Saturday's Child" C94
"Screaming Comedy Offered at Denham" D14
"Second Wind" E28
"The Seducers: A Fragment" B35
Selected Short Stories A13
"A Self-Made Ghost" E2
"Semiramis Was a Good Girl" E24

"Settings by Little Theaters Shown in Modern Art Display" D86
"Seven Foys Score Orpheum Success" D58
"Sex and Civilization" E7
"The Shattered Star" B1
Ship of Fools A18
"Ship of Fools" B36–38
"Shooting the Chutes" E5
"Silk Purse. . . ." C101
"Singer Wins Hearts of Denver Audience" D10
"A Singing Woman" E17
"The Situation in American Writing: Seven Questions" C32
"Skinner in Good Role as Scapegrace Hero" D59
"Society Gossip of the Week" D3
"Society Gossip of the Week by the Town Tatler" D1
"Some Every-Day Fare Relegated; Hospital Attaches Are Happy"
    D19
"Some Important Writers Speak for Themselves—Katherine Anne
    Porter" C78
"A Song (from the French of Clément Marot) [1496–1544]" C57
"The Source" B26
"Spaghetti Didn't Suit; Opera Stars Grieved" D52
"The Sparrow Revolution" E49
"Speech of Acceptance" C121
"Spirited Dances by Tots and Elders Feature Benefit" D73
"The Spivvleton Mystery" B41
"Splendor and Gaiety Mark Reception Tendered Governor by People
    of State" D11
"A Sprig of Mint for Allen" C97
"Stage May Lose Best Talent to Screen Thru Actors' Union" D102
"'A Stitch in Time' Scores at Denham" D57
"The Strange Old World" E58
"The Strangers" B30
"Striking the Lyric Note in Mexico" C4
"'Such a Life!' Says Saslavsky; 'Bullyragger,' Pupils Retort" D98

"Tabor Bill Features Bevy of Pretty Girls" D42
"Tabor Bill Has Chinese Touch—Wee Oriental Sings K-K-Katie"
    D50
"Tell Me About Adrienne . . . ." C105
"Tenor Scores Triumph in Opera Masterpiece" D26
"Texas by the Gulf of Mexico" C1
"That Tree" B16
"Theatergoers Like to Shiver Over Sins of Stage Heroes" D13

"Theaters Offer Good Bills—Playgoers Assured Treats" D47

"Theft" B12

Theft and Other Stories A26

"'These Pictures Must Be Seen'" E39

"Thespian Charms Party, Tho Late in Greeting Hostess" D64

"They Lived with the Enemy in the House" E52

"To a Portrait of the Poet" C15

"Touché" C43

"Transplanted Writers: A Symposium" C48

"Trouble Packed in Old Kit Bags of Two Charming Actresses" D17

"Two Ancient Mexican Pyriamids—the Core of a City Unknown Until a Few Years Ago" C10

Two Short Stories A27

"Two Songs from Mexico" C13

"Under Weigh" B33

"'Unlovely' Menfolk Are Seen at Denham" D51

"Valska, 'Tiger Vamp' Quite Tame Off Stage" D48

"Vampire Idea of Actresses Dispelled by Women of Stage" D39

"Varied Tastes Pleased by Saslavsky Concert" D96

"The Virgin and the Unicorn" E32

"Virgin Violeta" B7

"Virginia Woolf" E57

"Virginia Woolf's Essays—A Great Art, A Sober Craft" E57

"The Week at the Theaters" D2, 4

What Price Marriage A3

"Where Presidents Have No Friends" C9

"Who Will Be the Judge?" C64

"Why Does a 'Genius' Lose 'Pep' as Soon as Coin Rolls In?" D105

"Why I Write about Mexico" C11

"Why She Selected Flowering Judas" C56

"William Phips, Cotton Mather's Dear Machine" E40

"The Winged Skull" E51

"Winter Burial" C19

"With the Enthusiasm of a Boy Scout" E6

"The Witness" A12

"The Wooden Umbrella" C67

"Words on Length" C110

"A Wreath for the Gamekeeper" E68

"Wyoming Girl Tells of Hospital Service and Gay Paris Races" D88

"Xochimilco" C6

"You Are What You Read" C135
"Yours, Ezra Pound" E61